Even paranoids have enemies

'Even paranoids have enemies' is the reply Golda Meir is said to have made to Henry Kissinger who, during the 1973 Sinai talks, accused her of being paranoid for hesitating to grant further concessions to the Arabs. It is used as part of the title of this book to highlight the complex relationship between paranoia and persecution.

The book is divided into three parts. Part I addresses aspects of the complex psychological impact that experiences of external and internal persecution have on the individual. Part II brings together expositions on paranoid and persecutory processes in groups, institutions and bureaucracies. Part III discusses the social, political and cultural factors which give rise to these processes.

The theoretical viewpoints introduced and discussed come to life in the political, social and historical arenas where the politics of the Middle East, the pressures of Japanese society and the dynamics of the drug scene are used to illustrate and understand the issues involved in paranoid thinking and in persecution. The authors' perspectives, from psychoanalytic psychotherapy, psychiatry, politics, sociology, history and the arts, shed light on phenomena which are often taken for granted and show how our thinking on these matters has implications for social and ethical concerns, and for clinical practice.

Joseph H. Berke is the founder and Director of the Arbours Crisis Centre, London. **Stella Pierides** is Associate Director of the Centre, and both are psychoanalytic psychotherapists in private practice. **Andrea Sabbadini** is a psychoanalyst in private practice in London. **Stanley Schneider** is a psychoanalyst and Professor of Psychology at the Hebrew University and Michlalah, Jerusalem.

Contributors: Joseph H. Berke; David Edgar; Leonard Fagin; Calvin C. Hernton; Robert D. Hinshelwood; John Jackson; Otto F. Kernberg; Ilany Kogan; Robert Jay Lifton; Stella Pierides; Salomon Resnik; Andrea Sabbadini; Stanley Schneider; Vamik D. Volkan; Hisako Watanabe.

Even paranoids have enemies – new perspectives on paranoia and persecution

Edited by Joseph H. Berke,
Stella Pierides, Andrea Sabbadini
and Stanley Schneider

London and New York

First published 1998 by Routledge
11 New Fetter Lane, London EC4P 4EE

Simultaneously published in the USA and Canada
by Routledge
29 West 35th Street, New York, NY 10001

© 1998 Joseph H. Berke, Stella Pierides,
Andrea Sabbadini and Stanley Schneider in the collection
as a whole; individual contributions the contributors

Typeset in Times by Florencetype Ltd, Stoodleigh, Devon

Printed and bound in Great Britain by
TJ International Ltd, Padstow, Cornwall

British Library Cataloguing in Publication Data
A catalogue record for this book is available from the
British Library

Library of Congress Cataloging in Publication Data
Even paranoids have enemies: new perspectives on
    paranoia and persecution / edited by Joseph H. Berke
    . . . [et al.]
        p.   cm.
    Includes bibliographical references and index.
    1. Political persecution. 2. Persecution–Psychological
aspects. 3. Paranoia. 4. Psychoanalytic interpretation.
I. Berke, Joseph H.
JC585.E84 1998
616.89′7–dc21   97-26682
                            CIP

ISBN 0-415-15557-6 (hbk)
ISBN 0-415-15558-4 (pbk)

Contents

Contributors

Joseph H. Berke is an individual and family psychoanalytic psychotherapist. He is co-founder and Director of the Arbours Association and Arbours Crisis Centre, London, and a lecturer and teacher. He is the author of many articles and books on psychological, social, political and religious themes, including *Mary Barnes: Two Accounts of a Journey through Madness* (with Mary Barnes), *The Cannabis Experience* (with Calvin Hernton), *I Haven't Had To Go Mad Here*, *The Tyranny of Malice: Exploring the Dark Side of Character and Culture* and *Sanctuary: The Arbours Experience of Alternative Community Care* (co-editor). He is currently working on *Psychoanalysis and Kabbalah* (with Stanley Schneider).

David Edgar is Professor of Playwrighting at the University of Birmingham. He has written widely in journals and periodicals and published a book of essays, *The Second Time as Farce* (1988). His many plays include the adaptations: *Mary Barnes: Two Accounts of a Journey through Madness* (Royal Court, 1979), *Nicholas Nickleby* (Royal Shakespeare Company [RSC], 1980), and *Dr. Jekyll and Mr. Hyde* (RSC, 1991). His original plays include: *Destiny* (RSC, 1976), *Maydays* (RSC, 1983), *Pentecost* (RSC, 1994), *Entertaining Strangers* and *The Shape of the Table* (National Theatre, 1987 and 1990) and *Buying a Landslide* (BBC, 1992).

Leonard Fagin is Consultant Psychiatrist, Forest Healthcare National Health Trust and Senior Lecturer, University College, London. He developed one of the first community mental health centres in Britain and was a founder member of the Interdisciplinary Association of Mental Health Workers. A Fellow of the Royal College of Psychiatrists, he is currently on the executive of the Social and Community Section. He is the author of many articles on deinstitutionalization, unemployment and multidisciplinary work in mental health and family research in schizophrenia. His books include: *The Forsaken Families: A Study of Unemployment in Families* and *Stress and Coping in Mental Health Nurses*.

Calvin C. Hernton is a poet, writer, social scientist and Professor and Chair of African American Studies at Oberlin College, Oberlin, Ohio, USA, where he teaches African and African American Literature. He resided in London during the 1960s and was associated with the Caribbean Arts Mission and the Kingsley Hall Community project. He has published many poems and essays. His eight books include *Sex and Racism in America, The Cannabis Experience* (with Joseph Berke) and, most recently, *The Sexual Mountain and Black Women Writers*.

Robert D. Hinshelwood is a psychoanalyst, Clinical Director of the Cassel Hospital, Richmond, Surrey and Professor of Psychoanalysis at the University of Essex. He has sustained a long-standing interest in therapeutic communities and has worked to apply psychoanalytic ideas to groups and social systems. He is the author of many papers and books, including: *What Happens in Groups* (1987) and *A Dictionary of Kleinian Thought* (1989).

John Jackson is a businessman and naturalist. He is Chairman of Ladbroke Group plc, Celltech plc and a number of other public and private companies. He is also Chairman of Mishcon de Reya, solicitors and a joint publisher of *History Today*. He has lectured in the USA and the UK on the origins of modern cultural differences between North America and Europe and has written on the practice and philosophy of self-sufficiency.

Otto F. Kernberg is Director of the Personality Disorders Institute and the Cornell Psychotherapy Program at the New York Hospital–Cornell Medical Center and Professor of Psychiatry at the Cornell University Medical College. He is President of the International Psychoanalytic Society and a training and supervising analyst of the Columbia University Center for Psychoanalytic Training and Research. His numerous books include: *Borderline Conditions and Pathological Narcissism* (1975), *Object Relations Theory and Clinical Psychoanalysis* (1976), *Severe Personality Disorders: Psychotherapeutic Strategies* (1984), *Aggression in Personality Disorders and Perversion* (1992), *Love Relations: Normality and Pathology* (1995) and *Ideology and Leadership in Group and Organizational Conflict* (in press).

Ilany Kogan is a training analyst of the Israel Psychoanalytic Society and a lecturer and supervisor at the Psychotherapy Institute at Tel Aviv University Medical School. She is a member of the steering committee of the International Trauma Centre and of the advisory committee of the Holocaust Centre in Frankfurt, Germany (the Fritz Baurer Institut). During the past twelve years she has worked extensively with the offspring of Holocaust survivors and has published and presented many papers on their treatment in Europe and the United States. Her book, *The Cry of*

Mute Children: A Psychoanalytic Perspective of the Second Generation of the Holocaust, was published in 1995 by Free Association Books.

Robert Jay Lifton is Distinguished Professor of Psychiatry and Psychology, the City University of New York, and Director of the Centre on Violence and Human Survival at John Jay College of Criminal Justice. A pioneer in the new field of psychohistory, he has written extensively on issues of genocide, the Holocaust, nuclear warfare and Hiroshima and the impact of the cultural revolution in China. More recently, he has been researching the extremist Japanese cult, Aum Shinrikyo. His books include: *The Protean Self: Human Resilience in an Age of Fragmentation*, *The Genocidal Mentality: Nazi Holocaust and Nuclear Threat* (with E. Markusen), *The Future of Immortality*, *The Nazi Doctors: Medical Killing and the Psychology of Genocide* and *Death in Life: Survivors of Hiroshima* and, most recently, *Hiroshima in America: Fifty Years of Denial* (with G. Mitchell).

Stella Pierides is a psychoanalytic psychotherapist and Associate Director of the Arbours Crisis Centre, London, a supervisor, teacher and author. Co-founder and member of the Association of Arbours Psychotherapists' Borderline Workshop, and Arts and Psychoanalytic Workshop, her main area of work involves borderline psychotic conditions and her areas of interest include artistic creativity in the visual arts and in literature.

Salomon Resnik is a psychoanalyst who trained in Argentina and London and now lives and works in Paris and Venice. His main research interests are autistic children and psychotic patients in institutions. He is a former President of the Group-Analytic Society in France and the author of many books and papers, including *The Theatre of the Dream* and *Mental Space*.

Andrea Sabbadini is a psychologist and psychoanalyst. Former Director of the Arbours Training Programme in Psychotherapy and Honorary Psychotherapist at the Medical Foundation for the Care of Victims of Torture, he is currently Visiting Lecturer at Regent's College, London, Chairman of the British Psycho-Analytic Society's Book Club and Chairman of the series 'Psychoanalysis and the Arts'. He has published extensively in major psychoanalytic journals and is the editor of *Il tempo in psicoanalisi* (Time in Psychoanalysis) (1979).

Stanley Schneider is a psychoanalyst, Professor and Chairman of the Program for Advanced Studies in Integrative Psychotherapy, the Hebrew University, Jerusalem, Professor and Chairman of the Department of Guidance and Counselling, Michlalah, Jerusalem, Adjunct Professor, Wurzweiler School of Social Work, Yeshiva University, New York and co-founder and former Director of the Summit Institute, Jerusalem. He is the author of many books and articles on psychological and social themes and is currently working on *Psychoanalysis and Kabbalah* (with Joseph Berke).

Vamik D. Volkan, M.D. is a Professor of Psychiatry and Director of the Center for the Study of Mind and Human Interaction (CSMHI), University of Virginia School of Medicine. He is also a Training and Supervising Analyst with the Washington Analytic Institute, Washington, D.C. and a member of the Carter Center's International Negotiation Network. His two most recent books are *Richard Nixon: A Psychobiography* and *Bloodlines: From Ethnic Pride to Ethnic Terrorism.*

Hisako Watanabe is a paediatrician and psychiatrist. Former Director of the Department of Psychiatry, Yokohama City Hospital, she is currently Assistant Professor and Director of the Child and Adolescent Mental Health Unit, Department of Paediatrics, School of Medicine, Keio University, Tokyo, Regional Vice-President of the World Association for Infant Mental Health and President of the MIND CLUB: Forum for Mental Health in Yokohama.

Foreword

Vamik D. Volkan

In 1974, when the Cold War was still very much palpable, I drove through Bulgaria with my wife and two small children. One noticeable difference on Bulgarian roads was the absence of the colorful advertisements and neon signs typical in much of the western world. Instead, there was an abundance of huge billboards illustrated with figures whose fingers pointed at passers-by. Although the Bulgarian alphabet was foreign to me, I knew the billboards exalted the virtues of the communist system and 'ordered' people to behave correctly. Outside of Sofia, our progress was brought to a standstill by a policeman stopping all traffic. But he was not like the traffic police I was accustomed to in the US or other places who typically used the flashing lights of their patrol cars, bright orange cones, and large signs to stop the flow of cars. The Bulgarian policeman instead held a small cardboard sign that reminded me more of a lollipop which he moved up and down in slow motion. I perceived this policeman as a cartoon character; he seemed more a caricature of a traffic cop, but his power was nonetheless enormous. He was laughable but also scary.

Earlier that same day, as we crossed into Bulgaria, we encountered one of the customs officers, a mean-looking and unsmiling official. He checked our car thoroughly, looking under the hood and bending down to inspect the underside of our car. We had nothing to hide, but as we continued our drive through Bulgaria, the events of that day caused me to develop a fear of being stopped by a Bulgarian policeman, not unlike the cartoon-like traffic cop, and accused of some unknown crime. The unfamiliar external world was stimulating fearful responses in my internal world, making me very worried of sinister external powers. When we left Bulgaria and returned to the 'free world' my paranoia ended, though the memory of it remained.

From this simple experience, I felt an empathic connection with the internal world of those who live in unnurturing and persecutory environments long enough to assimilate the influence of such environments and develop paranoia in response. But unlike my brief encounter, others have observed this phenomenon over a far longer period. For example, Michael

Šebek, a Czech psychoanalyst, retained his remarkable observational abilities while living under his country's totalitarian regime. He reported his findings on the effects of totalitarianism in the evolution of a society into a 'pre-Oedipal anal universe' (Šebek 1992: 54) in which as Chasseguet-Smirgel (1984) stated, differences disappear and distinct structures are annihilated. What is created is an undifferentiated anal substance: 'The unified socialist architecture strikes us as gray undifferentiated material. The polluted air, dirty rivers, devastated landscape, decadence of language, and deterioration of "good" behavior that we associated with this structure are very close to the fecal world' (ibid.). Šebek goes on to describe how pre-Oedipal threats (threats that exist in the child's early dyadic relationship with his mother), which are much more fear-inducing than castration anxiety, are reactivated as totalitarian power 'spreads everywhere with vague limitations, controlling man from a distance' (Šebek 1992: 56).

In 1921, when Freud presented his ideas on group psychology, he did not focus on the influence of outer reality, and few have considered this approach in the intervening years. Essays such as Šebek's are therefore urgently needed to expand psychoanalytic inquiry concerning the interplay between the external and internal worlds of individuals and large groups and more specifically on individuals' and groups' paranoid reactions.

Like Šebek's work (1992) and Robins and Post's recent book *Political Paranoia: The Psychopolitics of Hatred* (1997), the editors of this volume expand the application of the term paranoid from the confines of clinical practice into societal issues. As clinical practice certainly indicates, it is not simply the influence of the external world that makes one paranoid. In the typical patient we note the individual's developmental difficulties and externalizations of aspects of self-representations and previously internalized object-representations as well as projections of unwanted elements onto the external world.

The editors of *Even Paranoids Have Enemies: New Perspectives on Paranoia and Persecution* have masterfully organized the contributors' chapters so that clinical findings on individuals are re-examined, updated, and integrated with observations of suspiciousness and enemy-making in organizations and large groups, including ethnic and national groups. The book thus delivers a spectrum of paranoid conditions that are above and beyond typical clinical material. Contributors offer an interdisciplinary approach – although psychoanalytic considerations are dominant – in order to understand suspiciousness, persecution, transgenerational transmission of trauma, the role of cultural, bureaucratic and technological influences on human experience, and other crucial issues.

In my own work on large-group psychology (Volkan 1988, 1997) I focus on the concept of identity – a relatively new approach in psychoanalysis.

I have suggested that the creation of social and political enemies, as well as friends, is a central part of human development. Early externalizations and projections, along with early internalizations and identifications, are involved in forming self- and object-representations. Enemies are needed in order to define our self-representations as well as the representation of our large-group identities. Enemies who attack us or in some way damage us are real, but an element of fantasy is also always present.

Mental health professionals who understand the dynamic links between what is real and what is fantasized, in collaboration with other scholars and practitioners who possess knowledge of and insights into human nature, can and should contribute to our understanding of 'normal' prejudice and its potential on the individual and group level to become irrational, consuming, and deadly. Those who have contributed to *Even Paranoids Have Enemies* have illuminated this area of investigation and stimulated the curiosity necessary to prompt further investigation. The abundance of new and exciting ideas that are presented between the covers of this volume requires that it be read in a serious manner.

REFERENCES

Chasseguet-Smirgel, J. (1984). *Creativity and Perversion*. New York: Norton.
Robins, R. and Post, J. (1997). *Political Paranoia: The Psychopolitics of Hatred*. New Haven, CT: Yale University Press.
Šebek, M. (1992). 'Anality in the totalitarian system and the psychology of post-totalitarian society'. *Mind and Human Interaction*, 4: 52–59.
Volkan, V.D. (1988). *The Need to Have Enemies and Allies: From Clinical Practice to International Relationships*. Northvale, NJ: Jason Aronson.
—— (1997). *Blood Lines: From Ethnic Pride to Ethnic Terrorism*. New York: Farrar, Strauss and Giroux.

General introduction

The word 'paranoia', originating from the Greek language (*para*: out of, beside; *noos*: reason, mind) denotes a condition of being out of, or beside, one's mind; it means malaise or disorder of the mind. The word *persecution*, originating from the Latin *persequi* (*per*: continually; *sequi*: to follow, pursue), refers to harassment, oppression, suppression, subjugation, tyranny and torture, especially on political, racial and religious grounds. Differences of opinion, nationality and creed are among the main inflammatory agents involved. Interestingly, the word persecution originally included a sense of vengeance – which may to some extent explain its entanglement with paranoia, but which highlights the issue of intolerance of difference and the consequent wrath of the persecutor. In this book, the authors consider perspectives on these words and on the ideas and concepts behind them, looking at them separately, as well as at their interconnections.

An international conference on 'Paranoia and Persecution', held in London in February 1995, gave the impetus for this book. Most of the contributors were active participants at the conference, which celebrated the twenty-fifth anniversary of the Arbours Association, a pioneering mental health charity. The Arbours Association was established in order to provide psychotherapeutic support and housing for people in severe emotional distress, and as an alternative to traditional psychiatric regimes.

The title of this book is a saying attributed to Golda Meir and it refers to the complex and ambiguous relationship between the internal and external factors involved in paranoia and persecution. During the Sinai talks, in November 1973, when Henry Kissinger had been pressing Golda Meir for further Israeli concessions, when Meir hesitated, he called her 'paranoid'. To this, she is said to have responded: 'Even paranoids have enemies'. Meir's reply pointed to the fact that even if she were paranoid, this would not alter the real situation in which she was – namely, that she and her country had enemies. Paranoia is no protection from persecution, nor is persecution immunisation against paranoia.

The aim of this book is to propose new perspectives on the concepts of paranoia and persecution. It will also differentiate between their expression on many levels, ranging from the intrapsychic to the macrosocial, as well as consider how they are intertwined. To do so not only informs and enriches our thinking on these matters; it has implications for social and ethical concerns, and for clinical practice.

This volume is divided into three parts. Part I addresses aspects of the complex psychological impact that experiences of external and internal persecution have on the individual person, the sensitive thinking required in order to understand them, as well as the delicate psychotherapeutic technique needed to assist them regain their lives. Part II brings together thoughtful expositions of paranoid and persecutory processes in groups, institutions and bureaucracies, as well as interesting enquiries into their roots. Part III highlights these processes in political, social and cultural domains and pinpoints some of the factors that give rise to them. This is the part where the theoretical viewpoints introduced, reconsidered and discussed come to life in the political, social and historical arenas; where the politics of the Middle East, the bearings of Japanese society, the dynamics of the drug scene as well as the manifestations of mechanical thinking in individuals and culture are used to illustrate and understand the issues involved in paranoid thinking and in persecution.

By the end of this book, we hope to have brought to light and illustrated at least some of the complexities involved in the concepts of paranoia and persecution, as well as the ambiguous currents that run through them. The authors' perspectives, arising from psychoanalytic psychotherapy, psychiatry, politics, sociology, history and the arts, as well as their own personal interests, illuminate anew an area much taken for granted.

Dinora Pines (1995) describes her experience with a patient from Russia who had given his KGB companion the slip when he was brought to London. The patient appeared to her to be obsessed by his fantasies about Baba Yar. He never gave her his home address or telephone number and always seemed to slip into his sessions in a shadowy and haunted manner. Pines's patient did not arouse any emotional response in her and she felt bored, only subsequently realising that she was in the presence of a person whose main internal difficulty was a 'falseness', a tendency to disallow emotional engagement and closeness. Her non-existent feelings towards him troubled her, keeping her thinking about his internal world until one day external reality erupted in her consulting room. After the murder of a Bulgarian dissident in Oxford Street, her patient disappeared. She never heard another word from him until she was shocked to read an obituary about him in the local newspaper. Pines writes:

> I felt very guilty about my previous indifference towards him, and my irritation with him for what seemed to be illogical precautions as to his

safety. Yet it also seemed to me, with hindsight, that he was right and I was totally wrong about his reality.

Her patient's past life experience differed enormously from hers and matters were further complicated by their cultural differences and his own psychological difficulties in being honest and open with those, such as his analyst, whom he perceived to be in a position of authority.

In its modern use the word paranoia is widespread, can be applied to individuals, social groups, institutions or even whole nations, and carries a multiplicity of meanings. It involves unfounded and exaggerated distrust and mistrust, suspiciousness, apprehension, fear and persecutory feelings. When we say that someone has paranoid thoughts we tend to think of that person as suffering from something unhealthy or abnormal. At the end of the spectrum of paranoid manifestations, the word as defined by psychiatric and psychoanalytic thinking becomes a term denoting a serious pathological condition; a predicament where one holds a coherent, consistent delusional system of beliefs which centres around the idea that one is grandiosely important in a religious, political, or sectarian way, and is for that reason persecuted, despised, betrayed or envied. The person in this situation, often assailed or prompted by hallucinations, behaves in a cold, aloof, argumentative, angry and superior manner which only serves to reinforce the system of persecutory beliefs.

The whole spectrum covered by the word paranoia is familiar. We are all aware of, and able, most of the time, to recognise – usually transient – paranoid phenomena in ourselves, others, society, history and culture and distinguish them from the extremes of dis-ease with the world. What is not often clearly discernible is the extent to which paranoid ideas and behaviour are connected to, or are the result of, external persecutory processes. Is the woman afraid to walk in the dark paranoid or is her fear due to the fact that she was attacked recently? Are cyclists wearing masks while cycling around London paranoid or are they protecting themselves from an environment that has grown too noxious? Perhaps more importantly, is a person who is truly being persecuted, and has awful feelings of people being after him in order to harm him, paranoid? Clearly, we need to be able to differentiate between a para-noia that is the result of ill-conceived thinking (out of one's mind) and a para-noia which is the result of processes going on outside of one's mind and control. We need to distinguish between the recipients of actual persecution who react to trying external circumstances and those who experience a paranoid ideation which interferes with a normal capacity to differentiate to an appropriate and flexible extent between real and exaggerated feelings, inner persecution. Although the term 'persecution complex' is almost synonymous with paranoia, there is a definite sense in which one can be persecuted without being paranoid.

Sigmund Freud understood the main mechanism of paranoia to be that of projection. He described how, in paranoia, unbearable and unacceptable impulses are defended against by projecting them outside. In his discussion of Judge Schreber, who underwent two major paranoid psychotic breakdowns, Freud (1911) identified homosexual needs as being at the core of such a process. However, Freud also linked paranoia to narcissism, the over-investment of psychic energy (libido) on the self, and issues of self-esteem and identity. He observed the oversensitivity of paranoid persons who tend to feel hurt at the slightest of provocations, their expectation that they will be abused and humiliated in all situations, their nursing of grievances and preoccupation with attacks and counter-attacks, beating and being beaten.

In a contemporary revision of Freud, Harold Blum (1994a) discussed the failure of the paranoid personality to properly negotiate the separation–individuation process and the patient's desperate attempts to re-attach himself to an object perceived as not constant.[1] The method at his disposal is to hold on to a relationship fused with hatred because it is considered better than no relationship at all. The hostility, hatred and rage which the paranoid patient directs at the external other are expressions of an inner blaming and haughty super-ego, which does not give the patient a moment of peace.

The effect of external persecution had also preoccupied Freud since the beginning of his working life – from his discussions of traumatic situations in hysterical patients, to his change in his seduction theory, to his tumultuous relationship with Ferenczi (Blum 1994b). In his paper on the Wolf Man, Freud (1918) discussed what would be essentially seen today as abuse and he connected his patient's beating fantasies to paranoia. According to Blum, however, it was Ferenczi who brought the issues of trauma back onto the stage of psychoanalytic thinking, through his elaboration and extension of Freudian thinking and his interesting observations of how this kind of persecution lives on in the mind of the child and reproduces itself in contexts all through the life of the adult self. It is now widely understood that many paranoid patients have been hurt, traumatised, humiliated, or, in other words, persecuted, in their early years of life (Frosch 1990).

The issue of differentiating actual from imagined physical abuse in childhood in the memory of patients has been crucial to psychoanalytic theory and practice from its inception. This problem has become particularly prominent during the past few years when Freud's abandonment of the seduction theory has been called into question and allegations of widespread early abuse have forced many analysts and therapists to reconsider their views on the subject. Such controversy, which may not find a comfortable resolution, is, of course, crucially related to the themes of paranoia and persecution under consideration.

Melanie Klein (1946), like Freud, concentrated on the internal psychic processes involved in cases of paranoia. In her description of the first few months of life of the infant, what Klein called the 'paranoid-schizoid position' involved the most primitive ways of coping with experience: splitting it into good and bad and projecting it outside. What is intensely desired by the baby, the mother's breast, for instance, under frustration can be projected outwards into the world and experienced by the child as fears of being devoured or poisoned. If this position is not sufficiently worked through to enable the child to have experiences of what Klein called the 'depressive position' (which is characterised by the capacity to tolerate ambivalence), then psychotic disorders may develop. The baby's aggression towards the mother's absent breast, whenever excessive and unmitigated, becomes a terrible threat experienced as coming from the outside world; which, as we know, is an essential feature in paranoia. Obviously, instances of actual physical neglect or wilful withdrawal of love, or feeding, or abusive behaviour from the parents confirm and reinforce what had started as a universal and ubiquitous unconscious fantasy.

From another angle, Morton Schatzman (1973) linked inner with external persecution, paranoia with actual assaults on a small child. He described the paranoid-inducing features of Dr Schreber's family. The father of Judge Schreber, whose disciplinary and educational techniques practised on his son matched his son's own bizarre symptoms, wrote many books advocating extreme forms of control over the nature of children. According to Schatzman, the unfortunate effect of such an 'education' is that the child would have to master enormous degrees of projection, repression, displacement, splitting and denial and that he would have no ego left to himself. In other words, it is difficult to see how such a child could have a single thought of his own without breaking some rule or other. Schatzman showed graphically the connections between such an 'education' and the symptoms of the most quoted paranoid schizophrenic in the history of psychiatry and psychoanalysis, Dr Schreber's own son, on whom he had vigorously applied his methods.

Internal and external persecution come together in the theoretical model of 'the paranoid process' – a set of developmental and defensive mechanisms which serve to delineate the individual's inner psychic world and his experience of his emerging self, while, at the same time, contributing to the shaping of his sense of significant objects in his experiential world (Meissner 1986). One of this model's core components, 'the paranoid construction', refers to a cognitive reorganisation taking place in an attempt to sustain a comfortable sense of self which, however, may be at the expense of reality testing. This process, in its extreme form, leads to the formation of a persecutory bond, where a link is established between, on the one hand, the paranoid individual and, on the other, his persecutors and the terrifying forces that threaten to engulf him. This can become a rigid construction that reinforces the spiral of paranoia–persecution–paranoia. Meissner understands this mechanism as offering a sense of cohesion and durability to a fragile self, though it often involves a high degree of pathology and victimisation. Instances of this process abound in individuals, institutions and groups (including whole nations) where views of internal and external situations are (ab)used to service a brittle sense of identity. Fully recognising this predicament, and the dangers involved, requires thinking about and tolerating our own conflictual parts.

Paradoxically, a certain degree of paranoia is desirable as it is a basis for discrimination (Segal 1994); when we let a new experience touch us, we acknowledge that it may be bad or good, which enables us to antici- pate danger. In leaders of an organisation, for instance, a certain degree of paranoid potential can be a useful resource, as opposed to a dangerous naivety that would prevent the leader from becoming aware of the situ- ations of activation of aggression in the group, or regression to primitive levels of functioning. Where the leader can be aware of, and apprehend risk and danger, there is the possibility of preparation for the group to face them and cope with them.

Does this apply to persecution as well? Is a certain degree of persecu- tion helpful or desirable? Persecution is linked with action, as opposed to paranoia which is linked with imaginative anticipation. Persecution involves action against someone who, usually consciously, will suffer as a result of it. While in acute paranoia internal catastrophes occur, which are experienced, as in the case of Schreber, as taking place in the external world, in persecution the outside world becomes the scene for the actual- isation and enactment of such a catastrophe imposed on others, as a defence against the internal catastrophe taking or having taken place. Any justification for persecution belongs to the realm of psychotic logic and behaviour, the realm where there is no differentiation between internal and external, fantasy and reality, feeling and action, waking reality and dream; where laws such as that of the talion (eye for an eye) apply, where there is no possibility of understanding, compassion or reparation. This is the logic of totalitarian regimes, as well as of those families where per- secution arises out of an ill-intended 'love' for the children, in the form of excessive 'education' or 'discipline', where the parents or leaders define as 'good' what seems good for them and impose their definition, eradi- cating the other persons in the process.

The result of such a persecution may be a situation where one is being persecuted without consciously realising it. We know that unresolved inner conflicts in the parents often visit their offspring. The frequency, however, and the extent of such a phenomenon merits a discussion of its own. On a wider scale, this is illustrated in modern Japanese society where unresolved psychic conflicts over the effects of the Second World War weighing on the parents affect the children in the form of immense cultural pressures to compete and succeed in educational, technological and financial areas. As a result of the difficulties of coming to terms with the narcissistic trauma of losing the war, a major portion of modern Japanese society is said to be gripped by a financial and technological will to power, which persecutes the individual in his family and social environment and obstructs a natural process of mourning and reparation.

Such a persecution, under the mis-name or misapprehension of education, moral values, social need or a higher good or purity as defined by those who impose it, is based on the kind of logic that, in its extreme forms, underpins totalitarian regimes such as National Socialism in Germany and Islamic fundamentalism in the Arab world, right-wing military dictatorships in Latin America or long-standing racial discrimination in the United States.

The effects of these policies have been seen and are still being witnessed all over the world in the present, the past, and, no doubt, in the future too. The list of severe oppressions is long and new examples, such as 'ethnic cleansing' in the former Yugoslavia or tribal massacres in Africa can be counted almost every day. In many ways all of these activities can be seen as enactments of the 'destructive narcissism' that Herbert Rosenfeld (1971) has described and which, as we have pointed out, can afflict whole cultures. As the Japanese Aum cult demonstrates, it is more than possible to put life-destroying, apocalyptic fantasies into practice. And, in a literal or desymbolised form, they become the 'end-of-the-world' vision often found in people who have been diagnosed as paranoid schizophrenic. In the service of rampant nationalism, whole groups, races or nations have been exterminated (Berke 1989).

Not many recipients of such malicious 'attention' live to tell their tales, to be heard, or indeed to work through their misfortunes. The concept of 'the paranoia of the persecuted', describes well the Gordian knot that results from the combination of real traumatic events – persecution and torture – with the delusional fantasies they are intertwined with. The intergenerational transmission of such a predicament, as witnessed in the analyses of children of Holocaust survivors, requires a painful, sensitive and affect-laden passage from a 'black hole' of silence to the light of understanding and real life.

Further, one twist of the logic of persecution has adverse repercussions in another way. Fear of the effects of totalitarianism and authoritarianism often leads to a phobic avoidance of all forms of authority and structure. The difficulty, or inability, to differentiate between effective, functioning authority and structure – in a family, a group, an organisation or a state – and authoritarianism may lead to chaos and collapse. Such a situation may deprive a group, or even a nation, of its chances of surviving. The fear of temptations faced by authority in regressive situations, that they will tip into paranoid functioning and an authoritarian stance, may lead, when extreme, into denial of authority in oneself and others, into diffusion of responsibility to 'democratic' committees, on the one hand, or passive obedience to any orders, on the other. Both situations being moved by appeal to, and exploitation of, the mass(es), or by mob decisions made in a head-less and mindless way, easily become breeding grounds for new destructive cycles of paranoia and persecution. The idea that these processes may have instinctual underpinnings which, together with evolutionary mechanisms, fuel tribal behaviour in a variety of human environments is compelling.

Perhaps it is in drama, on the stage, and that physical space which occupies the boundary between the actual and the imaginary, that some of these issues and dilemmas get the chance to be told, enacted and thought about in a collective and harmless way. At the same time, the playwright, the actor and the individual spectator are caught up in their own personal inner dramas which all contribute to create the external ones on the stage, through a complex process involving mechanisms of projection, identification, denial, displacement and transference. Certainly it is in drama – outside the area of psychotherapy – that we are given the space to reflect on the relationships between circumstance (role) and personality (character) and the fright that accompanies such reflection when their contrast seems insurmountable. Richard III's question: 'What do I fear? Myself? There's none else by' (Shakespeare, *Richard III*, V, iii, 183) is one that we need to keep asking ourselves. The cost of forgetting or denying ourselves the right to this question is enormous, both to the individual psyche, and to others who may suffer as a result of persecution spiralling out of control. On the other hand, the price we have to pay for asking it, that of keeping alive in ourselves the unavoidable tension between our love and our aggression, and the terrible pain that accompanies such awareness, not only makes us more tolerant of, and less persecutory to one another, but also enables us to remain alive and in character, that is, to be ourselves. Perhaps it is time now, while on the cusp of two millennia, when thoughts of new beginnings appear, to remember that old Greek saying, written in the ante-room to the Delphic temple of Apollo and adopted by Socrates as a basic principle for his teachings: 'Know thyself'.

NOTES

1 Readers not familiar with psychoanalytic language should note that the word 'object' denotes the internal representation of a person (whole object) or part of a person (part-object) in the mind.

REFERENCES

Berke, J.H. (1989) 'National Pride', in *The Tyranny of Malice: Exploring the Dark Side of Character and Culture*. London: Simon and Schuster.

Blum, H. (1994a) 'Paranoid Betrayal and Jealousy: The Loss and Restitution of Object Constancy', in Oldham, J.M. and Bone, S. *Paranoia: New Psychoanalytic Perspectives*. Madison: International Universities Press.

—— (1994b) 'The confusion of tongues and psychic trauma', *International Journal of Psycho-Analysis*, 75, 5/6.

Freud, S. (1911) 'Psycho-analytic notes on an autobiographical account of a case of paranoia (dementia paranoides)', *Standard Edition* 12: 3–79. London: Hogarth Press, 1955.

—— (1918) 'From the history of an infantile neurosis', *Standard Edition*, 17: 3–122. London: Hogarth Press, 1955.

Frosch, J. (1990) *Psychodynamic Psychiatry*, vol. 2. New York: International Universities Press.

Klein, M. (1946) 'Notes on some schizoid mechanisms', in *Envy and Gratitude*. London: Hogarth Press, 1984.

Meissner, W.W. (1986) *Psychotherapy and the Paranoid Process*. Northvale, NJ: Jason Aronson.

Pines, D. (1995) 'Paranoia and persecution'. Unpublished paper.

Rosenfeld, H. (1971) 'A clinical approach to the psychoanalytic theory of the life and death instincts: an investigation into the aggressive aspects of narcissism', *International Journal of Psycho-Analysis*, 52, part 1.

Schatzman, M. (1973) *Soul Murder. Persecution in the Family*. Harmondsworth: Penguin Books.

Segal, H. (1994) 'Paranoid anxiety and paranoia', in Oldham, J.M. and Bone, S. *Paranoia: New Psychoanalytic Perspectives*. New York: International Universities Press.

Part I

Psychological

Introduction

We have collected into this first part five chapters which, in their diversity, emphasize how persecutory phenomena develop and are experienced. We are aware, of course, that alongside such psychological components we always find interpersonal, social and cultural dimensions as well, and indeed Parts II and III of the book analyse such perspectives in more detail. Here, however, the authors have concentrated their attention on how different individuals face the pain of being threatened or attacked by internal (or better, internalized) objects and how they attempt to protect themselves from them.

The authors of this section come from different cultural, ideological and professional backgrounds. The first three chapters are by psychoanalysts from different parts of the world: Salomon Resnik is an Argentinian working in Paris and Venice; Andrea Sabbadini is an Italian who works in London; and Ilany Kogan is an Israeli. Robert Jay Lifton is an American psychiatrist and psychosocial historian and David Edgar a British playwright. The themes they cover in their respective chapters, and the angles from which they approach them, are somewhere at the crossroads between experiential and clinical, but are also radically different. Yet they have so many elements in common that it is possible to identify themes running through all of them which provide a rich and complex unity to the whole section.

In 'Being in a persecutory world: the construction of a world model and its distortions', Salomon Resnik refers to the concept of projection as Freud first applied it to the case of Frau P., a paranoid woman. In working with such patients Resnik finds it important to make use of the *climate* of the transference situation and the specific tonality of the atmosphere created in the therapeutic relationship. After providing an original review of the history of the concept of paranoia in psychiatric and psychoanalytic literature – from Kraepelin to Freud, Bleuler and Money-Kyrle – Resnik moves on to present some detailed analytic material from his work with four of his severely paranoid schizophrenic (as distinguished from Kraepelin's 'lucid paranoid') patients. He concludes that in the

contemporary western world even the 'normal basic personality' has paranoid components.

In chapter 2, 'From wounded victims to scarred survivors', Andrea
Sabbadini considers his psychotherapeutic work with refugees who have
undergone severe persecution and torture in their countries of origin.
He looks at these patients' predicament from the perspective of their
traumatic experiences of permanent loss, which he contrasts to the fundamental impermanence of their condition as refugees, and argues for the
centrality of mourning as part of the therapeutic process. He also considers
the problem of the recovery of painful memories, in that those who have
been severely traumatized are often trapped in the paradoxical need to
remember what they only wish to forget. As illustration, he offers analytic
material from his work with survivors of torture who present with symptoms of anxiety states, sleeplessness and terrifying nightmares. He
concentrates on issues of transference and countertransference, as such
processes, common in all analytic work, become significantly intensified
(often in the sense of displaying paranoid connotations) in relation to
victims of persecution.

In the third chapter, entitled 'The black hole of dread: the psychic reality
of children of Holocaust survivors', Ilany Kogan provides an original
framework to the experience of the Nazi genocide by focusing on its
effects on survivors' offspring, thus introducing a multigenerational
perspective to our understanding of the mechanisms of persecution and
paranoia. She believes that the commonly observed persecutory anxieties
of children of Holocaust survivors stem from their collective memory of
it, and are coloured by its imagery. The mechanism of identification with
either perpetrators or victims is of crucial importance, and of course it is
repeated in the transference situation with the analyst, as Kogan aptly
demonstrates through her clinical work. More specifically, she suggests
that it is what she calls 'primary identification' that facilitates the creation
of a *psychic hole* in the reality of these children, which then becomes the
source of persecutory anxieties and fantasies, often revolving around
themes of death and survival. Kogan believes that work with these patients
should involve a modification of more traditional psychoanalytic technique, to include *holding*, both as 'holding relationship' and as 'holding
interpretations', of which she gives here numerous and vivid examples.

Robert Jay Lifton further expands the analysis of such phenomena
by considering in his chapter, 'The "end-of-the-world" vision and the
psychotic experience', three different levels of experience: the external
event (for example, the bomb at Hiroshima); the shared theological imagery
(that organizes the event into an acceptable structure); and the internal
derangement (the personal Armageddon of psychosis). Mostly with
reference to the well-known case of Judge Schreber, Lifton re-examines our
theories of schizophrenia, looking both at Freud's emphasis on narcissism

in his understanding of paranoid mechanisms and at alternative interpretations, such as those of Macalpine and Hunter, Searles, Sullivan, Laing and others. He concludes that the schizophrenic's self, flooded with death anxiety, disintegrates into 'a lifeless life', where existence itself is equated with the constant threat of annihilation.

Finally playwright David Edgar, in this section's concluding chapter 'Only pretend: the dramaturgy of paranoia', reminds us that acting implies pretence, or even deceit, and that all drama, as Shakespeare demonstrated, expresses a fundamental duplicity: tragedy is about broken promises, and comedy about ineffective disguise. At the core of drama as a medium Edgar places the contrast between character and role. The same might be said about the internal dramas of persons diagnosed as mental patients: once their 'inner objects' are projected on to an outside tableau, the characters and roles portrayed often take on a life of their own. Edgar demonstrates this development in his play about the 'resurrection' of the psychotic painter Mary Barnes, especially in the scene where she acts out the various parts of the Crucifixion while simultaneously painting it. In the dramatized escape story about the South African lawyer Albie Sachs, who was detained for six months without trial, Edgar depicts an instance of extreme persecution and privation. Here a circumstantial role has become more important than one's own character. Edgar uses this play to express his concerns about the tendency to see oppression as a psychological concept, as if it had no existence outside the mind of the person experiencing it. Metaphors, he concludes, have real meanings even if they should not be taken literally, and we must allow the presence of the visionary and the utopian in our lives if we are to have any chance of reducing political paranoia and the real persecution from which it flows.

Chapter 1

Being in a persecutory world
The construction of a world model and its distortions

Salomon Resnik

In order to write meaningfully about paranoia, it is necessary to go back to the origins of the concept of projection. The first use Freud makes of the term 'projection' is in his 1905 paper 'Analysis of a case of chronic Paranoia' in which he describes the case of Frau P., a woman of thirty-two, married and with a child of two. In her middle twenties she became confused and depressed. A few months after the birth of her child, she showed the first signs of paranoia: she became uncommunicative and distrustful, showed aversion to her husband, brothers and sisters, and complained about her neighbours. According to her, the neighbours were beginning to be rude and inconsiderate towards her. She thought people had something against her, though she had no clear idea what. Then she added that people in general began to show no respect for her and to do things against her. She complained that she was being watched by people in the street, who were able read her thoughts and so knew everything about her. One evening she thought that she was being watched while undressing, thereby adding an erotic element to the picture of her unwilling exhibitionism. She was describing a transformation in her world, which from our point of view could be seen as a distortion of the world-picture.

In addition, she experienced strange symptoms in her body. One day, when she was alone with her housemaid, she had a sensation in her lower abdomen, and thought that the girl had at that moment an improper (i.e. sexual) idea. These erotic sensations increased, and she felt her genitals 'as one feels a heavy hand' (*dixit* Freud). Then she began to develop horrifying sexual hallucinations of naked women showing the lower part of the body – the pubic region, and pubic hair, sometimes with male genitals. All this delusional somatic distortion added to her distorted transformation of the world. Here we have through Freud's description an excellent picture of the beginning of a delusional universe.

She went to Freud for treatment in the winter of 1895. Freud notes that her intelligence was undiminished in spite of all her delusions and hallucinations. Influenced as he was at that time by Breuer's technique, Freud

was aiming at removal of the hallucinations and treatment of her persecutory feelings in a case which he diagnosed as paranoia.

Freud was still placing his hand on his patients' foreheads (he was
following the Mesmer tradition of magnetism) in order to help them to
remember and to associate, and in this way make contact with their unconscious fantasies and fears. He suggests that some of Frau P.'s delusions
and hallucinations were to some extent based on actual facts – for instance,
the first hallucinated images of a woman's abdomen appeared in a hydro-
pathic establishment, a few hours after she had in fact seen a number of
naked women at the baths. Freud showed interest in her memories about
the past; the patient responded by mentioning scenes from her adolescence, at age seventeen or eighteen, when she had felt ashamed of being
naked in her bath in front of her mother, her sister and her doctor. Then
she was able to associate her brother with a scene at the age of six, when
she was undressing in the nursery before going to bed; in that situation
she had felt no shame. Freud suggests that she had omitted to feel shame
as a child, and therefore that she repressed her sexual play with her
brother (voyeurist and exhibitionist experiences). The repressed feelings
returned as shame in her delusional, hallucinated, erotic compulsion.

The patient spoke also about her depression, which she related to a
quarrel between her husband and her brother. She regretted that after
the quarrel her brother, of whom she was fond, would no longer come to
their house, for she missed him very much. Frau P. thought at one point
that her sister-in-law reproached her with managing things in such a way
as to make it impossible for her brother to come back. However, the
patient was later able to meet her brother again, but could not talk to
him clearly, and she thought that he would understand her suffering since
he knew the cause. My impression from Freud's account is that the patient
was certain that there remained between her brother and herself some
image related to their infantile sexuality which should be kept secret
between them. Freud says that he was able after a time to help his patient
talk about the various sexual scenes with her brother; these were related
to the physical sensations in her abdomen. According to Freud, after this
abreaction, the hallucinatory sensations and images disappeared; this
enabled him to formulate the idea that the hallucinations were no more
than parts of the content of repressed sexual experiences in childhood.

Frau P. spoke constantly about her 'inner' voices and 'inner' hallucinations – one of them used to say 'Here comes Frau P.' At other moments
the voices would repeat what she was reading in a book (this recalls Echo
and Narcissus).

Freud thought that these voices had their origin in the repression of
thoughts related to self-reproaches about her traumatic childhood sexual
experiences: the voices were symptoms of the return of the repressed, and
also a compromise between the resistance of the ego and the strength of

the returning wishes. Freud writes at this point of 'distortions' following Frau P.'s experiences with her hallucinated voices – distortions of her feelings and perceptions.[1] The patient felt criticized by her inner hallucinated persecutory world. Her only relief lay in her mental space, once the inner persecutors moved from the internal to the external world. But then she felt that people 'outside' were making mocking and critical remarks about her: 'There goes Frau P.' was felt to mean that everybody in her environment was pointing at her in full knowledge of her infantile sexual fantasies and experiences. This atmosphere of criticism and mockery became unbearable, but it was the price she had to pay for her projections. It is in fact in this paper and thanks to this clinical case that Freud describes publicly for the first time the concept of 'projection', the birth of which I shall now go on to discuss.[2]

According to the Strachey translation, 'in paranoia, the self-reproach is repressed in a manner which may be described as *projection*'. This 'repression' is a particular one in that it consists of the erecting of a defensive symptom of distrust of other people. Freud uses the term projection as a *pro-ject* – a way of ejecting (*Verwerfung*[3]) the persecuting voices (the self-reproach) outside onto/into the world; the movement is much clearer in the original German text, where this kind of repression (*Verdrängung*) is a transfer from the inner to the outer world – Frau P.'s persecuting inner voices were repressed (*verdrängt*) into the Other, into persons in the outer world. It is clear to my mind that Freud's original formulation, whereby in paranoia projection takes place *into* other people, *into* objects is a precursor of Melanie Klein's notion of projective identification.

I must draw the reader's attention to the fact that in the German text of his paper, Freud uses the expression *Wiederkehr des Verdrängten* (*Gesammelte Werke*, 1, p. 401), translated as the 'return of the repressed'. In the word *Wiederkehr* there is a play on *wieder* (again) and *kehr* (turn round); in terms of time, there is the idea of *returning* – and in terms of space, the space of the transference, it becomes a kind of turning-round-again acrobatics of the mind, recalling the expression 'athletics of the mind' used by Bion. This latter expression comes in fact from the French surrealist poet, Antonin Artaud, in his *Les Tarahumaras* (1955). In my reading of Freud, I can imagine a playful and living metaphor through which by projection the *Verdrängte* appears reversed and turned into the animate creatures of the outer world. We cannot, however, go to the extent of postulating that the psychotic loses his *entire* self in this way and becomes a non-being. Indeed, the feeling that one is turning into a zombie, a mixture of life and death, implies that part of the self is always there to look at a shadowy world, like the giant overwhelming shadow of Nosferatus imposing itself on what remains of the living self.[4]

AN ECOLOGY OF DELUSION

I find it important in my clinical work to make use of the *climate* of the transference situation and the particular tonality of the atmosphere – whether it is monotonous or changing, for example. The German psychiatrists who follow the phenomenological approach use the concept of *Stimmung* , which in reference to some French authors I will translate as *climatique de la rencontré* (the 'climatics' of the encounter). I should add that my aim is to understand the climatic of the transference, not so much in terms of quantity but essentially in terms of quality – the nature of the climate. For example: is the 'weather' cold, dry (dryout of feelings), or is there at any particular time a frozen atmosphere which might change into a warm and humid one? With specific reference to paranoia, this is what I would call an ecology of delusion. It often happens with very chronic pychotic patients who are emotionally frozen that when they improve and an opening for communication appears, the new de-frozen climate may be experienced as a catastrophic state of de-glaciation in which the danger of a prehistoric flood bursts out. I am suggesting through these metaphors the same idea as Freud had expressed in his recently discovered metapsychological paper (Freud 1915). When time that had been blocked or frozen, with regression to glacial time (Resnik 1994), begins once again to flow, this is often conveyed through a frenentic incoherent movement of an alienated and paralysed ego which greedily desires to experience warmth and freedom, but is not yet able to control this new 'transformation' with the appropriate degree of de-glaciation. This is equivalent to a wound which had been bleeding but is now covered with scar-tissue; when a *mental* blood-clot becomes de-coagulated, the fear is that the resultant 'mental bleeding' will prove impossible to stem.

The atmosphere of the psychotic's disturbed and nightmarish vision of the world appears in an exemplary fashion in paranoid schizophrenia. In Kraepelin's classic description, the disturbed element is essentially the extreme obsessiveness and cold lucidity of the patient, in which opinions turn into unshakeable convictions. It is as though a lucid zombie turns into a 'living' *statue*, a hard substance impermeable to any intimation of otherness. The particular *climate* of the paranoid psychotic patient is one in which people in his environment become paralysed and frightened and sometimes unable to breathe properly. We know through the psychoanalytic experience with psychotic patients that such individuals are themselves very frightened, but unable to tolerate their fear. They need to get rid of it through violent projection into other people, as I shall show below.

Freud was able in his draft to Fliess (which is earlier than the paper in which he describes the case of Frau P.) to transmit a picture of the *climate* of his time concerning paranoia and paranoid patients. He writes:

'The purpose of paranoia is to fend off an idea that is incompatible with the ego, by projecting[5] its substance into the external world' (Freud 1950a: 209). He goes on to say that two questions arise – one is the 'transposition' of this feeling (or relocation, removal in the sense of moving house), and the other is whether it applies to other cases of paranoia. For Freud, transposition or projection is a very common psychic mechanism. He seems here to be concerned with a quantitative increase in paranoia of an otherwise normal phenomenon. But in Frau P.'s case he speaks also of distortion of perception – and therefore of a qualitative or *substantial* aspect. Freud suggests also the idea of a clinical differentiation between normal and pathological projection, in which case projection has its place in normal life; it is only abnormal or distorted projection which participates in the pathological or deluded perception of the world.

In another paragraph of the draft paper, Freud discusses the relationship between hypochondriasis and projection. I myself regard hypochondriasis as a *projection into the body* of something which is unavailable for the mind. The old French psychiatrists used to talk of somatic paranoia in serious cases of hypochondriasis. Moebius, who is mentioned by Freud in the draft, said that people tend to deny what is endogenous, and transform it into exogenous. For example, a paranoid patient will say that he is being poisoned or hypnotized (or controlled, damaged, possessed) by somebody else. I would add the transformation of endogenous into exogenous could also be seen as a way of locating an inner climate 'outside' and transmitting it there. The hypochondriac patient shares with the paranoid the fact that there appears to be something external to the mind which makes him ill. In the same way as the paranoid patient puts fear into others, making them afraid of him, the hypochondriac gets rid of unbearable bodily anxiety or anguish (*Angst*) through projecting it into other people – thereby making *them* worried and upset.

In addition to making others upset, the origin of the hypochondriac syndrome lies precisely in the need for the patient to get rid of some unbearable fear of death from mind into body, and then into others (into their *minds*). For the hypochondriac, the body must be felt to be external to the mind. This means that he requires a 'perfect' splitting between mind and body, so that unbearable paranoid or depressive feelings in the mind can be projected/ejected (*verwerft*) into an organ. Thereupon, he can feel free to consult as many physicians as he likes in order to undergo all sorts of 'analyses' – except of course psychoanalysis.

HISTORY OF THE CONCEPT OF PARANOIA

In order better to understand the history of the concept of paranoia, it is important to go back to Freud, whose draft paper on paranoia was an original contribution, coming as it did precisely at the time when in German psychiatry Kraepelin's definition of paranoia was being widely discussed. According to the latter, paranoia is defined as a 'permanent' and 'fixed' state of mind, with conservation of splitting of a 'normal–obsessive' part of the personality which remains coherent and cold, together with the idea of an extreme obsessive orderliness. Eugen Bleuler agrees with Kraepelin about this inflexible quality of the original system in which logic is deployed under the shadow of a referential world (delusions of reference).

The concept of delusion of reference is important, and corresponds in German to *Eigenbeziehungen* and *Beziehungswahn*. These symptoms are the same as those noticed in Frau P. when she expressed her pathological 'free' associations (and free dis-associations) projectively and in a split-off way about her neighbours talking around/about her.

Freud discusses paranoia in connection with the affective disturbances that he was trying to understand 'psychoanalytically'. He was more concerned with understanding (*verstehen*) this kind of patient than giving explanations (*Erklärung*). I make this distinction in a similar way to that of L. Binswanger, who was later to become interested in the phenomeno-logical approach in psychoanalysis.

I find that Freud's paper on Frau P. is a very early and intuitive discovery concerning psychotic phenomena and in particular the way in which the persecutory world is experienced. In his draft paper, Freud describes paranoia as a pathological mode of defence, like hysteria, ob-sessive neurosis and hallucinatory confusion (this is more of a French conception regarding chronic paranoid patients). Freud says that people *become* paranoid (therefore he is thinking in terms of a secondary para-noia rather than a primary one).

Freud gives a further example in which he manages to transmit some-thing of the climate of a paranoid patient, and in so doing he anticipates the concept of transference psychosis. He describes the case of an unmar-ried woman of thirty, who had a sexual encounter with a lodger living in their home. When she went to tidy his room, while he was still in bed, she 'obeyed' him when he called her to come close and then put his penis in her hand. There had been no apparent sequel to this, and soon after-wards the man had left. A few years later, the girl fell (mentally) ill. She began to develop unmistakable delusions of observation and persecution (here is the *Eigenbeziehungen*): she thought that the women neighbours were pitying her because of the experience with the lodger, as though she was still waiting for the man to come back. She hallucinated that those women neighbours were mocking her, and saying all kinds of things to her about the man. This state was described by Freud as initially tempo-rary, with bouts of remission, but then it became permanent. Following Breuer's idea, Freud attempted to reinstate in her the memory of the scene, but he failed in this, in spite of the fact that he used 'concentration' hypnosis on her. My reading of Freud, particularly when he writes that the patient was merely 'obeying' the lodger, albeit sexually, is that the patient was describing a hypnotic compulsive state. The patient refused to see Freud again, because it upset her too much – and Freud concludes that he was upsetting her paranoid defences too much. He adds that the patient did not want to be reminded of her repressed intentions. Freud then asks the excellent question of why she became paranoid rather than hysterical or obsessive. He thought that she was blaming herself for being a 'bad' woman, which shows how the early Freud had an intuition about the existence of something he was much later to call the persecutory super-ego. Freud seems to suggest that the patient was avoiding an upsetting inner judgement by ejecting it into the outer world (*Verwerfung*) – that is, she was projecting her upsetting 'concrete' inner persecution. Freud uses the expression 'projecting its *substance*'. In the *Imago* text,[6] the German term is translated by *subject-matter*. We may feel that Freud's preoccupation was more to do with concreteness in thinking and also with body experiences of the mind. I would add that Freud's use of the term 'substantial' makes sense since this kind of patient creates a 'substantial' change in the family climate and in the neighbourhood – this is part of what I shall call an ecological language.

In 1957, when I worked in the famous Parisian mental hospital (Hôpital Sainte-Anne), I gave a lecture in the Salle Magnan on the conception of the world in paranoid psychosis, and on the possibility of making a diagnosis of the beginnings of the schizophrenic process. In other words: when do the vision and the 'climate' of the world change from neurotic to psychotic? When and where does this 'substantial' change occur? How indeed are we to understand the paranoid-schizoid conception of the world and its corollary, autophilic expansion? To answer these questions, I find it useful to go back to Eugen Bleuler's description of the moment and the circumstances in which the normal structure of the world becomes distorted and pathological. In his classic work *Dementia Praecox or the Group of Schizophrenias* (1950) he gives an interesting example: 'A paranoid patient had once *misunderstood* the proper name of the village in which he [*sic*] had asked the parson for help. In spite of repeated proof to the contrary, she persisted in the use of her own distorted name of the village' (1950: 133). In this example, Bleuler shows a healthy side of the patient asking for help, and a paranoid-obsessive part in combat with itself trying to *impose* its own distortions on reality and its *substantial* personal alienated/alienating contribution to the formal reality principle. When I gave my lecture, I was trying to understand (*verstehen*) and to discuss the phenomenological aspects of the perception of the world, in order to clarify in the discussion the whole picture – or as I would say, the landscape and the climate – of a distorted, changing world. For instance, at which point in time does a dia-logical or heterogeneous conception of reality (based on otherness) become homogeneous and uniform in a persecutory sense – 'all the neighbours are mocking me', 'the noise made by that car horn is a message aimed at me'? I find it easy to imagine now that some *misunderstanding* about perceptions and sensations can at a particular moment turn into an *unmistakable certainty* in the mind of the nascent paranoid person, in his need to 'expand' the substance of his feelings and ideology.

Money-Kyrle (1961) writes of the construction of a world-model and the distortions which such a model may undergo. He speaks of externalization of unknown distortions in the inner world, implying projection (projective identification) in a multiple way. He adds that the world-model could be represented as a *solar system*, with the ego as the sun surrounded by objects and persons as planets. This model, according to him, could be representative of a *monistic and egocentric period* in a small child. It corresponds also to a paranoid-schizoid model of the mind, and this feeling is no mere metaphor – in his delusional belief, the egocentric person loses the principle of otherness, and therefore the existence of other people's systems of the world, and the possibility of sharing common meanings and symbols.

For Money-Kyrle, following Freud, there may be a complete regression to the phase of subjective monism before ideas and other symbols begin to refer to anything beyond immediate experience. Money-Kyrle goes on to describe the intermediate shades of perception and reason.

I would add that at the beginning of a psychotic transformation of the world, the egocentric conception of the small child tries to impose its shadow on the present light of the adult world, in such a way that the structure of the world changes. It loses meaning in the usual sense of being a confrontation between different ways of being and thinking, and changes a 'multi-planetary' metaphoric universe into a single egocentric or ego-cosmic conception of daily life.

The French psychiatrist of Italian origin, B. Ball (who practised in the 1870s), spoke of 'autophilic' tendencies, in which the subject believes that everything which occurs in his environment refers directly and solely to him. This was an intuitive formulation of what Bleuler was later to call 'delusions of reference' (*Beziehungswahn*).

Let me now quote from some clinical material in order to illustrate the issues raised in this chapter. One of my patients, whom I shall call Miss Milton, whom I treated in the Cassel Hospital (Richmond, UK) in the 1960s, was sitting facing me. She stared at me, her eyes 'pointing' at me, and suddenly said : 'Are you saying I'm crazy ?' (I had not yet uttered a word.) She went on to say, 'I heard a voice calling me crazy first in my own head, then coming from your head' – this is a clear endogenous hallucination which changed into an exogenous one in the way in which Freud described projection (see p. 20). After a pause, she went on, 'Now it's changing. Now, the voice isn't coming from you alone. It has turned into many little voices coming from all around me and saying "crazy, crazy" in a gentle way.' The fragmentation of the inner/outer persecuting voice into numerous sound particles turned the *atmosphere* around her into a circular surround of sound and space, in which everything was related to her. The persecutory model of the world corresponds to a self-centred and auto-philic (Ball) structuring of the landscape and an expansive substantial invasion of her paranoid *milieu* or inner climate. It is as though the patient was 'throwing' (*Verwerfung*) and projecting (*Projektion*) the inner persecutory voice which says she is crazy into my head, whereupon it became split up into numerous little voices. These voices were softer – and so less dangerous – but they expanded to fill up the whole of the surrounding space and to alter its meaning. The patient changed her 'big' persecutory object into multiple 'little' persecutors – and this was apparently better for her. She was thereupon able to 'breathe' better in this changed atmosphere of small paranoid particles.

It seems to me that in paranoid transformations or distortions of the world-model, the individual loses his capacity to deal with alternatives and with otherness. Everything becomes contaminated by the lack of the capacity to metaphorize correctly and to symbolize experience. In other words, the patient loses the capacity to digest and transform experience in a syntonic hetero-centred way. For the paranoid patient such as Miss Milton, the world becomes more and more concrete, in the sense of a particular *subject-matter* dominating a world of thought. Her violent splittings and projections in the inner world were unconsciously ejected into the outer world. Thereafter, the entire picture of the landscape changes and becomes like a nightmare.

I believe, as Bion himself suggested, that during an acute breakdown, there is a catastrophic experience[7] in which the ego and the self, as a living substance, breaks into bits and pieces. In this case, fragments of inner experience ejected into the landscape become confused with Nature and with other people, in such a way that the subject can no longer recognize the usual form of the world. Further, some 'magical' phenomena can begin to occur – for instance the idea or fantasy of arborescence of thoughts and feelings becomes equated with a 'real' tree and its branches which look at and talk to the subject. This has to do with the projection of hallucinated objects, part-objects or fragments. I use the term '*fragments of inner reality*' in order to make it clear that during the catastrophic experience or the acute psychotic phase which precedes schizophrenia or paranoid states, parts of the broken self impinge on '*segments*' of outer reality, changing it into a bizarre landscape with consequential bizarre sensations and perceptions. An arborescent thought projected into a tree or into a forest can change into an army (like Birnam Wood in *Macbeth*); the concrete identification of an inner object or idea or image with the outer landscape is a kind of 'camouflage'.

Another of my patients, Leonardo, described an acute catastrophic breakdown in which the world suddenly started to change and turn into a real nightmare. One summer day in the south of France he was walking with a girl-friend, and felt that he would like to show her that he could defy the sun and the moon. But this mythological Sun–Moon couple reacted in a powerful and dreadful way against him. He wanted to eclipse the moon during the night, but the sun reacted together with the moon, and sent a terrific tempest against him. He began to 'see' that a dreadful shadow coming from the sun was invading the whole sky. A terrible storm took place, which made him feel defeated in his challenge to the sun-god. When he recovered, he became interested in 'stars' of theatre and television; he particularly admired the famous Italian actor Carmelo Bene. There followed a period in which he felt *himself* to be populated inside by several star-figures such as Buddha, Jesus, Khrishnamurti, and Carmelo Bene. One day during a session he told me that in his inner cosmic world the stars were talking all at the same time and competing amongst themselves, as in the tower of Babel. This was driving him even more insane, until he found a way to gain some relief. His way of resolving this dilemma was to buy photographs or images of his 'stars', including Christ. He placed these on the desk in front of him, and immediately felt relief. As the voices disappeared from inside himself, the images began to talk to him. This reversal of inner hallucinated voices into outer images enabled him to integrate aural hallucinations with visual ones, giving him what amounts to a more complete picture of his personal living landscape.

Another example comes to mind, that of a young female patient whom I shall call Laura. She described walking the streets of Florence with her father when she was sixteen years old; suddenly above the city she saw a great flash of light, which she experienced as a gigantic short-circuit. After this, while travelling by train, again in the company of her father – to whom she was very attached – she became aware that things were changing around her – this was another kind of short-circuit, this time in human relationships and the way in which other people appeared to her. She remarked that people were not being spontaneous, and were not showing their real faces. Her impression was that people sitting in front of her in the train were wearing masks. Then she 'realized' that everyone in the street outside was also wearing a mask. This led her to believe that everything around her was false; her total picture of the world changed. She became the centre of her world, and began to be convinced that everybody was hiding their real self from her. This was a projection outside into the surrounding environment of her own changing personality and her feelings of depersonalization (she was becoming a 'stranger' to herself). Both being depersonalized and de-realized (she did not recognize the world as being identical to what it used to be) was accompanied by an increasing inflexibility of her personality, as though she herself was wearing a hard and inflexible mask. Some of her friends, who noticed her sitting in the park with her dog, described her as a kind of immobile and immutable statue – even her dog looked as though it was petrified. She held on to her dog by the leash, as if she nevertheless wanted to keep some kind of link with the dog (the petrified infantile self). I could imagine the leash today as a kind of *filum* through which some 'electric current' of life and communication was supposed to flow.

When she consulted me, at the Verona mental hospital (Santa Giugliana), she was already twenty-seven years of age. She appeared to me to be a beautiful and apparently sensitive girl – though in a 'statufied' state. After a long silence, she began to look towards the ceiling. I asked her what she could see. She replied, 'an electric wire'. Then she added: 'There is a light coming from the wire, and the voice of a woman who is afraid.' I asked her who this woman could be, and she told me that the woman resembled her mother, very critical of Laura's illness and disappointed that she was not going on with her studies. I learned that her father was a university lecturer and her mother a famous painter. Laura had one older brother, and a sister two years younger than she. At one moment, she looked at the little table in the consulting room, upon which there was a microphone, with its trailing lead. She looked around, and saw her own psychiatrist, Dr D., and some of the nurses she knew from the ward in which she was staying. I told her that there was some truth in what she was saying – there was a real wire on the table, and probably her voice was being recorded, just as mine was. (This was indeed the case, and she had been informed of this, and also of the fact that some of the staff would be on the other side of the one-way mirror.) It was then that I recalled what her doctor had told me about the light she had seen over Florence when she was sixteen, when the sort of 'short-circuit' had occurred. I said that of course she did not know me; she understood that I was a consultant, but I was a stranger to her, and therefore unknown and dangerous inside her, so that she had to get rid of me and all the people listening through the wire as quickly as she could. That was why she saw the hallucinated wire near the ceiling (through projective hallucination). Through her eyes and her ears, she got rid of a persecutory link with the outer world (the microphone lead or wire) which was putting her in contact with a persecutory world, even though she knew we were supposed to help her. The short-circuit in the session meant that the initial transference with me and the staff together, was very important for her, an 'illuminating' experience – but dangerous at the same time. After that she remained immobile in her statufied state. She did not move a muscle, and this motionless state made me feel that she was paralysing her own feelings and e-motions, changing them as it were into a-motions. In my view, psychotic patients with strong paranoid feelings need sometimes to stop the world moving in order to defend themselves from a catastrophic relationship. However, since this takes place inwardly also, Laura's own feelings became petrified in order to avoid mental pain and unbearable persecution. Laura is a classic case of paranoid schizophrenia, which she had been suffering from for several years (since adolescence) – but she did desire very much to get back into contact with life, both inner and outer.

I saw her after this with her family, and her father recalled being very much in communication with his daughter, particularly in Milan when she was very little; something broke inside herself when they moved house, in order to live in Florence. The father remembered another episode from Laura's childhood: she wanted to approach her mother, who was busy with her painting. Her mother pushed her away in an apparently violent manner; Laura was very upset, as though paralysed, and all she could say was: 'You are not my real mother, my mother is somebody else.' Thereupon Laura broke off all relationships with her mother, and became more and more distant with her.

I met Laura several times in the presence of her doctor and some staff nurses. They showed me (with her accord) one of her drawings, called 'The Lady from the Past'. We were able to work through this painting; it appeared that this idealized woman (who was very well dressed and looked like a queen) represented the mother who was emotionally open towards her and not rejecting as in the episode from her childhood. I understood then that she was reluctant to accept a maternal transference with the institution and myself, because she did not want to be disappointed and rejected once again. This was particularly true of me, since I was not able to see her very often.

As her treatment progressed, she was able to become more permeable and less inflexible, and she wanted to return home in order to attend her father's birthday party. The staff were reluctant to authorize this, because she had attempted to commit suicide on a previous similar occasion (i.e. as she was beginning to show some improvement). I find that when such patients become more in touch with their feelings and wish to go 'outside', they require great care and sometimes increased medication in order to contain unbearable feelings. This occurred with Laura too. She was full of vitality but confused at home, and did indeed attempt to kill herself, by 'throwing out of the window' all her strong yet unbearable emotions – but fortunately her defenestration was not fatal, even though she had severe fractures. We then recalled that in one of the meetings with the family, the mother had told us a dream in which Laura's little dog threw himself out of a window. We understood that the mother had destructive unconscious fantasies concerning her daughter – she was always jealous of the close relationship between Laura and her father, and envious of her beauty and intelligence in periods of remission. We decided that if Laura wished to leave the hospital, it was unwise for her to return to her parents' since the mother was unconsciously envious and abortive. My impression was that the mother in fact had never wanted the pregnancy, and indeed desired to abort; she had only agreed to go through with it because the father was very keen on having a child.

The world for Laura was still hostile; she felt that her 'maternal world' did not accept her entirely. Perhaps her infantile demands and the feeling of being 'pushed out' and rejected by her mother did not deserve any real 'improvement' on her part.

Herbert Rosenfeld, in his papers on envy and destructive narcissism, shows how resentful and competitive patients prefer to destroy any chance of being helped; they refuse to give up 'the flag of revenge'.

Henry was a patient whom I had in analysis for several years since adolescence. He developed a particular hatred for anything which could represent a 'link', contact or communication. While still young he had developed a 'gift' for rapidly taking watches to pieces and dismantling all sorts of electric cables. He could not stand 'energy' and the flux of life; transmission of feelings was unbearable for him. In the transference situation, he was very gifted at 'dismantling' any sort of link between us in spite of another part of himself which very much desired to be helped and to establish a link with the world and with his own feelings.

I met him for the first time when he was nineteen years of age. He was in a catatonic state, absolutely blocked. He described himself as living in 'the iron age'; he felt that his body was a lump of iron, which had only the shape of a human body – he described it as being a 'heavy iron box' – inside which he felt imprisoned, but at the same time protected. He needed to be inside some heavy matter, because he was convinced that the 'cosmos' was about to swallow him up, and lift him off the earth and up into the sky. He wanted to be rid of this heavy armour, and of his iron mask, yet he felt that without it he would be in grave danger. He described himself as being not only swallowed up, but magnetically attracted to what he called the cosmos. I understood this to mean something like an enormous greedy mouth indistinct from the celestial vault.

Henry's autophilic tendencies were particularly strong, and his delusions of reference – his *Eigenbeziehungen* – were stronger along a vertical axis than in the horizontal one. If we go back to the specific meaning of the verb *ziehen* we note that it has the sense of 'pulling' (as in a magnetic pull); in Henry's case, this attraction was accomplished by strange forces or by strange expressions on the faces of other people. In the initial stages of his breakdown, Henry felt that people were interested in him – attracted

to him – or that he was being drawn to them. Later, he felt that plane-
tary forces were having the same effect on him – and this was when he
felt in danger of being swallowed up. I want at this point to emphasize a
degree of difference in his delusions. It began with a transformation of
the world from hetero- to auto-centred; then his delusional experience of
reference, and his suppositions and interpretations concerning this,
resemble what Sérieux and Capras (1921) called *délire d'interprétation*.
In my lecture in the Sainte-Anne hospital, I tried to develop a hypothesis about the different stages of transformation from a normal model
of the world into a distorted one. There is first of all an awareness of
de-realization: the external world has changed (at a particular moment,
the internal world also becomes strange to the patient himself – de-person-
alized). What is changing is his feeling of reality and of the structure
of the world – everything seems to be related to the patient, as though
his personality has become the centre of the whole universe. Thereafter,
the patient interprets what is going on in a delusional way as being influenced by other people in his environment or by ordinary or extraordinary
forces of nature.

With the treatment, Henry became less persecuted by these cosmic
forces; he became aware that there was hardness on the outer crust of
his body, and softness inside. He realized that his attacks – dating from
when he was a young boy – against any electrical or mechanical links
were an attack on his own 'nervous system', transmitting painful and
unbearable feelings and sexual sensations which he could not face up to
because of their relationship to his incestuous fantasies concerning his
mother. This endogamic incestuous link with his mother made him feel
his father to be an enemy and implacable judge; he would sometimes feel
me to be a judge and he would hate me for it, especially once he began
to go out with a girl-friend.

One day I asked him if he would authorize me to mention his case
material in one of my books (under a different name). He acquiesced,
and I asked him what name he would like me to use; 'Karl', he replied.
To explain this choice, he told me that before he was born, his mother
wanted him to have that name; but in one of his dreams the meaning of
Karl became much clearer (the dream occurred after I had in fact quoted
from his material in a paper). In his dream, Karl was a Nazi soldier
attacking and destroying the French and the Jews. Thanks to his associations and our efforts at understanding, we became aware that 'Karl' got
inside my book in order to attack and destroy all the work that I had
done with Henry. I find that Herbert Rosenfeld's ideas on destructive
narcissism (and my own analysis with Herbert Rosenfeld) helped me to
understand this disturbing period in Henry's analysis and in my countertransference (Rosenfeld 1971; 1975).

CONSTRUCTION OF A PERSECUTORY WORLD

These cases – Miss Milton, Leonardo, Laura and Henry – illustrate the construction of a persecutory world and the transformation of inner and outer landscapes and climate at the moment when the psychotic break-down changes the model of the normal world. I am attempting to show, following Melanie Klein's idea, how in the case of Henry the delusional tendencies and omnipotent magical transformation of the world is rooted in infancy – rooted in some basic misunderstandings, unconscious misperceptions and misconceptions as Money-Kyrle suggested. I would add that such misperceptions and misconceptions come not only from the child but are shared also by his parents. In the transference situation with Henry, I could understand – in the aftermath – that I misunderstood Henry (or I understood him only partially) when he first told me about Karl. It was only when he helped me through his dream that I was able to overcome my own misunderstanding, as well as his own. Thus we were able to link interpersonal transference with the intrapsychic one, and to understand together that Henry and Karl were two split-off parts of the same person-ality, and that two conceptions of the world were locked in combat within his Self. This helped me to understand my own countertransference and my position as witness, judge and fellow-actor in the drama that we were experiencing in our intimate transferential landscape.

During a supervision with Dr Bion before he left England for California, I recall reporting some clinical material of psychotic patients. I mentioned that I was particularly concerned about the factual elements which acted upon the mind of schizoid or paranoid personalities. What results is a model of perception and mis-perception, or of understanding and mis-understanding, which can play a major role in the genesis of the illness. I mean by this a confrontation between external and internal reality in a traumatic situation. For example, Freud, in his paper on President Schreber (1911) was concerned about the divorce between what was reported in the biography and the *raison d'être* of his breakdown. In other words, Freud was interested in the real facts or events which might have precipitated the psychotic regression. We know from Ida Macalpine's study that Daniel Paul Schreber was the son of a distinguished family, and that his father Daniel Gottlob Moriz Schreber, of Leipzig, the son of an advocate, was a famous physician and lecturer at Leipzig University, where he founded an Institute of Gymnastics and Orthopaedics. He was an educationalist and social reformer, with a quasi-apostolic mission 'to bring health, happiness and bliss to the masses through physical culture'. The father published a number of books, in which he attempted to convince 'the world' that his medical ideology of bringing health through concrete physical activity was sufficient, even though it left no room whatever for any emotions or romantic conception of life. It would appear that the young Daniel Paul Schreber had to deal with – from his early childhood on – a persuasively mechanical and rigidly moralistic concept of life. I would think that his inner world of childhood fantasy and playful tendencies was very stifled; the only way to develop his personality was probably in terms of a concrete and rigid truth which played no doubt some role in his identification with his grandfather, the advocate – hence his study of law and his later becoming a judge, so identifying himself partly at least with a rigid paternal super-ego. This may well have implied for him a continuation of his father's system of values, that of a moralistic (ethical?) mission – to save mankind. The father's mechanistic ideology of life left no space for emotional or personal social life. In Freudian terms, his concrete body ego made no allowance for a living place for his mental or psychic ego: in this conception the human being could be no more than a physical being, and so it was only from his body that Daniel Schreber could find a solution to the mental and social vicissitudes of his life. This charismatic father-conception of life with no room for mental space made Daniel's life very restricted, as though his body was confined in some kind of straitjacket. For the young Schreber, the father's inflexible law became a part of his professional attitude towards daily life, with no room for fantasy in everyday reality – only in his inner, personal, eccentric reality. One could suggest that his delusion was a way of solving the problem of how to identify with a rigid, obsessional and paranoid father – it was only through his delusion that he was able to have creative fantasies. I would suppose that he found it impossible to introject a good and flexible image of a paternal super-ego or inner father, which would allow him to take responsibility for the paternity of his own life and his own system of ideas. This may be the reason why he did not himself have children – other than in his delusion, as a woman identified with his maternal inner object or maternal super-ego.

For Schreber, the only way to be alive and creative was on the one hand to identify with his mother – a delusional identification which enabled him to be pregnant during his major breakdown, when his body was transformed into that of a woman able to procreate; and, on the other hand, the only possible alternative father figure that he could introject as different from his own father was Professor Fleschig, during a psychotic transference (the concept itself did not of course exist in psychoanalysis at that time). Daniel Schreber 'introjected' an idealized delusional father figure, thus allowing him to change his very nature and become pregnant – but pregnant with what? One could see his autobiography not only as a self-analysis and an attempt at self-healing, but also as a book-child to which he was able to give birth – an important book, an important child. The only way the paternal super-ego would allow him to live was through his physical body – and this is precisely what he uses in his delusional transformation when he becomes a woman.

One could hypothesize, as we follow Schreber's life through the different versions extant – his own, that of Freud, and the other major studies – that, just as in any delusion or other psychotic illness, there was something concrete in his family and social life which stimulated his own psychotic tendencies. In this sense, the concept of transference in psychoanalysis enables the psychotic or neurotic patient to experience his inner and outer world in a different context, with another person who is neither his father nor his mother; this will eventually allow him to question his early models of object relations, his conceptions and misconceptions, his understandings and misunderstandings (Money-Kyrle 1961). Delusional ideas of a persecutory kind have their roots in real facts, some of which can be very disturbing, and this may well increase the normal schizoid or paranoid fantasies of the child, particularly an already sensitive and perhaps disturbed child.

In his *Cogitations* Bion says:

> The supreme importance of transference lies in its use in the practice of psychoanalysis. It is available for observation by analysands and analysts. In this respect it is unique – that is its strength and its weakness; its strength, because the two people have a 'fact' available to both and therefore open for discussion by both; its weakness, because it is ineffable and cannot be discussed by anyone else. The failure to recognise this simple fact has led to confusion.

(Bion, 1992: 363)

I would agree that patients and analysts are both witnesses to this co-participating fact, but is not, however, ineffable for me. It has something to do with a concrete social context in which two beings, patient and analyst, each bring into the analytical setting their own cultural 'baggage' and system of values. When I say not necessarily ineffable, I refer also to the body language in the transference of patient and analyst, and the climate they are able to create. For me, the climate of the analytical setting in each session and the analytical process is a language in itself, in which old patterns of family and cultural atmosphere are brought back into the here and now of the transference situation.

In this sense, I appreciate some of the analytical approaches to the understanding of the family and its impact on its members. One could also extend some of these hypotheses to countries and cultures, and to the political climate – which sometimes can be a concrete pathogenic fact in its impact on the health of individuals. Melanie Klein wrote a paper 'On mental health' in 1960, in which she tried to integrate her ideas on primitive emotional development and different models of object relations with various social settings. In this paper, Klein speaks of the persecutory mother and the good idealized mother; the latter can help the child faced with the persecutory one. We could make the same comment about a persecutory father (Schreber's own) as opposed to the good or idealized father he was attempting to discover inside or outside of himself. It is interesting, too, to supplement this with sociological approaches of cultural anthropology which study the reasons and models of normality and abnormality at different times in the history of mankind and through different cultural backgrounds.

For example, some years ago, when I read Kardiner's conclusions (1957) on the 'basic personality' of our culture, I realized that about fifty years ago the attributes of the 'normal' person in the western world required the individual to keep within the necessary rules of existence and co-existence in a manner which I would call *obsessive*. It seems to me that the 'basic personality' has changed over the past few years and has become the *paranoid* one. I developed this thesis in the lecture to which I have referred in the Sainte-Anne hospital in Paris (the lecture was given in November 1977). Here I shall simply mention the fact that nowadays the combination of being persecuted and living in a persecutory world has become even stronger. Nationalist and fundamentalist political and religious positions have increased even more the distortions in the 'normal' model of the world.

We already know that many politically ideological activists and militants find themselves facing a crisis whenever they stop their activities. In order to avoid depression – both paranoid and 'depressive' depression[8] – some psychopathic personalities need to find another motivation for action. The ideology apparently changes (at least in part), but the dominant model of the world remains persecutory, to which by their own behaviour they actually contribute.

The clinical cases I have mentioned to illustrate my theses in this chapter are paranoid schizophrenic patients. The classic 'lucid paranoia' as described by Kraepelin is only rarely met with in everyday clinical practice – but we can find it in many contemporary political and religious leaders. I was able to treat analytically a few cases of lucid paranoia – but these were patients who came to me ostensibly for quite other reasons – for example feelings of depression or impotence. At first, they did not give the impression of being deluded, but I was able, for example, to follow up observations one of them made about the noise made by the ventilator in my consulting room: he said that it was 'driving him mad' – not only was the ventilator preventing him from talking freely, but he felt that his own voice was being literally taken away by the noise or *changed into* a noise. Thankfully, from time to time the noise would turn back into a voice.

I am convinced that in specific situations some of these 'lucid' paranoid patients are able to manifest their clearly delusional transformation of outer and inner reality. It is unfortunate that very few such patients actually come into psychoanalysis.

NOTES

1 Freud uses the term 'distortion' to suggest the idea of a mistaken perception or a wrong interpretation of reality. This has to do with what Money-Kyrle was later to call 'misperception' and 'misunderstanding'.
2 In an earlier draft of the paper, sent to Fliess, he goes into it more fully (Freud 1950a, Draft H, *Standard Edition*, 1: 206).
3 The French psychoanalyst Jacques Lacan uses the term *Verwerfung* (repudiation or foreclosure) as a specific projective or 'rejective' mechanism which he terms *forclusion*. According to Lacan, this mechanism lies at the root of the psychotic experience, and consists in the primary ejection of a fundamental 'signifier' (for example, the 'name of the father' – an internal object ? – as a rejected phallus) which is thrown outside, into the external world – i.e. out of the subject's symbolic and imaginary world.
4 See the 1930 film by Murnau *Nosferatu*.
5 Strachey notes that this is the first appearance of the concept of projection, and indeed of the term itself, in Freud's writings. (Note on p. 209, Draft H, *S.E.*, 1.)
6 *The Origins of Psycho-Analysis*, translated by Eric Mosbacher and James Strachey, 1954.
7 This is Kurt Goldstein's term, in order to differentiate it from catastrophic change, which is a later appellation concerning the psychoanalytical transference.
8 In paranoid depression, the dominant factor is the claim against society or members of it, who are felt to be the 'cause' of the depression. 'Depressive' depression concerns one's own responsibility for one's own ambivalent feelings as the 'cause', and as such is closer to what Melanie Klein called the depressive position.

REFERENCES

Bion, W.R. (1992) *Cogitations*. London: Karnac Books.
Bleuler, E. (1950) *Dementia Praecox or the Group of Schizophrenias*. New York: International Universities Press. His monograph on dementia praecox first appeared in the original German in 1911.
Freud, S. (1896) 'Analysis of a case of chronic paranoia', *Standard Edition*, 3: 174–85, part of 'Further remarks on the neuro-psychoses of defence', in German 'Weitere Bemerkungen über die Abwehr-Neuropsychosen' *Gesammelte Werke*, 1, Frankfurt: S. Fischer Verlag.
—— (1911) *Psychoanalytic Notes on an Autobiographical Account of a Case of Paranoia (Dementia Paranoides) Standard Edition*, 12: 9–82.
—— (1915) *A Phylogenetic Fantasy: Overview of the Transference Neuroses*, ed. Freud, S. (1950a) 'Extracts from the Fliess papers', *Standard Edition*, 1: 175–280, at p. 209. I. Grubrich-Simitis, trans. A. and P.T Hoffer. Cambridge, MA: Harvard University Press.
Kardiner, H. (1957) *The Individual and his Society*. New York: Columbia University Press.
Klein, M. (1960) 'On mental health'. In *Envy and Gratitude. The Writings of Melanie Klein*, vol. 3. London: Hogarth Press and the Institute of Psycho-Analysis.
Money-Kyrle, R. (1961) *Man's Picture of his World*. London: Duckworth.
Resnik, S. (1994) 'Glacial times in psychotic regression', in V. Schormen and M. Pines (eds) *Ring of Fire: Primitive Affects and Object Relations in Group Psychotherapy*. London and New York: Routledge.

Rosenfeld, H. (1971) 'A clinical approach to the psychoanalytical theory of the life and death instincts: an investigation into the aggressive aspects of narcissism', *International Journal of Psycho-Analysis*, 52: 169–78.
—— (1975) 'Negative therapeutic reaction', in P. Giovacchini (ed.) *Tactics and Techniques in Psycho-Analytic Therapy*, vol. 2. New York: Jason Aronson.
Sérieux, P. and Capras, J. (1921) *Traité de Pathologie Médicale*, VII, vol. I. Paris: Maloine et fils.

Chapter 2

From wounded victims to scarred survivors[1]

Andrea Sabbadini

... e quindi uscimmo a riveder le stelle.

[... and out we came and saw the stars again.]
>   Dante Alighieri, *La Divina Commedia*, *Inferno*,
>   XXXIV, 139

In this chapter I shall discuss some aspects of the psychotherapeutic work with victims of torture which I have carried out for a number of years at the Medical Foundation for the Care of Victims of Torture.

This institution, described as being 'at the sharp end of human rights', provides medical treatment, social and legal assistance, crisis intervention and long-term psychotherapy to survivors of torture and their families. Its orientation is humanitarian before being political, in the sense that those coming for help might belong to any political group, or to none at all. However, as is stated in one of the Medical Foundation's brochures, torture 'is not simply the exercise of sadism by individual torturers. It is often used by governments to suppress dissent by coercion and terror. Concentrated in the torturers' electrode or syringe is the power and responsibility of the state'. Through deprivation, or psychological, pharmacological and physical methods, the torturers deliberately try to extract information or confessions, intimidate individuals or even whole populations.

Some survivors escape to countries such as Great Britain in search of protection from further persecution or to recover from their experiences. The Medical Foundation assists those who seek its services in providing the evidence they require in order to obtain asylum as political refugees and in offering, free of charge, the specialized medical and psychological help they need to heal the deep scars left in their bodies and minds by the traumatic experiences they have suffered. Many survivors of torture just need to talk of their dramatic experiences with a sympathetic listener who can accept and believe them without feeling excessive horror, anxiety or pity; such 'testimonial therapy' has at times a powerful cathartic effect. At other times, longer-term psychotherapy becomes necessary.

The centre, founded in 1985 in north London by Helen Bamber, treats about two thousand patients a year, coming from all over the world. It has a paid staff of administrators and practitioners (including caseworkers, general doctors, psychiatrists, physiotherapists and psychotherapists), but it mostly relies on the services of a large number of honorary professionals like myself.

A frequent focus of discussion at the Medical Foundation for the Care of Victims of Torture is whether the word 'victims' should be replaced by the word 'survivors'. Both sides have valid arguments: those in favour of the term 'victims' insist that it is appropriate to acknowledge the clients' experience of themselves as having been selected for torture, humiliated, scapegoated and victimized, to recognize their sense of failure, guilt, passivity, powerlessness in the face of major traumatic violence perpetrated against them. They feel that not calling them victims would be tantamount to ignoring their wounds and denying their suffering. On the other hand, those in favour of the term 'survivors' point to the fact that those who reach the Medical Foundation are a minority who have – for whatever combination of circumstances, including personal strength, social resources and sheer favourable fortune – succeeded in leaving behind themselves torturers, prisons and repressive countries, and in arriving, not unscarred but alive, on the doorstep of an institution created to offer them at least some of the physical and psychological help they need. A compromise solution would be to see ourselves as engaged in helping scarred survivors to become aware of, and tolerate, their wounded victim parts; and in helping victims to heal their wounds, get back in touch with their inner resources and thus become true survivors.

If I were to compare psychotherapy with victims of torture and with other patients, I would say that in neither of these situations I consider my intervention as being a form of treatment.[2] In both I let myself be guided by similar sets of theoretical, technical and ethical principles, and in both I strive to keep an empathic, non-directive attitude within a consistent, reliable, safe setting, using interpretations (including those relating to the transference and countertransference) as my main therapeutic tools. However, the setting at the Medical Foundation is considerably different from the one I normally use in my practice. In particular, the possible presence of an interpreter in the room transforms the one-to-one relationship into a tryadic, 'oedipal' one; the use of the face-to-face position on two opposite chairs (instead of the therapist sitting behind the patient lying on the couch) alters the quality of some interactions and the content of certain fantasies, especially around issues of control, dependency and sexuality; the absence of a financial component to the therapeutic contract affects the relationship, in the sense that at times either patient or therapist may feel less committed to it; and, last but not least, the once-weekly frequency of sessions allows a kind of interpretative work which is different to what tends to emerge if the meetings are more frequent, especially in terms of the opportunity of understanding transference and countertransference phenomena.

I will not dwell here on the various theoretical and clinical concepts which are relevant to psychotherapeutic intervention in this field, such as 'massive psychic trauma', 'post-traumatic stress disorder' and 'survivor's guilt', as all of them are already abundantly covered in the psychiatric and psychoanalytic literature. I would like, however, to point out that progress in the psychotherapy of these patients requires taking into account another important phenomenon which I here suggest to call 'paranoia of the persecuted'. By this I refer to the risk that real traumatic events may go unnoticed as they get confused with delusional fantasies, with which they are often intertwined. For instance, a therapist may be tempted to attribute to psychopathology her patient's accurate perception that he is in reality being followed by secret agents, if that same patient also claims that a television film on the KGB contains a coded message addressed to him (a psychotic delusion of reference). Or, vice versa, a therapist might believe in the historical accuracy of *all* the events her traumatized patient reports in therapy, while in fact some of them are the fruit of his own paranoid fears. In other words, real persecutors are no protection from imaginary ones, much as paranoid delusions are no protection from real enemies. More specifically, identifying possible psychopathology pre-dating persecution, imprisonment and torture, and differentiating its consequences from those of the later traumatic experiences, constitutes a problematic area in the diagnostic, prognostic and therapeutic aspects of this work. Such work involves, I believe, careful, progressive and often painstakingly frustrating attempts at construction and reconstruction of the past, to be carried out jointly by therapist and patient. In this respect the relative importance of the therapeutic alliance (as a separate phenomenon from the transference) constitutes perhaps another difference from more traditional psychoanalytic therapy.

I would like to stress here the importance of *loss* for understanding the experience of survivors of torture. 'There is a tendency', writes John Bowlby in his monograph on the subject, 'to underestimate how intensely distressing and disabling loss usually is and for how long the distress, and often the disablement, commonly lasts' (Bowlby 1980:8). Facilitating the mourning process – bereaving the loss of country, home, relatives, body organs and functions, and sense of self – and thus re-empowering people who have been deprived of their identities, often takes absolute priority in our therapeutic approach. Furthermore, problems often manifest themselves psychologically as feelings of urgency, insecurity and impermanence, due to the survivors' social status of stateless refugees. Such problems can be explained as resulting from a need to compensate for multiple losses – of family and friends and comrades, of physical health, of psychological integrity, of social identity, of political purpose – and to restructure internal, as well as external, lives in ways that take such losses into account. The following is just one of the countless examples I could present of the devastating effects that loss can have on people's lives.

Jamila is an Asian woman in her late twenties, whose husband had been a long-term psychotherapy patient at the Medical Foundation with a colleague. Though not a victim of torture herself, Jamila had to endure traumatic years throughout her childhood. In particular, she had to witness her psychotic mother's several suicide attempts and eventually to stare, powerless to intervene, at her mother burning herself to death in front of Jamila's eyes, when she was a nineteen-year-old. She lost her much beloved father, who died of a heart-attack, only two years later, and she had to suffer separation from the closest of her sisters, now a refugee in another country. I believe these losses, though taking place relatively late in her life, played a major part in her current problems: severe anxiety attacks, various phobias, frequent bouts of depression, a desperate sense of loneliness despite her husband's affection, lack of confidence in herself. Jamila felt insecure as a result of her social isolation and lack of support from the extended family, to which she was used in her country, before having to emigrate to Britain where she was in much more precarious financial, social and cultural conditions.

Loss, unlike separation, is *permanent*, while the adaptation to new external reality, and the sense of new identity that people have to acquire as refugees, is by its nature *impermanent*. Their Home Office papers only give them 'Temporary Admission' or 'Exceptional Leave'; their accommodation is not secure; their new relationships are often just instrumental ones; their future, when not bleak and hopeless, is uncertain. A large amount of mental pain, fragility and confusion to which survivors are exposed is the result of this contrast between the permanency of their past losses and the impermanency of their present emotional, personal and interpersonal situation. Of course it may be inappropriate to generalize the centrality of loss for the understanding of all problems facing these patients, insofar as we refer to events dissimilar in their nature, or even when similar, likely to be experienced for a variety of complex personal and cultural reasons in different ways by different people. However, I am convinced that the idea of loss, especially when its finality is met by the sense of impermanence suffered by so many refugees, can help us make better sense of the social predicament and the physical and mental pain of many survivors of traumata.

Another crucial aspect in the experience of survivors of torture is the painful tension between the need to remember and the wish to forget. Memory has the function of reinforcing our identity by providing us with a sense of continuity through time and by connecting our experiences with those of other people within a social community. *Re-membering* can be seen as the opposite of *dis-membering*, which is, literally or metaphorically, one of the purposes of torture. However, memory of past events, like perception of the external world, must also be selective. It is equally important for our sense of self – for its integrity and its continuity – that our minds dispose of some experiences by forgetting them, as it is that they retain others over time.

Leaving aside neuropathological conditions that may affect our memory, psychological well-being also involves the faculty of establishing and maintaining the correct mnemonic balance between what is being remembered and what is being forgotten. For instance, a certain amount of painful experiences must be remembered for us to be better equipped to protect ourselves from the danger of similar experiences being repeated (e.g. a child should remember having been scalded by a hot radiator in order to avoid touching it again), while other unimportant or unpleasant events should be forgotten or repressed to make sufficient room available in our minds, as it were, for more important or favourable experiences. Events which are irrelevant to us or have an emotionally negative connotation, in other words, have to be selectively left behind and overcome. When this does not occur, as for instance in the case of abnormally prolonged mourning, individuals become stuck in a pathological condition from which they may find it difficult to emerge, feeling haunted by the painful memory of their loss.

Let us now replace the cognitive concept of memory with the emotional one of *internal representation* of the specific events to be remembered or forgotten. Such internal (or internalized) objects are sometimes acceptable to the ego and can then be integrated into the mental space, which will then have to undergo some restructuring in order to accommodate them. Other internal objects, and their relationships, will also be reorganized, all of which inevitably has implications for the person's emotional life. Sometimes, however, especially when the events to be internalized as internal objects and object relations are of a traumatic nature, the ego will find their presence intolerable and will use whatever defence mechanisms it has at its disposal to project them outside, displace them elsewhere, radically distort them in order to deprive them of their threatening connotations, or even altogether deny their existence; as a result, their integration will be made difficult or impossible. In other words, on the cognitive level we have events which can be remembered or forgotten, and on the emotional one we have mental representations of those events as internal objects and object relations which can be integrated or else distorted, split off and denied.

Joe, a seventeen-year-old African boy, came with depressive anxiety and a variety of psychosomatic complaints. He had lost his mother at birth and his father had been killed in the civil war when Joe was only five years old. An uncle looked after him for a while, but then put him in a children's home, where he was treated brutally. He was then forcibly conscripted into the army when he was still little more than a child, but he somehow managed to desert from it. Around that time, Joe also lost his older brothers, murdered during the war. At sixteen Joe was arrested in a church, where the police had opened fire on the crowd and slaughtered many civilians suspected, on the flimsiest of excuses, to be hostile to the government. In prison he was forced to stand in an overcrowded cell, starved, tortured and severely beaten on his head, chest and genitals. He was sure he was going to die. However, within a couple of months his uncle managed to bribe some prison guards with the money obtained by selling Joe's house, which was then also lost to him. Joe escaped, hid in a hen-coop for days and eventually was put on an airplane that took him to England.

This, more or less, is what he consciously remembered. This, more or less, is also what he wanted to forget. He felt that he could not adjust to his new life in London, settle down, concentrate on his studies, enjoy playing football, find a girlfriend, eat and sleep properly, unless he pretended that all his traumatic experiences had never taken place. From the beginning, an important aspect of the therapeutic work consisted of helping him come to terms with his past, painful as it was, so that his own experiences at least would not be lost like practically everything else he had ever had, but could to some extent be integrated into his present life. Even if he wished to forget, he knew that he needed to remember in order to retain a sense of self and continuity with his personal, family and social history. This eventually allowed him to take a more hopeful attitude towards his future, which at first had seemed so bleak to him.

As a result of the severe beatings and tortures Joe had suffered while in prison, he had also lost his health and much of his confidence in his physical appearance and sexuality, though in his case attribution of these problems to torture was made more complicated by the fact that concerns about the body are typical in all adolescents. In England he found a relatively safe, but unstable status as a refugee: his papers were only temporary ones, and he feared he might be sent back to his country any day; the flat he was sharing, and the hostel where he was later sent, did not feel like home; he could not study full-time as he would have liked to, due to his position as a refugee. Even more importantly, he did not dare get involved in deep long-term relationships – with the exception of his caseworker, myself and our interpreter, whom he described as his 'new family' – because they may have come to a sudden end, as they had so often in the past. Practically since birth, he had learnt that in order to survive he could rely only upon himself; this, while allowing him to develop a prematurely autonomous personality, also involved a painful loss of carefree childhood, a factor responsible I think for his intense depression in adolescence. Because of all this, Joe felt he could not plan or even envisage any future for himself, as any boy of his age should have a right to do, because he had nothing solid enough in the present to build it on. In his therapy, Joe experienced the occasional changes of time or cancellations of sessions, or the summer break, as traumatic events, because for him any evidence of something being impermanent brought about the fear of yet another loss.

Many surviving victims of torture find themselves, like Joe, literally torn between the wish to forget the traumatic experiences they have undergone at the hands of their persecutors and the need to remember such experiences in order to come to terms with, accept and integrate them in the rest of their lives. Psychotherapy, when such a conflict is brought to it, will become the arena where this struggle is represented, often in a dramatic form, and where it can, more or less safely, be at least partially resolved. Finally, one of the functions of psychotherapy is to help people remember, accept their losses and come to terms with as much as they can.

I would now like to present and discuss another case in some detail.

Harim is a middle-aged Asian man, well-educated, intellectually sophisticated and fluent in several languages. He had been a successful businessman until he was arrested and dispossessed of his wealth by his country's dictatorial regime that suspected him of political activity. Harim was kept in prison for over three years, during which time he was systematically tortured, both physically (beatings on his head and legs, electric shock) and psychologically (deprivation of all contacts with the outside world, mock executions, continuous threats and humiliations, having to listen to the amplified crying of other tortured prisoners throughout the night). After release, obtained by bribing his jailers, he managed to flee to London, where he was reunited with his wife and daughter.

Harim impressed me as being an open-minded man, physically and emotionally strong, if battered by his ordeal, and still full of inner resources. His left wrist, that had been twisted by his torturers, still hurt; his feet still felt sore for having undergone *falaka* (a common, and enormously painful, form of beating under the soles); and he still suffered from excruciating headaches, resulting from the blows he had received. He was particularly concerned about his loss of memory relating to the events that had taken place when he was in gaol. Harim was shocked to realize that while in the past he had a prodigious memory (for instance, he could remember by heart hundreds of telephone numbers), he could now only vaguely recall his period in prison. Various episodes pertaining to those years were recollected only superficially, or confused with one another, or compressed in a retrospectively short period of time.

Yet Harim 'knew' somehow that much must have happened which he could not remember and he felt that unless he got it back – and he asked me to help him with this task – he could never be himself again. His past *was* himself, and he could not afford to lose such an important, if terribly traumatic, part of it. As a result of several months of psychotherapeutic exploration and analysis, more conscious memories gradually began to emerge and his years in gaol began to take a more coherent shape for him. Harim described how he would often be taken to a pitch-dark, windowless room, tied to a chair with his arms stretched behind his back until they became numb, a blinding spotlight directed into his eyes, a man interrogating him, while the torturer would apply increasing physical pressure to make him answer the interrogator's questions. If he fainted, he would be woken up by cold water, or thrown back into his cell.

What mostly worried him were his sleeping problems and recurring, terrifying, confused nightmares. Full at first of faceless bodies, knives and blood and screams, these nightmares were gradually replaced by more detailed dreams, with real people in identifiable places. A still vague but important dream in which '*He had a weapon in his hands and was fighting back*' was followed a few months later by a nightmare: '*He was all in arms with some of his comrades in the mountains, fighting his enemies. Later, he was in a prison cell with two of his friends. A guard opened the door and threw in a man who had been tortured, his guts sticking out. Harim couldn't see his face. The guard laughed and said that this man had been beheaded.*' This nightmare led Harim to remember the time when a guard had announced that thirty-six hours later he would come back and take two of the fifteen men crowded in the cell to be executed, but without indicating who they were going to be. Two or three of the prisoners started shouting and hitting themselves and lost control of their bowels.

Some time later, Harim told me that, on the previous night, he had had his first dream for a long time which was not a nightmare, and from which he had awakened without screaming. In the dream '*There were some people having an argument. He intervened and settled it, and everybody was pleased with him.*' I noticed tears in his eyes, as he explained that he was worried about his housing situation; he had been told that the Council would make him and his family homeless unless he agreed to sign a contract for a rather dilapidated flat without central heating. He felt humiliated by the request, upset by the sense of loss (he used to have power, money and a large villa), and overwhelmed by his responsibility towards his wife and daughter, whom he could no longer provide with what they needed. As to himself, he had been in prison, and now he was free: he felt – and he said this with a mixture of pride and sadness – that he could now adjust to anything. As Harim could begin to remember his ordeal, he also regained his sleep and natural good humour, his anxiety gradually gave way to a more relaxed attitude to everyday living and he could begin to look forward to the future again.

In his sessions, I was mostly a silent witness who helped by allowing Harim to share with me the intolerable load of his suffering. In the context of an external reality charged with such enormous traumatogenic power, transference interpretations would have often been useless or even inappropriate. However, it was obvious to me that specific transference and countertransference dynamics were in operation between us. Harim's attachment to me stemmed from his close relationship to his parents, always described by him as loving, wise and just. His good early experiences in childhood must have been the necessary, if not by themselves sufficient, conditions that helped him survive his recent ordeals, and to form an altogether positive rapport to the world (however disappointed he must have felt by its darkest manifestations) and to others, including myself. This original basic trust made Harim feel safe enough in the transference and allowed him to reveal to me details of his experiences which at times amounted to very confidential information about the involvement of his country's government in systematic terroristic activities against its political opponents. The consistency, regularity and friendly atmosphere of our sessions, as well as my careful listening to, and gentle interpretation of, his anxieties also played a part in building up his confidence in the therapeutic process, especially as my attitude to him was in such stark contrast with what events in the previous few years had taught him to expect from people in a position of authority and power.

While negative or hostile transference feelings against myself were not prominent in Harim's relation to me, I know from my work with other survivors of torture that they can easily internalize the torturer – through the defence mechanism of *identification with the aggressor* – or else emotionally equate therapists with their persecutors; consulting rooms with dark prison cells; interpretations with their interrogators' attempts to extort information; silence in a session with the cowardice of the bystanders who had let them be arrested. The therapist, in other words, can himself easily become in the patient's, as well as in his own mind (through the mechanisms of *projective* and *introjective identification*), a persecutor, or a victim, or a passive bystander. Even if it will feel unpleasant for both patient and analyst, this is an inevitable and even welcome aspect of the therapeutic process, for it eventually allows analysands to express and come to terms with their own anger, resentment, aggressiveness and hatred. However, the emergence of the negative transference should not be prematurely encouraged and special tact should be used in the timing of interpretations with patients who have suffered severe traumatizations, the scars of which will require a long time to heal.

Another most delicate and difficult aspect of analysing people like Harim concerns the countertransference. The genuine wish to be helpful in therapists who choose to work with victims and survivors of torture is always mixed with a sort of morbid curiosity for the extremes of human cruelty and endurance to it. The identification of the therapist is always both with the patient ('How would I have responded to what she was put through?') and the persecutors ('How can I be sure that I could never do to another human being what these people have done to her?'). Furthermore, it is particularly hard to establish a correct professional attitude and, more specifically, to maintain the always precarious balance between an excessive distance from, and an excessive proximity to, such analysands. Therapists will either emotionally remove themselves from their patients' inner worlds in the attempt to defend themselves from a pain which they feel is intolerable; or, alternatively, they will be drawn too close to it and be tempted, possibly through an unconscious sense of guilt, to indulge in unrealistic rather grandiose or even omnipotent reparative fantasies of rescuing and saving them. Therapists might then idealize their patients if they see them as survivors or heroes, or take a protecting or patronizing attitude if they see them as victims. In these cases therapists end up enacting, as opposed to understanding, their own compassion through mostly useless efforts to provide humane compensation for what has been suffered.[3]

In relation to Harim, I felt the necessity to resist two different countertransference temptations. The first one concerned the timing of my interventions and revolved around my need to find out about, and make sense of, the horrific experiences he had undergone. I soon became aware, however, that my guiding principle should not be my wish to know but his need to tell me, and that he could only do so when he felt emotionally ready for it. My second effort was to avoid dealing with my sense of impotence by replacing what I could offer him – that is: a consistent setting, attentive listening, empathic understanding and meaningful interpretations – with some ill-defined form of practical support. For instance, I nurtured (and resisted) fantasies of inviting him on holiday with me, of introducing his daughter to mine, of paying for the telephone he could not afford. I am convinced that acting out such fantasies would have only resulted in the contamination of our therapeutic relationship, and ultimately in the destructive undermining of the only help – limited but important to him – that as a psychoanalyst I could give him.

In conclusion, in this chapter I have tried to present some of the issues involved in working psychotherapeutically with severely traumatized patients, such as the surviving victims of torture I have described. A careful evaluation of the potential in these patients for what I termed 'paranoia of the persecuted', of their desperate sense of permanent loss, of their ambivalent relationship with memories some only want to forget, of their need to be listened to and believed, of the recreation of frightening and confusing scenarios in the context of transference and countertransference dynamics, are all features of this most painful, but also most rewarding work. In the course of many discussions, my colleagues and I have often questioned the value and the limitations of our therapeutic tools in helping people who had been so violently abused. Yet I am convinced that, as we accumulate more experience in this relatively new area of therapeutic intervention, we should hopefully improve our ways of contributing with other professionals in supporting, containing and healing our patients' suffering, and in making the unbearable more bearable to them and to ourselves.

NOTES

1. An earlier version of this article was published in *The British Journal of Psychotherapy*, 1996, vol. 12: 513–20.
2. I have discussed elsewhere (Sabbadini 1991) my objections to the use of the term treatment in relation to psychoanalysis.
3. See also, in this connection, Sandler's notion of 'role responsiveness', whereby the patient allocates new roles to himself and the analyst in an effort to bring about in reality, through manipulation of the analyst's countertransference experiences or even enactments, 'the self-object interaction represented in his dominant unconscious wishful fantasy' (Sandler, Dare and Holder 1992: 91).

REFERENCES

Bowlby, J. (1980) *Attachment and Loss*, vol. III. Harmondsworth: Penguin Books.

Sabbadini, A. (1991) 'Treatment', *Journal of the Society for Existential Analysis*, 2: 2–7.

Sandler J., Dare, C. and Holder, A. (1992) *The Patient and the Analyst. The Basis of the Psychoanalytic Process*, second edition. London: Karnac Books.

Chapter 3

The black hole of dread

The psychic reality of children of Holocaust survivors

Ilany Kogan

In this chapter I want to explore the cycle of persecution and paranoia which is typical of Holocaust survivors and their offspring, as it is reflected in the therapeutic relationship.

The unrememberable, as well as unforgettable, persecution of Holocaust survivors' parents is often the source of their children's paranoid fantasies, which they feel compelled to enact in their own lives, as well as in the treatment situation. The paranoia of these children becomes in therapy the persecution of the therapist.

By acting out paranoid fantasies and delusions connected to the parents' traumatic past in their own lives, Holocaust survivors' offspring attempt to endanger themselves in order to conquer death, and thus become survivors like their parents. The persecution of the therapist consists of creating a stressful emergency situation in which they often put him in the role of the saviour.

The acting out of their paranoid delusions in the treatment situation (acting in) includes the attempt to castrate the therapist's analytic prowess by rejecting him and often breaking the therapeutic relationship.

Through my clinical experience, I became aware of the extent to which the children's affliction was caused by various modes of traumatisation, which were unconsciously used by persecuted, damaged parents. For example, the traumatised parent often became his child's actual persecutor, through a defensive identification with the aggressor. Children were treated as if they were reincarnations of the Nazi oppressors. Children who were slated to replace offspring who had died in the Holocaust were made to feel especially responsible for their failure to literally reproduce the dead, and hence were identified by their parents with the Nazis who had killed them.

Another way of traumatising their own offspring was by using their children as a vehicle for repetition of the trauma. Since the aggressive, destructive aspects connected to the parents' own traumatisation often endangered the parents' own physical and psychic survival, they were projected upon the child who was thus used as a life-saving device. This placed a great burden of depression and guilt upon the child, who often felt that there was no chance of hope or of a future.

The persecuted parent, though himself a survivor, was often identified by the child with the traumatic message which he unconsciously conveyed – that the world is an evil, unsafe place, full of pain and suffering, without hope or future. This message often shaped the child's paranoid attitude towards life, and could be examined through his persecutory attitude to his therapist.

Thus the persecution of the parent often became the paranoia of the child who, in turn, persecuted his therapist. By turning his therapist into his victim, the child unconsciously tried to convey to him how he felt as a victim of his persecutor parent, while being identified with the victim aspect of his parent. At the same time, by rejecting the therapist, because of his identification with the aggressive, persecutory parts of the parent, the child attempted to turn the therapist into his persecutor, expecting from him anger and retaliation.

From my clinical work, I realised that the psychic reality, the complex pattern of unconscious thoughts, feelings, expectations, anxieties and defences which these patients brought into the analytic situation was of an intense, persecutory nature, being coloured by the imagery of the Holocaust. This was communicated through the patients' use of words as well as their actions which carried unconscious symbolic meanings from their parents' past. The transference relationship often became a stage where unconsciously expressed themes of survival and death were acted out. The patients were protagonists in the drama of their parents' past, alternately playing the roles of victims and persecutors, and assigning complementary roles to me. Thus, the transference was not only full of meaning and history belonging to their own lives, but also full of the meanings and history of their parents' traumatic past. It is through my observation in the immediate transference relationship of the need of these patients to live out their parents' past that I realised the profound psychic impact of the parents' massive traumatisation on the psychic reality of the child.

The psychoanalytic literature dealing with children of survivors has described the mechanism employed in the transmission of the Holocaust to them as early, unconscious identifications which carry in their wake the parents' perception of an everlasting life-threatening inner and outer reality. Laub and Auerhahn (1984) in their paper 'Reverberations of geno-cide: its expression in the conscious and unconscious of post-Holocaust generations' stressed that the child feels compelled to experience the parents' suppressed themes, thereby echoing what exists in his parents' inner world.

In my work with Holocaust survivors' offspring, I have examined these identifications from the point of view of the transference relationship. In the transference, I have often been the object of a powerful process of fusion between the patient and his therapist, which psychoanalytic litera- ture referred to as 'primitive identification', and which is typical of Holocaust survivors' offspring, the patient not being able to differentiate between himself and me. It is this process of fusion which enabled us to explore the lack of differentiation between the patient and his damaged parent.

PRIMITIVE IDENTIFICATION AND THE PSYCHIC HOLE

The phenomenon of 'primitive identification' leads to the loss of the child's separate sense of self. This occurs especially in cases in which the child is exposed to his parents' severe traumatisation at a very early stage in his life, when the introjection–projection mechanism is dominant. The child experiences the traumatisation of those close to him, especially the mother, almost as if happening to himself, because he is totally absorbed in his parent's feelings at a time when he lacks an adult's ability to organise, conceptualise and articulate this kind of traumatisation (Greenacre 1967).

'Primitive identification' occurs on the fantasy level as well as in reality. Identification in fantasy occurs when, in his interminable effort to under- stand his parent and thus help him, the child tries to experience what the parent has experienced by recreating in fantasy the parent's traumatic experiences and their accompanying affects (Auerhahn and Prelinger 1983).

The living out of these fantasies in reality occurs when the child attempts to recreate the parent's experiences in his own life through concrete acts. In such cases, persecutory anxieties may grow into delusional fantasies of paranoid proportions, which include a loss of differentiation between self and others, past and present, inner and outer reality. These delusional fantasies may lead to a violent acting out which often shows a loss of differentiation between death wishes and frightening external events. I have illustrated this phenomenon which has been described by Bergmann (1982) and labelled 'concretisation' in many of my case studies (Kogan 1995b).

I would now like to put forward the hypothesis that the phenomenon of 'primitive identification' facilitates the creation of a 'psychic hole' in the psychic reality of these children in a later developmental stage. This 'hole' is the source of extreme persecutory anxieties and paranoid delu- sions.

This 'psychic hole' does not belong to the category of 'blankness' – negative hallucination, blank psychosis, blank mourning, all connected to what Green (1986) calls the problem of emptiness or of the negative.

Neither is it an 'absence of psychic structure', as it is seen by Cohen and Kinston (1983). The 'psychic hole' I am referring to is similar to the phenomenon of the 'black hole' in the field of physics. The 'black hole' is a body which sucks into it whatever gets close to it, by force of gravitation. The 'psychic hole' can also be seen as a body. It is the encapsulation of intense paranoid fantasies connected to the parents' traumatic past, which have an impact on the patient's entire life.

The uniqueness of the 'psychic hole' in cases of Holocaust survivors' offspring is in the way it is formed and the way it leaves its traces in the unconscious. In contrast to the 'psychic hole' created in the self by the denial or repression of one's own traumatic experiences, the 'psychic hole' in these cases is formed through the denial or repression of the trauma by their parents (a trauma which, by means of 'primitive identification', becomes attributed to themselves), as well as through the offspring's repression of the traces of the trauma. (I believe that in cases in which the parents have succeeded in working through feelings of mourning and guilt connected to their traumatic past and in conveying their history to the children in a healthier way, the children tend to experience much less a 'psychic hole' in their psychic reality and they are less tormented by their fantasies of the past.)

The child experiences the piece of parental history which is missing as a persistent wound in his psyche, a gap in his emotional understanding. This 'unknown' or 'unrememberable' part of parental history is what fixates the child's self to the parents' past, and is the source of persecutory anxieties which often grow into paranoid delusions and are then externalised in his present life.

I will present here some examples of such delusions stemming from the 'unknown' past of parents. In a case study (Kogan 1987), Kay, a young woman, the adopted daughter of a Holocaust survivor whose stepfather had been castrated by Mengele's doctors, communicated with me (in the first phase of treatment) through infantile drawings. One of her pictures, bearing the title "Electricity", was of a man with a wiry flower emerging from his head. Only later in analysis, when she was able to communicate with me in a verbal manner, were we able to understand her unconscious fantasy: the flower of death symbolised her stepfather's traumatic experience of surviving death by spending an entire night standing naked in the cold between the electric wires of the concentration camp.

Only now did we understand Kay's attraction to falling from heights as an attempt to enact her torment connected to her stepfather coming close to death and surviving it. Falling, for her stepfather, would have meant touching the wires, electrocution and certain death. Kay went to the top of a high building, intending to throw herself over and convinced she would survive it. Kay's delusional, paranoid fantasies of magically and omnipotently conquering death endangered her life.

The first phases of this analysis, which revolved around Kay's suicidal wishes and her fear of acting upon them evoked in me intense persecutory anxieties. The sense of emergency created by the image of a constantly looming, impending death, aroused in me primordial feelings of distress which I had to overcome in order to help my patient.

Another example of a life-threatening delusional fantasy of paranoid proportions may be found in the case of Isaac (Kogan 1991). Isaac, a young man, is a Holocaust survivor's son, who shot and wounded his father during the latter's attempt to save him from suicide.

Only by becoming aware, through the therapeutic relationship, of my persecutory anxieties evoked by the violent nature of his acting out, was I able to understand his paranoid fantasies connected to developing an emotional attachment to me.

In the later phases of analysis we understood Isaac's violent behaviour as an enactment of his delusional fantasies of his father's past. Discovering the fact that his grandfather was killed by Nazis when Isaac's own father was only a small, helpless child helped us to realise that by calling his father on the night that he wanted to commit suicide, Isaac attempted to give his father the opportunity of becoming a saviour and thus expiate his lifelong guilt. The other side of this paranoid delusion was that by wounding his father, Isaac was in fact identifying with the Nazi aggressor and thus leaving the child (himself) to an endless life of misery and guilt.

Children of survivors' fantasies often revolve around themes of death and survival. Since the wish to die, as well as to conquer death, was so much part of their parents' lives, it remained present in the lives of the children. The conflictual emotions and unconscious wishes regarding living or dying were often conveyed to the children through non-verbal communication, or through the parents' 'Mythos of Survival' (Klein 1981; Klein and Kogan 1986). This Mythos consists of personal myths and fantasies created by a person who was traumatised by the Holocaust. Thus the struggle with thanatic forces, which was often expressed through the compulsion to repeat the parent's traumatic experience in order to master it, became a compelling need in the children's lives.

I believe that the only way to transform the compulsion to repeat (which, in these cases, is often an expression of the death drive) into a cognitive mode is by helping the children find the meaning of the trauma in their parents' history. Looking for roots in parental history is not only an attempt to make the trauma comprehensible, but also an attempt to bind the death instinct by enclosing it in a meaningful construction. By working through this meaning and differentiating between their own lives and that of their parents, the patients may eventually achieve mastery over it.

THE HOLDING RELATIONSHIP

Working with children of Holocaust survivors, I was often confronted with the dilemma of how to modify the analytic technique so it would be effective in creating in my patients the willingness to look for the roots of the trauma in their parents' history. I believe that the generally accepted procedure in psychoanalysis, that of interpretation which conveys understanding and insight, is not valid in the first stages of work with these patients. It is my experience that, since these patients live on the brink of what Winnicott called an 'unthinkable anxiety' (Winnicott 1965), the analyst must support the patients' ego until they feel safe enough to discover and work through the traumatic past of their parents. In order to help Holocaust survivors' offspring mobilise their life forces and discover the source of their trauma in the parental history, I, together with analysts like Grinker (1975), Knight (1953) and Zetzel (1971), advocate 'holding' as the main therapeutic agent. I have chosen Winnicott's term of 'holding' (Winnicott 1965) for describing the way the analyst attempts to help the growth of the patient's self, because it is the closest to the mother's way of facilitating the development of the infant's self at the beginning of life. I refer here to 'holding' on two levels: through the 'holding relationship', as well as through the 'holding interpretation'.

By 'holding relationship' I mean a nurturing, confiding and reflecting relationship which is characterised by an intense emotional attachment and deep empathic communication, mainly on a non-verbal level. The non-verbal communication is often based on 'over-sensitive rapport' (Khan 1979): the analyst has to know how the patient feels and what he is thinking without the patient clearly communicating these feelings and thoughts in words. A very important quality of this relationship is the awareness that the satisfaction of some concrete needs might be necessary at this stage.

For example, I had often to change my usual procedure (I adapted the analytic setting to the needs of the patient) without immediately interpreting the patient's underlying, unconscious wishes. In a case study (Kogan 1990), the daughter of a Holocaust survivor's mother who lost her child in a car accident due to her reckless driving, I agreed to see the patient sporadically, i.e. on 'her terms' for a period of three months until she was able to come back to analysis on a regular basis.

It is mainly through this empathic communication which takes place on a non-verbal level that the analyst can convey his caring and involvement to the patient and thus provide him with some security in analysis, as well as in life, leading to the strengthening of his psychic forces.

The 'holding relationship' also includes a survival test, when the patient's struggle to face the traumatic past of parents begins to surface, and with it the enactment of the patient's paranoid fantasies in analysis.

The paranoia and dread of the patient now becomes the persecution of the therapist in a different way.

The persecution consists of the attempt to destroy the analyst's prowess by rejecting him and castrating him in his analytic role. At this point, the analytic relationship is often in danger of being broken.

I would like to describe my recurring reaction, my feelings of hurt, rejection and impotence during this difficult phase. First, I attempt to explore my countertransference feelings, and often find that my narcissistic hurt is due mainly to the patient's rejection, especially as we have both made an emotional investment in the treatment which has been going on for a considerable amount of time.

Following this, I often feel helpless when confronted with the patient's persecutory attack. By working through my feelings, I realise time and time again that my feelings of impotence and lack of hope during this period are in fact my patient's own feelings in confronting the past, which were powerfully projected onto me and with which I was identifying. My gradual awareness of this fact helps me arrive at the conclusion that surviving the patient's attack, i.e. my continuing to function as an analyst without retaliating, is vital for the patient's well-being (Winnicott 1971). This helps me remain 'alive and whole' and resume my therapeutic role.

I will here present an example of the patient's paranoia actualised in the therapist's persecution. In a case study (Klein and Kogan 1986; Kogan 1989a) I describe the analysis of a survivor's daughter. Her mother suffered a lot through the Holocaust, and survived it with a badly injured leg that left her limping. She also suffered from rheumatic fever which later developed into a heart complaint. The birth of her daughter still further deteriorated her physical and psychic well-being. When Gabrielle came to treatment, we were able to reconstruct, with the help of analysis, her abandonment by her mother during the first year of her life. Gabrielle left analysis after three and a half years when it was discovered, through psychological tests, that her infant daughter had suffered a trauma when left in the care of an inadequate babysitter. It was only after I worked through my hurt, caused by Gabrielle's rejection, that I realised that this was the patient's way of acting out her paranoid fantasy of being able to destroy me by her abandonment (the way she imagined she had damaged her daughter or her mother), or alternatively letting me destroy her by allowing her to leave analysis carrying a great burden of guilt upon her shoulders. This realisation helped me understand the necessity of showing Gabrielle that I could 'survive' her rejection and that she should not destroy the therapeutic relationship without giving us a chance to save it. I thus invited Gabrielle to return to analysis for a few sessions, during which we attempted to understand the reason behind her abandonment of analysis in light of her unconscious fantasies. As a result of these sessions, the therapeutic relationship was mended and strengthened, and was never again broken during the entire period of analysis.

Another example of the enactment of the patient's paranoia in analysis and my reaction to it is found in the case of Isaac, which I described above. During a crucial phase of the treatment, Isaac left analysis and thus broke the therapeutic relationship. Here too, I at first felt hurt and angered by Isaac's rejection. In spite of trying to help Isaac understand the unconscious reasons underlying his wish to abandon analysis, I did not succeed in convincing him otherwise. Only by working through my persecutory anxieties – my feeling impotent in my analytic role – did I realise that Isaac may have been trying to 'wound my therapeutic arms', in the same way that he wounded his own father who attempted to save him from suicide. This helped me survive his aggressive attack. I pointed out to Isaac that, in spite of his rejection, I would always be available to help him should he want to return to analysis and continue the search for his own self. This conveyed a feeling of devotion and strength to Isaac, which helped him decide to return to analysis later, when he felt the need.

In the various cases of second-generation patients whom I have treated, I have noticed that in this phase, when the patient comes back to therapy, the therapeutic relationship is mended and the treatment continues after a shorter or longer break.

The analytic work up until now paves the way for conveying empathy and understanding in a more mature form, through words.

THE 'HOLDING INTERPRETATION'

In contrast to insight, which is the result of a correct interpretation, the result of the 'holding interpretation' is a 'feeling'; while 'insight' correlates with seeing, 'feeling' correlates with touching. Thus, the 'holding interpretation', though being on the adult level of words, may be experienced by the patient as being touched. I believe that this 'holding' through words may have a mutative impact by helping the patient mobilise his life forces.

My interpretations convey not only the fact that I understand the patient's confrontation with the trauma, but also, like the mother who holds a distressed baby in her arms, they convey a life-giving embrace.

I will now present an example from a case study to illustrate the 'holding interpretation'. This episode was followed by working through the actual trauma and its differentiation from the persecutory fantasies which, in these traumatic circumstances, could have become paranoid delusions connected to the parent's traumatic past.

The case study (Kogan 1989b), involves Rachel, a thirty-year-old woman, an artist, the daughter of a Holocaust survivor who lost his entire family (parents, sisters, a wife and a child) during the war and emigrated to the US after it ended.

While she was in analysis with me, Rachel, after an abortive love affair, finally found someone with whom she was quite in love, but there was a great deal of ambivalence in the relationship. One night, while making love, her lover, Jacob, died in her arms of a heart attack. Rachel was totally distraught. She felt that she was a murderess and wanted to kill herself, but decided to call me for an emergency session. I saw her and listened to the detailed account of what happened that night, a terrifying story which she described in a voice devoid of emotion. Becoming fully aware of her tremendous guilt feelings and the danger of her becoming convinced that she really was a murderess, I decided to point out to her the other polarity of hate, namely love. I reminded Rachel that Jacob had died a graceful death in her arms; that death, which can be so agonising and lonely, occurred to him in an embrace during an act of love; that his death resembled his birth – he was born from a woman and died, in the midst of love, inside of one.

It was this interpretation which helped Rachel decide to go on living, not to run away either from life or from analysis. Perceiving me as an ally in her struggle for life, she was able to work through her unbearable feelings of 'persecutory guilt' (Grinberg 1964) which were reinforced by the trauma transmitted to her by her survivor father. My interpretation helped her undo the connection between her reaction to the actual trauma and her early delusional fantasy of being a murderess connected to her father's past. 'Before I came here, I kept thinking that I killed him,' said Rachel, 'and I couldn't live with that. Your words made me see the whole picture in a different light.'

I believe that it is Eros, the life force, which is conveyed through the analyst's words which often stems the tide of Thanatos, the death force. I feel that my knowledge and understanding of the power of Thanatos has greatly enabled me, through the use of the 'holding interpretations', to help my patients achieve a deeper appreciation of life. This is not to say that Thanatos disappears from their lives, but that it has been tamed by the life force and is under its control.

The potency of a supportive, nurturing environment combined with the 'holding interpretation' to strengthen the life forces and bring about substantial and durable improvement is documented by various case studies which I have described in my book *The Cry of Mute Children – A Psychoanalytic Perspective of the Second Generation of the Holocaust* (Kogan 1995b). The concrete 'holding' of the relationship, as well as the verbal 'holding', strengthen the patients' mental organisation to the point where they halt the flow of fragmentary re-enactments of delusional paranoid fantasies which may be life-threatening.

The result of the 'holding interpretation' is a decrease of the paranoid fears of the patient and the persecutory anxieties of the therapist. Since the patient mobilises his life forces, he is less threatened by death and destruction and, as a result, his paranoid fears diminish. Feeling less the stress of an emergency situation revolving around life and death, the therapist's persecutory anxiety also decreases. With the weakening of his paranoid attitude and rejection towards the therapist, there is a modification of the therapist's own sadistic tendency to retaliate and to become himself the persecutor.

The construction of an unbroken narrative – one that fills in the gaps of the child's knowledge, that permits the saying of what has been unmentionable, that interweaves the knowledge of the past and present with the realities and horrors of the Holocaust – permits the child of survivors gradually to gain some comfort with what has been split-off with unacknowledged affects and fears. The events and narratives that were the starting point of the traumatic wound of the child are reconstructed so that the split-off and diffusely re-enacted memory fragments from a persecutory world are elucidated and, as a result, paranoid feelings decrease even more.

This quest for information, whose purpose is that the patient give up living in the shadows of the past, is a difficult experience for the survivor's child. The missing piece of the parent's history is connected to the child's feelings of shame and guilt, and its integration can only occur now, when his self is strong enough to tolerate the pain and the repressed affects associated with it.

The quest for knowledge also serves the purpose of differentiation and the creation of a new and separate self. On this level it may be accompanied by torment and anxiety. Consciously, the child is afraid that his questions about the past will force the parent to re-experience painful, traumatic memories, which may threaten his psychic survival. Unconsciously, the child experiences his wish to know his parent's history as a step towards differentiation and a relief from the burden of the past, which he feels might be potentially destructive for the parent. This search is usually facilitated by the holding atmosphere in analysis, and by the patient taking the analyst on as an ally in this quest.

In some cases, the story doesn't emerge easily, but has to be actively sought after. The therapist's supportive attitude helps the patient find that part of history that will fill the 'hole' by searching for concrete details from his parent's past (e.g. Kay asking for her father's book of memoirs in order to read, amongst other things, about his castration by the Nazi doctors; or Sarah (Kogan 1995a) breaking into her mother's locked cupboard in order to steal her diary and find out some information about her mother's past as an adolescent during the Holocaust).

Both of us, analyst and patient alike, eagerly await the story which emerges from this quest and, after its rendition and its working through, living in a real world becomes possible for the patient. The terrifying 'hole', which was a source of intense torment, has been filled by a more comprehensible, although very painful story, completing the circle. Thus, the 'holding relationship' and the 'holding interpretation' break the unending cycle of persecution and paranoia between patient and therapist and eventually between parent and child, paving the way towards the construction of a new, more cohesive self.

REFERENCES

Auerhahn, N.C. and Prelinger, E. (1983). 'Repetition in the concentration camp survivor and her child', *Int. Rev. Psycho-Anal.*, 10: 31–45.

Balint, M. (1968). *The Basic Fault*. London and New York: Tavistock Publications.

Bergmann, M.V. (1982). 'Thoughts on super-ego pathology of survivors and their children'. In *Generations of the Holocaust*, ed. M.S. Bergmann and M.E. Jucovy. New York: Basic Books, pp.187–311.

Cohen, J. and Kinston, W. (1983). 'Repression theory: A new look at the cornerstone'. *Int. J. Psycho-Anal.*, 65: 411–22.

Green, A. (1986). 'The dead mother'. In *On Private Madness*. London: Hogarth.

Greenacre, P. (1967). 'The influence of infantile trauma on genetic patterns'. In *Psychic Trauma*, ed. S.S. Furst. New York and London: Basic Books.

Grinberg, L. (1964). 'Two kinds of guilt – their relations with normal and pathological aspects of mourning'. *Int. J. Psycho-Anal.*, 45:366–71.

Grinker, R.R. (1975). 'Neurosis, psychosis and borderline states'. In *Comprehensive Textbook of Psychiatry*, ed. A.M. Freedman, H.I. Kaplan and B.J. Saddock. Baltimore: Williams and Wilkins.

Khan, M.M.R. (1979). 'The role of polymorph-perverse body experiences and object relations in ego integration'. In *Alienation in Perversions*, ed. Clifford Yorke. London: Hogarth and the Institute of Psycho-Analysis.

Klein, H. (1981). Yale Symposium on the Holocaust. Proceedings, September 1981.

Klein, H. and Kogan, I. (1986). 'Identification and denial in the shadow of Nazism'. *Int. J. Psycho-Anal.*, 67: 45–52. In *Pyschoanalyse im Exil – Texte Verfolgter Analytiker*, ed. Stephen Brose and Gerda Pagel. Würzburg: Königshausen and Neumann (1987), pp. 128–37.

Knight, R. (1953). 'Borderline states'. *Bulletin of Menninger Clinic*, 17: 1–12.

Kogan, I. (1987). The second skin'. *Int. Review Psycho-Anal.*, 15: 251–61.

—— (1989a). 'Working through the vicissitudes of trauma in the psychoanalyses of Holocaust survivors' offspring'. *Psyche, Zeitschrift für Psychoanalyse und ihre Anwendungen* 1990, 6: 533–45.

—— (1989b). 'The search for self'. *Int. J. Psycho-Anal.*, 70: 661–71.

—— (1990). 'A journey to pain'. *Int. J. Psycho-Anal.*, 70: 629–40. Reprinted in *Libro Anual de Psicoanalisis* (1991).

—— (1991). 'From acting out to words and meaning'. *Int. J. Psycho-Anal.*, 73: 455–67. In *Psychoanalysis in Europe*, Bulletin 39, autumn, 1992, pp. 3–21.

—— (1995a). 'Love and the heritage of the past'. *Int. J. Psycho-Anal.*, 76: 805–23.

—— (1995b). *The Cry of Mute Children – A Psychoanalytic Perspective of the Second Generation of the Holocaust*. London and New York: Free Association Books.

Laub, D. and Auerhahn, N.C. (1984). 'Reverberations of genocide: its expression in the conscious and unconscious of post-Holocaust generations'. In *Psychoanalytic Reflections on the Holocaust: Selected Essays*, ed. Steven A. Luel and Paul Marcus. New York: University of Denver and Ktav Publishing House Inc.

Winnicott, D.W. (1965). *The Maturational Processes and the Facilitating Environment*. New York: International Universities Press.
—— (1971). 'The use of an object and relating through identification'. In *Playing and Reality*. London: Tavistock Publications.
Zetzel, E.R. (1971). 'A developmental approach to the borderline patient'. *Amer. J. Psychiat.*, 127: 867–71.

Chapter 4

The 'end-of-the-world' vision and the psychotic experience

Robert Jay Lifton

End-of-the-world imagery takes us to the heart of contemporary threat, psychological theory and man's ultimate role in his own and society's destiny. In order to understand this, three levels of experience must be distinguished.

There is, first, the external event, such as the bomb at Hiroshima. Second, there is the shared theological imagery, or eschatology, that renders such imagery acceptable as it is imbued with meaning which gives it structure. Finally, there is the internal derangement – the intrapsychic disintegration or personal armageddon of psychosis found especially but not exclusively in certain schizophrenic disorders.

All three of the elements are present in the Hiroshima experience. There is an overwhelming external event and there is an internal experience, something like internal breakdown or overwhelming psychological trauma. There are, as well, immediate and lasting struggles with belief systems, which start from the moment of encounter with the external threat.

The same is even true in regard to schizophrenia. We generally think of schizophrenia as a strictly internal derangement, but it too is subject to external influences, and to the struggle for some kind of meaning structure. Hence, the content, style and impact upon others – the dialogue or nondialogue between schizophrenic people and society – vary enormously with historical time and place. Correspondingly, the end-of-the-world imagery of schizophrenia is strongly affected by historical and technological contexts[1].

In pursuing the nature of the threat in schizophrenia, we do well to turn to Freud. Freud was mostly a conquistador of the neuroses, and was not, as he often pointed out, a psychiatrist professionally weaned on schizophrenia. He did theorize considerably on psychosis, though his concepts have been looked at more critically here than in relationship to neurosis. But we do well to try to understand what he was after, and for that purpose we must turn once more to the problem of narcissism and its relationship to schizophrenia.

Schizophrenia is the example par excellence of Freud's invocation of narcissism to account for what we would speak of as intrapsychic disintegration (Freud 1914: 74). He was quite explicit about doing so on behalf of libido theory. Freud understood schizophrenia to result from a reversal of the path of libido: 'The libido that has been withdrawn from the external world has been directed to the ego'. Adult 'megalomania' of schizophrenia was then 'a form of "secondary narcissism" ... superimposed upon a primary narcissism,' which Freud considered a 'half-way phase between autoerotism and object-love,' during which the young child directed his libido toward his own body (Freud 1911: 60–1).

Freud first introduced the concept in connection with his analysis of the mechanism of paranoia: his stress on the 'homosexual wish' behind paranoia and delusions of persecution, and the relationship between narcissism and these homosexual tendencies. The celebrated 'Schreber case,' based upon this distinguished jurist's *Memoirs* of his paranoid psychosis, was the basis for Freud's elaborate conceptual web: Schreber's 'passive homosexual wish fantasy,' directed toward his physician, as the 'exciting cause' of the psychosis; the prior 'father-complex' behind this erotic longing: the unacceptability of the proposition 'I (a man) love him (a man)' leading to the contradictory proposition 'I do not love him, I hate him,' and then, via projection, 'He hates me'; and the attachment to the ego of 'liberated libido' so that it is used 'for the aggrandisement of the ego' (megalomania), based on a developmental *'fixation at the state of narcissism'* (Macalpine and Hunter 1955: 372–4).

Two later psychoanalytic students of the Schreber *Memoirs* take issue with Freud and stress instead the theme of 'soul murder' and associated issues around death and continuity. Indeed, Schreber, in explaining the soul murder he believed perpetrated on himself, speaks precisely within our own paradigm:

> the idea is widespread in the folk-lore and poetry of all peoples that it is somehow possible to take possession of another person's soul in order to prolong one's life at another soul's expense, or to secure some other advantages which outlast death.
>
> (Freud 1911: 55)

Macalpine and Hunter tell us that soul murder or theft of soul substance meant 'denying the Schreber family, i.e., himself, offspring because the life substance which God gives to all human beings to perpetuate themselves was taken away,' so that 'Schreber, being without children, was excluded from the eternal cycle of life.' Not only the self was being annihilated, but so was all possibility of larger human connection.

They saw in this an explanation for Schreber's 'end of the world' fantasy, as well as his delusion that he was immortal: 'A person without a soul, i.e., life substance, cannot die.' Schreber's delusion of world catastrophe is required for him to become the ultimate or 'sole survivor to renew mankind' (Macalpine and Hunter 1955: 379).

Schreber's 'procreation fantasies,' which were indeed prominent, were a component of the total sense of annihilation conveyed in the image of soul murder. Macalpine and Hunter point out that Freud could 'make nothing' of that image, but that its combination of prominence and yet obscurity in the *Memoirs* is 'perhaps evidence that it was the centre of his psychosis.'

PARANOIA AND THE DENIAL OF DEATH

Years later Harold Searles made similar observations on the basis of his painstaking therapeutic work with schizophrenics. He was struck by the fact that the 'very mundane, universal factor of human mortality' seems to be a major source of anxiety in 'this overtly most exotic of psychopathological processes' (Searles 1965: 488–9). He came, in fact, to believe that people 'became, and . . . long remained, schizophrenic . . . largely or wholly . . . *in order to avoid facing*, among other aspects of internal and external reality, the fact that life is finite.' Important to this denial is a combination of actual death encounters (a loss, through death, in childhood of a parent, nursemaid, or sibling 'of the deepest value to him'); and a pervasive sense of life as unlived and, one might say, unlivable (parents will die before he can ever feel related to them, or he himself is in middle life with little expectation of 'fully living'). In the absence of the experience of promise of vitality, death can only be anticipated as premature, and therefore radically threatening.

Consequently, the schizophrenic inserts into his lurid delusional system 'a kind of colourless rider-clause' – an ingredient which represents a denial of the finitude of life. It contains the idea that 'People don't die . . . but in actuality are simply "changed", "moved about from place to place" . . .' More than that, the schizophrenic is likely to feel himself 'totally responsible *for* death itself,' to feel either that he carries 'the seeds of mankind's destruction in his own breast' or that he is (via his delusions) God or else hears (via his hallucinations) God's voice and has become his agent in such matters. Searles points out that this compensatory omnipotence aims at the related claim of immortality. The schizophrenic makes that claim in a variety of ways, but behind it is the fact that 'many if not all of them are unable to experience themselves, consistently, as being *alive*.' Feelings of immortality are enhanced because 'One need not fear death so long as one feels dead anyway; one has, subjectively, nothing to lose through death' (Searles 1965: 492, 500, 495). (We are again reminded of the Musselmänn, for whom death is not really death.)

Searles suggests here that both the inner death and the claim to immortality are ways of defending against the inability to accept actual death.

While this can certainly be true, I would, from the standpoint of our paradigm, put the matter in a slightly different way. The inner death or absence of vitality on an immediate level parallels severed larger connections on an ultimate level. Immortality must be literalized – and therefore rendered delusional – because it cannot be symbolized (rendered psychically real). Behind both experiential deadness and literalized immortality is something close to Schreber's 'soul murder,' something close to perpetual dread of annihilation.

All this brings us back to our critical distinctions between such annihilation and Freud's view of narcissism. Freud attributed the severity of schizophrenic symptoms to the predominance of narcissism. He spoke both of 'fixation points for the libido' at its earliest (narcissistic) phases of development, as well as regression to this primitive narcissism 'to which dementia praecox returns in its final outcome' (Freud 1915: 421). Indeed, Freud placed schizophrenia among the 'narcissistic neuroses,' which he considered virtually untreatable by psychoanalysis precisely because the predominance of narcissism prevented the necessary 'transference' between analyst and patient (in contract to 'transference neuroses,' such as hysteria, obsessive-compulsive states, and phobias, in which psychoanalysis is more specifically indicated precisely because that transference is more readily achievable).

More generally, Freud associated narcissism with immortality, injury, and even death. The attitude of affectionate parents toward their children is to be understood as 'a revival and reproduction of their narcissism, which they have long since abandoned.' And, 'At the most touchy point in the narcissistic system, the immortality of the ego, which is so hard pressed by reality, security is achieved by taking refuge in the child' (Freud 1914: 90–1). Here Freud almost comes to a principle of symbolized immortality, but must subsume any such imagery to infantile-instinctual sources – so that 'Parental love ... is nothing but the parents' narcissism born again ...' Freud is employing the concept of narcissism to connect with *his* immortalizing principle, that of libido, on the one hand, and *anyone's imagery* of immortality, on the other.

Thus, in one of his final writings, Freud equated what he called 'narcissistic mortifications' with 'early injuries to the ego' (Freud 1939: 74). These 'injuries to the ego' are death equivalents, perhaps mainly imagery of annihilation. But if any psychic injury is to be equated with 'narcissistic mortification' (literally the death of narcissism), then narcissism becomes nothing short of a psychic life force, a kind of accumulation of libido that provides the energy for, and confidence in, self and world necessary for ongoing existence. Thus, with narcissism, Freud has it all ways. Narcissism, along with its vicissitudes, comes to substitute for breakdown and death on the one hand, and the symbolization of continuing life on the other.

Yet, even if Freud substituted narcissism for disintegration, his use of the word pointed to a consistent feature of schizophrenia having to do with a breakdown in self-world relationship which we have called radical uncentering and ungrounding, Lidz has called egocentricity, Bleuler called autism, and which is at the heart of the classically described phenomenon of 'ideas of reference' (and its twin, 'ideas of influence'). 'Things seem to have hidden meanings, neutral individuals are suddenly animated with strange ideas and designs, curious connections between feelings and perceptions are experienced . . . [and] everything experienced is measured as to its possible relevance for the individual.' Suspicion of possible relevance then proceeds to the 'idea of reference,' the individual's cognitive certainty 'that this or that object, person, event, or transaction (an upheaval in a distant country, a public statement reported in the newspapers, a conversation between two strangers) is directed at, and has special meaning for, him. That shift to the 'idea of reference' can be understood as 'the cardinal characteristic of psychotic experience' (Bowers 1968: 348–55). At that point in acute psychotic experience, one can observe the 'depatterning' and 'destructuring' of the sense of self. This point of psychotic break, according to Harry Stack Sullivan, followed upon 'a disaster to self-esteem' and was 'attended subjectively by the state . . . of *panic*' (Sullivan 1962: 198).

We would understand the moment, in terms of death equivalents, to be one in which the fear of annihilation gives way to the experience of disintegration.

That shift to the fixed idea of reference is also the movement into paranoia. We have discussed, in connection with the Schreber case, our own death-centred revision of Freud's libido-centred (struggle-against-homosexuality) view of paranoia. A survivor-like 'suspicion of counterfeit nurturance' characterizes much of paranoia. That interpretation is consistent with Lionel Ovesey's suggestion that 'the . . . power (aggression) motivation . . . is the constant feature in paranoid phenomenon . . . and . . . the essential related anxiety is, therefore, a survival anxiety.' What Ovesey means by survival anxiety is close to what we mean by death anxiety or fear of annihilation; and he understands this anxiety to result from a sequence of frustrated dependency, extreme aggression, and symbolic distortion, until the feeling 'I want to kill him' becomes converted to 'He wants to kill me' (Ovesey 1955: 163–73). All this is connected with disintegrative imagery at the onset of psychosis, and its relationship to questions of meaning.

An additional issue for a death-related approach to the sense of threat in schizophrenia has been the 'end-of-the-world' fantasy, also first discussed in relationship to the Schreber case. The meaning of this fantasy was at issue in Jung's questioning of the application of libido theory to schizophrenia (which had much to do with Freud's invocation of narcissism in defence of that theory). Jung's point was that the fantasy expressed the psychotic's withdrawal of all interests from the external world, not just his sexuality, and argued, on that basis, for a more general (more than a merely sexual) understanding of the entire concept of libido (Selesnick 1963: 350–6). In a more death-centred age, however, we would expect to encounter harsher views of the meaning of this fantasy.[2]

Related to the question of threat is the relationship of depression to schizophrenia. Recent work has emphasized the close association of the two, and especially the presence of severe depression both at the time of schizophrenic breakdown and immediately following reintegration or recovery from psychosis. It would seem that depression is prominent at the transition points in and out of psychosis – or perhaps more specifically in and out of paranoia (Donlon 1976: 1265–74).

Some writers have gone further and emphasized the 'depressive core' in schizophrenic patients, or spoken of the condition itself (at least in certain instances) as 'a depressive equivalent' (Levin 1971: 219–29). In discussing their differences, we have emphasized the question of blame. We could in fact understand the paranoid shift into psychosis in terms of an equation put forward by Sullivan: 'It is not that I have something wrong with me, but that he does something to me.' Sullivan in fact considered the 'essence' of this 'paranoid dynamism' to be 'the transference of blame' (Sullivan 1956: 146).

But why the shift? Actually, nobody knows for certain. Searles, however, has suggested an interesting possibility. He says of the schizophrenic that 'the losses which he has already experienced have come too early in his development, and in too great magnitude, for him to have been able to integrate them.' Under those extreme conditions were he 'to experience his sense of loss fully ... he would experience a feeling, not of "loss" in the mature sense, but of disintegration of the total self.' His defence is to assert omnipotence, 'his conviction that he has suffered no loss, and that it is unthinkable that he could ever suffer loss, for he is the whole world' (Searles 1965: 497).

We spoke of depression itself and its mimetic death as a means of avoiding a feeling of loss. The implication here is that schizophrenia carries the avoidance of that feeling to greater extremes, or, one could say, invokes greater deformations in the service of that avoidance. No one can say whether it is a question only, or even mainly, of losses – though that assumption is very much in keeping with our view of depression as the essence of mental disturbance. There does seem to be, as we have emphasized, the special dimension of 'soul murder' or disintegrative death equivalent in schizophrenia, whose ultimate origin is unclear, and can indeed include genetically transmitted vulnerabilities. But from the standpoint of psychological origins, we must ask whether schizophrenia requires an added dimension of 'attack' or annihilative threat from the environment (what could be classified as physical or psychological brutality), or whether loss itself – if sufficiently early and extreme – is enough to set in motion the full-scale disintegrative process.

We have already discussed death-related questions of meaning, both in terms of the subjective experience of, and shared feelings about, the schizophrenic condition. We have seen both to be permeated by death imagery, even if rarely so formulated.

Kraepelin's physicalistic view of schizophrenia (as an organic disease – on the order of pneumonia, syphilis, or diabetes, differing from them only in its inexorable progression) contained imagery something close to that of physical death. Bleuler and Freud viewed schizophrenia in ways consistent with a sense of physical death. All three contributed greatly to a process of humanization of schizophrenia, of viewing the condition as a potential form of human reaction to vicissitudes of living. Here an early figure was Adolph Meyer, followed by such determined therapist-investigator gladiators as Sullivan, Fromm-Reichmann, Searles, Boss, Minkowski and Laing. With them, one can characterize the imagery of schizophrenia as human struggles writ large, struggles around inner death and faint vitality. With the later Laing, the imagery around the schizophrenic is that of a visionary who will teach us new ways of seeing, new forms of transcendence that will, so to speak, deliver us from our own psychic deaths. Then along comes Thomas Szasz to view schizophrenia as a kind of 'deadly conspiracy' among psychiatrists to confine and otherwise brutalize their patients: 'Kraepelin invented dementia praecox, and Bleuler schizophrenia, to justify calling psychiatric imprisonment 'mental hospitalisation' and regarding it as a form of medical treatment' (Szasz 1976).

Concerning subjective struggles for meaning in schizophrenia, we have implied that the movement into psychosis can be understood as, first, a near-total breakdown in meaning characterizing the sense of disintegration, followed by a reassertion of disordered (psychotic) meaning structures (including pathological self-reference, delusions, and hallucinations). But we have said little about the crucial part played by guilt in these struggles. While the importance of guilt has certainly been evident to those working closely with schizophrenics, its *conceptual* place in the condition has on the whole been neglected.

GUILT AND PSYCHOSIS

Guilt begins with the developing sense that one is responsible for, indeed the cause of, the annihilation that threatens. Self-blame is inevitable in those who become schizophrenic. This is partly because there is truth in it: something in the very young child does evoke threatening responses. And even when the self-blame is pathetically 'inappropriate,' some early imagery is necessary to the development of the adult concept of responsibility. The trouble is that in the extremity of the schizophrenic's perceived environment, that sense of guilt readily arouses the feeling that one has no right to be alive at all. And unlike the situation in neurosis and in depression, that feeling becomes literalized, so that *one's very existence may be perceived as a transgression.* 'There is the primary guilt of having no right to life in the first place, and hence of being entitled at the most only to a dead life' (Laing 1959: 176). It is quite appropriate to collude, or even initiate, one's own 'soul murder.' As Schreber himself wrote:

> The voices which talk to me have daily stressed ever since the beginning of my contact with God (mid-March 1894) the fact that the crisis that broke upon the realms of God was caused by somebody having *committed soul murder:* at first Flechsig [his doctor] was named as the instigator of soul murder but of recent times in an attempt to reverse the facts *I myself have been 'represented' as the one who had committed soul murder.*
>
> (Macalpine and Hunter 1955: 55; last italics mine)

Thus, the voices (or the psychosis) followed upon the soul murder, and they now accuse Schreber himself of that crime.

Guilt contributes greatly to the schizophrenic's collusion in the murder of his self, but he also feels guilty for having done so. While we may speak of the first form of guilt as static and the second as animating (part of an impulse to stop the 'murderous' process and bring the self back to life), the distinction can be peculiarly difficult to make in schizophrenia. For the guilt becomes part of the twisted or kinky quality of the condition, part of the circle of mockery and self-mockery. It is also readily totalized.

These patterns are perhaps most evident in catatonic reactions. The patient remains motionless. To act – to *move* – is to risk annihilation. But he also may feel that it is wrong, evil, to act or move. Indeed, such patients may 'feel that if they move, the whole world will collapse or all mankind will perish.' The sense of guilty taint becomes part of the grandiosity and delusion, as well as of the implicit end-of-the-world imagery. Yet, mixed in with the guilt and grandiosity, there can be a kind of mocking and self-mocking challenge: I dare you to make the move; it is my will against yours; I warn you that if I move there will be trouble, big trouble; it's not only wrong for me to move – it's wrong for *anybody* to move; by not moving I'm exposing all of the hypocrisy, terror, and guilty taint of others' movements.

The guilt, in other words, is part of the labyrinth – part of what Laing called 'schizophrenese.' In depression, we spoke of the imbalance between static and animating guilt. In schizophrenia, it is not only a matter of imbalance but of further convolution and totalization of both forms of guilt. Still, as Searles and others have shown, one has to tease out the animating possibilities in schizophrenic guilt and shame – notably around what one has done to one's self, and to one's life, and what, should one change, these might become.

This kind of exaggerated behaviour – and now we move beyond the question of guilt per se – has to do with a desire to exorcize the psychosis, or, more generally, the pain and confusion of existence. The imagery is something like: If I can be as crazy as possible, maybe I can shake everyone and everything up sufficiently to put things right. That implies either exorcizing one's own craziness, or influencing the world sufficiently to make it as crazy (or as sane) as one feels oneself to be. And that kind of impulse can attach itself specifically to destruction: If one imaginatively destroys – or actually kills – enough people, a sufficient portion of the threatening-persecuting world, evil and confusion can be eliminated and replaced by goodness and lucidity (Stein 1967: 274).

But psychosis also means safety; in our terms, protection from annihilation. One is reminded of a patient's plea: 'Please, please, let me be crazy again' (Roth 1970: 58) and, of another in the process of recovery: 'When reality started coming back, when I realised where I was and what had happened, I became depressed' (Bowers 1968: 353).

Beyond the protection madness affords, and the despair over failed efforts at its exorcism, that madness can have positive attraction for the patient. There are many descriptions of ecstatic states associated with schizophrenia, often but not always just preceding the psychotic breakdown. These include religious and mystical revelations, in the case of Schreber, the experience of 'miracles,' of extraordinary lucidity, and of creative release. These have been described as peak experiences' (after Maslow), 'a sense of heightened awareness,' 'altered experience,' or 'altered states of consciousness.' They tend either to be associated with, or give way to, full-blown psychosis. These 'peak experiences' have many features of what we have called experiential transcendence. And indeed they can be just that, when they occur in the transient psychoses of relatively integrated people. In such situations, the combination of psychotic and peak experience can, as Don Jackson once wrote, serve as 'growth experiences.' The psychosis-cum-peak-experience can provide a sense of death and rebirth. That is the sort of thing Ronald Laing had in mind in advocating 'living through' one's madness.

That sequence is relatively unusual. Much more frequent is the association of psychosis-cum-peak-experience with the kind of desymbolization and deformation we have been discussing. For a peak experience to qualify as what we called experiential transcendence, you have, so to speak, to 'come back.' And that is what the schizophrenic usually cannot do.

Indeed, even the heightened awareness tends to be associated with anxiety – often as one patient put it, 'horror and ecstasy' (Bowers and Freedman 1966: 240–8). That is, the peak experience, in the absence of the capacity for symbolic ordering, seems to favour 'the progression of the psychotic state and the formation of delusions' (Bowers 1968: 354).

Since this state is accompanied by 'hypervigilance,' it may well be a psychobiological response to perceived threat, as some believe. If so, however, the response tends all too often to be inseparable from the threat itself, that of annihilation or the experience of disintegration. In any case, our point here is that the schizophrenic person can experience imaginative pleasure that is inseparable from his immediate disintegration – pleasure that may well herald his more fundamentally despairing and 'deadened' state.

Questions of meaning enter directly into a theory of schizophrenia. As Lyman Wynn, a leading investigator of psychological patterns in the families of schizophrenics, emphasizes, '*Feelings* of meaninglessness or pointlessness as *subjectively* experienced by the persons (in the families) themselves.' What is shared is 'a disbelief in the possibility of connected, subjectively meaningful and satisfying experience.' In one group families 'appear to have no stake in looking for meanings'; in another there is 'profound skepticism about achieving meaning' (Wynn 1968: 287). Wynn also emphasized what he called 'pseudo-mutuality,' by which he means an insistence upon a facade of harmony at the expense of both individual differentiation and, one may say, actuality (Wynn *et al.* 1958: 205–20) as suggested by the example of a mother of a schizophrenic:

> We are all peaceful. I like peace even if I have to kill someone to get it ... a more normal, happy kid would be hard to find. I was pleased with my child! I was pleased with my husband! I was pleased with my life. I have always been pleased. We have had twenty-five years of the happiest married life and of being a father and mother.
>
> (Wynn 1968: 26)

Beyond the extremity of denial and numbing we encounter a 'grotesque counterfeit ... of meaning and relation' (Schaffer and Wynn 1962: 44). The violent imagery is significant, suggesting a willingness often encountered in these families, and not just on the part of one member, to annihilate psychically whoever threatens the counterfeit structure. In these families there may be 'shared dread of meaning and relation, manifest in the systematic destruction of meaning, the routine elimination of implication, and the insistence on fragmentation of experience.' Wynn and Margaret Singer, on the basis of a series of projective tests given to family members, have been able to predict the specific form of thought disorder and degree of disorganization of the schizophrenic member, and to match 'blindly' individual patients and their families (Wynn and Singer 1963: 199–206) They understood themselves to be studying 'family constellations' around styles of communication, especially patterns of handling attention and meaning; styles of relating, especially erratic and inappropriate kinds of distance and closeness; affective disorder, especially unacknowledged feelings of pervasive meaninglessness, pointlessness and emptiness; and overall structure of the family, especially around pseudomutuality and related distortions. In other words, their work describes the family transmission of specific features of what we have been calling desymbolization and deformation.

Family transmission of desymbolization can be experienced as a life-or-death matter. The suffocating pressures of 'pseudomutuality' in the absence of vital symbolic exchange can leave the schizophrenic person with an either/or equation, 'When I become born, Mother becomes dead' – 'As though life may be in only one person; if it is in me, it is not in Mother; if it is in Mother, it is not in me.' This is a kind of absolute conflict over survival priority, in which full vitality (autonomy, separateness, and the psychic action of genuine symbolization) is equated with murdering another, sometimes with an intensity that 'for the outsider had all the fascination of a fight unto death' (Monke 1963: 22-35).

And the process can be 'deadening' (numbing) all around, since the family member who receives little response from a schizophrenic feels that 'I as a subject have no object, I too am without life, for nowhere in that moment am I in the process of exercising the process of "taking in" the process which designates life' (Monke 1963: 33).

It is worth quoting further Monke's sensitive representation of the transaction between the schizophrenic person and someone near him, as the sequence vivifies our own paradigm:

'Affect flatness' is the appropriate response to that situation which in the first person can be referred to as, 'I've had it with you.' It applies when 'I perpetually fear that you will engulf me as your object or, reciprocally, fear that should I venture to be so much a somebody that I would affect you, you would disappear as the object and I, because of having no object, would be again a non-somebody.' It would maintain when 'I give up my congenital right that you permit me enough of a psyche so that I as a 'somebody' would be a subject who affects you as object.'

When the above preposterous proposition maintains, I, in reaction to it, would cease 'affecting.' I would so behave that there would be nothing in me which you would recognize as affecting you, and there would be nothing in me which you would sense as something which you could affect.

In poetic metaphor, I would speak of this defensive and protective manoeuvre *as a withdrawing of the psychic self onto the other side of a thick, plate-glass window through which one can see all about the world but through which the act of affecting does not occur either from the patient to the world or from the world to the patient.* By this manoeuvre to the other side of the big plate glass, the dreadful stresses are success-fully avoided.

(Monke 1963: 31)

Of course genetic family transmission is also important. The genes' 'encoded information' and 'potential instruction' to the organism undoubt-edly contribute to the deformations of schizophrenia. Recent adoption studies seem to demonstrate significantly greater incidence of schizo-phrenia where a biological parent is schizophrenic and the adopted parents are not, as compared to situations in which an adopted parent is schizo-phrenic and the biological parents are not (Rosenthal and Kety 1968). These studies, however, and especially their conclusions about genetic causation, have been questioned by investigators of family process (Lidz 1976: 402–11), who, in turn, point to new evidence of psychological trans-mission (Wynn, Singer and Toohui 1976: 413–51). Nowhere is the old intellectual bugaboo of dualism more harmful than in pursuit of the nonquestion of heredity versus environment in the causation of schizo-phrenia. Even the 'concept of interaction (of genetic and environmental factors) does not capture the unified complexity of development' (Cancro 1975: 356).

In that 'unified complexity' we may assume that only certain kinds of environments (a family, as already mentioned, but also of class and of subculture and larger culture, and perhaps certain forms of timing and even random experience) are likely to activate the potentially harmful, genetically influenced combination of traits that result in schizophrenia. None of this alters the fact that the schizophrenic response is mainly one of psychological manifestations. For instance, Manfred Bleuler rejects somatic theories of schizophrenia, such as 'a brain lesion . . . or a pathology of metabolism, precisely because he is attached to biology and to general medicine . . . [and] all the somatic theories of schizophrenia are open to the most severe criticism from biologists' (Rosenthal and Kety 1968: 9). At the same time the structural-psychological disorder would seem to 'have strong biological roots,' to be related to 'elementary perceptual processes' (Reiss 1978: 184).

Genetic potential and family environmental influence converge on impaired capacity for symbolization, particularly symbolization of vitality and consequent vulnerability of a fundamental kind to imagery of death and death equivalents.

There is some evidence to suggest that those who are vulnerable to schizophrenia on genetic and, possibly, environmental bases belong to society's more creative segment (Cancro 1975: 357–8). It would seem that death imagery either does one in or lends itself to imaginative achieve-ment – depending upon one's capacity to order it to hitch on to the formative-symbolizing process. And that process itself may have grey areas in which the breaking of old forms in the service or original synthesis is barely distinguishable from their break*down* in the service of schizophrenic disintegration.

SOUL MURDER AND PARANOIA

Once more Schreber has something to tell us. He was a gifted, imaginative man, who had been a distinguished jurist prior to his breakdown, and one reads his memoirs with respect for his intellect as well as sympathy for him in his suffering. Concerning the source of Schreber's paranoid schizophrenia, remarkable evidence has recently been uncovered concerning his father, a physician and educational reformer obsessed with principles of posture and obedience in child-rearing. He developed a series of Draconian devices that literally strapped and bound children to the prescribed straight-arrow position, both during sleep and while awake and sitting. ('It is made of iron throughout,' the inventor proudly declares, 'preventing any attempt at improper sitting.') Dr Schreber advocates, in one of his influential books, that the child in question should not only be immediately punished when violating rules, but required 'to stretch out its hand to the executor of the punishment' in order to prevent 'the possibility of spite and bitterness.' Dr Schreber was, in fact, a visionary who aimed at combating the decadence and degeneracy of youth and all vestiges in parents of what these days is called permissiveness. And 'his aggressive efforts aimed toward the development of a better and healthier race of men' (Niederland 1959: 160).

By his own admission, Dr Schreber applied his belts, vises and straps to his own children, probably more systematically to his two sons, one of whom committed suicide, while the other became the famous case – the three daughters apparently remained nonpsychotic. Clearly, Dr Schreber's child-rearing approaches, especially toward his sons, must have included every feature that research on schizophrenic families has emphasized, and more. We would focus on the threat of annihilation he posed for his boys, his carrying out that threat in the form of his Draconian procedures (in ways that must have been perceived by the boys as actually experiencing annihilation), and his own visionary commitments about a new race of men that sound not too different from his son's delusional system: 'The father, with no little apostolic grandeur, strives for the development of better health and hygiene in an earthbound way, as it were; the son and his delusional elaboration of these precepts does so in an archaic, magical way' (Niederland 1959: 165).

But there is more. Dr Schreber's idiosyncrasies spilled over into an actual psychiatric syndrome. He was described once (on the basis of information given to a psychiatrist) as having 'suffered from compulsive manifestations with murderous impulses'; by his biographer as having experienced a 'protracted, chronic head condition' either connected with an accident in which a ladder fell on his head in his gymnasium or 'possibly a severe nervous breakdown'; and by his daughter as having experienced a strange disease of the head. All this developed during his fiftieth or fifty-first year (he died at the age of fifty-three from an intestinal disorder), just about the age at which his son underwent his first psychotic break- down. At the very least he suffered from an unusually severe obsessive neurosis, and more likely from a paranoid psychosis not unlike that of his son. The inherited factor could be considerable; the psychological influence is surely catastrophic.

Morton Schatzman points to Schreber's persecution by his father, and argues from a general 'transactional theory' of paranoia as originating in some form of persecution (Schatzman 1971: 177–207). The theory may be almost correct, but neglects the symbolizing process – the recreation of whatever persecution has been undergone – from which the paranoid process takes shape. Without that symbolizing stress we could not address questions of why a paranoid psychosis occurs at a particular time and in relationship to a particular set of events.

Again, it is not a question of either genetic or familial transmission alone, but rather a 'unified complexity of development.' To understand more about its operation, more about schizophrenia, we probably need to study patterns over several generations on the one hand, and their rela- tionship to desymbolization and death imagery on the other.

The 'soul murder' or inner disintegration of schizophrenia gives rise to extreme forms of numbing and deformation throughout the functioning of the self. At the immediate level, the schizophrenic feels himself flooded with death anxiety, which he both embraces and struggles against. At the ultimate level, his absence of connection beyond the self leaves him with the feeling that life is counterfeit, and that biological death is unaccept- able and yet uneventful because psychic death is everywhere. Equating his very existence with transgression and the constant threat of annihila- tion, he makes his mocking compromise, the lifeless life.[3]

NOTES

1 See my 'The Image of 'The-End-of-the-World': A Psychohistorical View,' in S. Friedlander, G. Holton, L. Marx and E. Skolnikoff (eds), *Visions of Apocalypse: End or Rebirth?* New York: Holmes & Meier.

2 Elias Canetti, a literary man rather than a psychiatrist, emphasizes Schreber's wish to be 'the only man left alive,' and concludes, much like Ovesey, that paranoia 'is an illness of power in the most literal sense of the words.' For him, survival is 'the moment of power' par excellence, and can indeed become in certain heroes and despots, 'a dangerous and insatiable passion' (Canetti 1962: 227).

3 This chapter appeared, in part, in my book, *The Broken Connection*, reissued by the American Psychiatric Press, Washington, DC, 1996.

REFERENCES

Bowers, M.B. (1968). 'Pathogenesis of Acute Schizophrenic Psychosis: An Experiential Approach,' *Archives of General Psychiatry* 19.

Bowers, M.B. and Freedman, D.X. (1966) ' 'Psychedelic' Experiences in Acute Psychoses,' *Archives of General Psychiatry* 15.

Cancro, R. (1975). 'Genetics, Dualism, and Schizophrenia,' *Journal of American Academy of Psychoanalysis* 3.

Canetti, E. (1962). *Crowds and Power*, New York: Viking.

Donlon, P.T. (1976). 'Depression and the Reintegration Phase of Acute Schizophrenia,' *American Journal of Psychiatry* 133.

Freud, S. (1911). *Psycho-Analytic Notes on an Autobiographical Account of a Case of Paranoia (Dementia Paranoides)*, S.E. Vol. 12, London: Hogarth Press.

—— (1914). 'On Narcissism: An Introduction,' *S. E.* Vol. 14, London: Hogarth Press.

—— (1915–1917). *Introductory Lectures on Psychoanalysis*, S.E. Vol. 16, London: Hogarth Press.

—— (1939). *Moses and Monotheism*, S. E. Vol. 23, London: Hogarth Press.

Laing, R.D. (1959). *The Divided Self*, London: Tavistock Publications.

Levin, S. (1971). 'The Depressive Core in Schizophrenia,' *Philadelphia Association for Psychoanalysis Bulletin* 21.

Lidz, T. (1976). 'Commentary on "A Critical Review of Recent Adoption, Twin, and Family Studies of Schizophrenia: Behavioral Genetics Perspectives".' *Schizophrenia Bulletin.*

Macalpine, I. and Hunter, R.A, eds. (1955). *Daniel Schreber: Memoirs of My Nervous Illness*, London: William Dawson.

Monke, J.V. (1963). 'On Some Subjective, Clinical and Theoretical Aspects of the Acute Psycotic Reaction,' in *Acute Psychotic Reaction*, eds. W.M Mendel and Leon J. Epstein, Psychiatric Research Report of the American Psychiatric Association, Washington, DC.

Niederland, W.G. (1959). 'Schreber: Father and Son,' *Psychoanalytic Quarterly* 28.

Ovesey, L. (1955). 'Pseudo-Homosexuality, the Paranoid Mechanism, and Paranoia,' *Psychiatry* 18.

Reiss, D. (1976). 'The Family and Schizophrenia,' *American Journal of Psychiatry* 133.

Rosenthal, D. and Kety, S., eds. (1968). *The Transmission of Schizophrenia*, Oxford: Pergamon Press.

Roth, S. (1970). 'The Seemingly Ubiquitous Depression Following Acute Schizophrenic Episodes: A Neglected Area of Clinical Discussion,' *American Journal of Psychiatry* 127

Schaffer, L. and Wynn, L.C. *et al.* (1968). 'On the Nature and Sources of the Psychiatrist's Experience with the Family of the Schizophrenic,' *Psychiatry* 25.

Schatzman, M. (1971) 'Paranoia or Persecution: The Case of Schreber,' *Family Process* 10.

Searles, H. (1965). *Collected Papers on Schizophrenia and Related Subjects*, New York: International Universities Press.

Selesnick, S.T. (1963). 'C.G. Jung's Contributions to Psychoanalysis,' *American Journal of Psychiatry* 120.

Stein, W.J. (1967). 'The Sense of Becoming Psychotic,' *Psychiatry* 30.

Sullivan, H.S. (1956). *Clinical Studies in Psychiatry*, New York: W.W. Norton.

—— (1962). *Schizophrenia as a Human Process*, New York: W.W Norton.

Szasz, T. (1976). *Schizophrenia: The Sacred Symbol of Psychiatry*, New York: Basic Books.

Wynn, L.C. (1968). in *Family Processes and Schizophrenia*, eds. E. Mishler and N. Waxman, New York: Science House.

Wynn, L.C., Ryckoff, I.M., Day, J. and Hirsch, S.I. (1958). 'Pseudo-mutuality in the Family Relations of Schizophrenics,' *Psychiatry* 21.

Wynn, L.C. and Singer, M.T. (1963). 'Thought Disorder and Family Relations of Schizophrenics: II. A Classification of Forms of Thinking,' *Archives of General Psychiatry* 9.

Wynn, L.C., Singer M.T. and Toohui (1976). 'Communication of the Adopted Parents of Schizophrenics,' in *Schizophrenia 75. Psychotherapy, Family Studies, Research* eds Jorstad and Ugelstad, Oslo: The University of Oslo Press.

Chapter 5

Only pretend
The dramaturgy of paranoia

David Edgar

In the mid 1970s I began work on a stage adaptation of Mary Barnes and Joe Berke's book about Mary's journey through madness at Kingsley Hall, the alternative therapeutic community set up by R.D. Laing and others in east London in 1965 (1973). I wanted to begin with a bold statement, and was struck by Laing's remark that he found it impossible to conceive of any mad person he had met being more seriously deranged than Richard Nixon.

Accordingly, the first draft began with an edited version of Nixon's notorious East Room farewell to his staff, punctuated by explanatory slides which applied the symptoms of schizophrenia to his meanderings, from delusions of grandeur and paranoia to hebephrenia, incongruence and disturbance of affect. It wasn't terribly hard to do, and perhaps for that reason it was quick to bite the dust.

In fact, there was a more appropriate Nixonian analogy on offer, which was to be exposed in Bob Woodward and Carl Bernstein's description of Nixon's final days (Woodward and Bernstein 1976). The night before he resigned, according to Henry Kissinger, Nixon had wandered through the White House saying farewell to portraits of past Presidents. In this superficially loopy activity, the 37th President was to be echoed by the wife of the 42nd, a fact revealed by the same journalist. For it was Bob Woodward, in his book about the early days of the 1996 presidential campaign (Woodward 1996), who revealed to the world that Hillary Clinton had been advised by a spiritual mentor to imagine herself in conversation with Eleanor Roosevelt.

As Mrs Clinton was also advised to talk to Jesus (an activity known in religious circles as praying) it didn't seem to me much of a scoop. Of more interest was a motto the First Lady had picked up from a friend in Alcoholics Anonymous, 'fake it till you make it', with its implication that internal change can follow and inhabit outward behaviour. For this slogan follows the George Burns aphorism that honesty is the most important quality in an actor: 'if you can fake that, you can fake anything'.

It was not ever thus. When drama began, it almost certainly consisted of the direct expression of felt emotion in the special context of the initiation rite and the sacrificial ritual. As drama became formalised into theatre, expression gave way to representation, possession to pretence, rites to rituals and actual sacrifice to the symbolic. But theatre has not entirely lost sight of its origins: which accounts for the number of plays which involve ceremonies of various kinds, set in the unfamiliar and often magical places in which rites of passage occur.

Writing a play about a schizophrenic is a complicated activity; not least when the person concerned is paranoid herself but also has that effect on other people. Mary Barnes has little in common with Richard Nixon, but they both provoked the suspicion that they knew more of what they were up to than they let on. And in representing such behaviour, I faced the question that Shakespeare faced in writing Edgar in *King Lear*, Prince Hal in the *Henry IV* plays and Hamlet: were they genuinely sad, bad and mad or were they – like George Burns – faking it? And if so, could they tell?

Concerned as it is with the public representation of private human behaviour, the theatre has much to do with the concerns of psychiatry. Dealing as it must with extremes, it is inevitably much exercised with paranoia, persecution and the circumstances which give rise to them. Metaphorically, the very act of performance is often taken to imply not only pretence but also deceit: the Greek word for actor is 'hypocrite'. However, this metaphor is inaccurate; in fact, in a literal sense, the professional actor is not aiming to deceive. He or she is inviting the audience to participate in what Coleridge memorably defined as a 'willing suspension of disbelief', a game which relies on both sides knowing, accepting and sharing the rules. As Philip Sidney wrote, no one believes they *are* the gates of Thebes; for Dr Johnson, 'the spectators are always in their senses' (Styan 1963: 235). Coleridge defined what he was describing more delicately: 'the true stage-illusion in this and in all other things consists – not in the mind's judging it to be a forest, but in its remission of the judgement that it is not a forest" (ibid.). And while members of the public may affect to treat soap operas as documentaries, and journalists may use the names of soap star and part interchangeably, there is very little confusion in the minds of the actors themselves.

But to say that the drama has nothing to do with dissemblance would be disingenuous. That Johnson refers to our senses and Coleridge to remission implies that, in order to work, the dramatic experience must embrace parts of the consciousness that other forms of communication don't reach. At the very least, the suspension of disbelief means that we are volunteering to place ourselves in the grip of an illusion.

And while the actor is not intending to deceive the audience, a great deal of the drama is about the actor's character deceiving other people.

It is possible indeed to define the two great traditional dramatic genres in two simple actions, in both of which duplicity is at the very core: ultimately, all tragedy is about broken promises, and all comedy ineffective disguise.

It's for this reason that dramatists devote so much attention to developing devices to reveal to the audience what characters are unwilling to reveal to each other. Denied the novelist's facility for psychological description and inner monologue, dramatists have had to invent an array of devices to make the internal external. The two most obvious examples are the soliloquy and the aside, both of which are designed to allow the character to reveal his or her deceits to the only people who won't snitch on them.

The questions raised by these techniques are interesting. The conventional wisdom about Shakespearian soliloquy is that soliloquising characters tell the truth. On the other hand, it is the truth as they see it. Shakespeare didn't know about the unconscious, but he knew that we lie not only to each other but ourselves. Thus when Iago justifies his malice by asserting that Othello has bedded his (Iago's) wife, we suspect this isn't true. More importantly, we know that it is by no means a full explanation of Iago's actions.

In *Richard III*, the actor's problem is not whether the character is speaking the truth, but who he is speaking it to. Are Richard's gleeful celebrations of his villainy delivered to a judge (a plea), a priest (a confession), himself (a diary) or a combination of the foregoing (as in the film *Double Indemnity*)? In his book on playing Richard (1985), Antony Sher describes his own ingenious solution. For Sher, it is in fact a seminar: Richard is demonstrating his villainy to a school of potential Richard IIIs. It is particularly important incidentally that Richard is *not* speaking to himself, as this self comes into some contest towards the end. In his last great soliloquy Richard sees the ghosts of those he has killed, wakes, and faces the question he has been evading since the start: 'What do I fear? Myself? There's naught else by./Richard loves Richard; that is, I am I.' Having finally discovered the thing that really frightens him, the poisoned void of his own self, Richard has nothing left to do but implode.

Earlier in the same play, there is another example of the hidden complexities of the soliloquy-equals-truth model. The imprisoned Duke of Clarence wakes from a dream and describes his nightmare vision of his own death. His gaoler is happy to reassure him: it was but a dream. Ten minutes later, Clarence is horribly murdered. The dream in fact was a prediction.

It was also, of course, a manipulation of time. There is – famously – no literal flashback in Shakespeare. There is however a portmanteau of devices to reveal the future and the past and to demonstrate their impact on the present. The presence of supernatural beings almost always implies a time-jump: the ghost of Hamlet's father is in effect a flashback (and a great deal more effective in revealing backstory than the lumpenly lengthy perorations which do the same job in *A Comedy of Errors* and *The Tempest*). The witches in *Macbeth* are predictors of the future, and in their last great scene they show rather than tell how the barren Macbeths will be succeeded by other people's children.

But they are of course much more than just an expositional device. Like Hillary Clinton's Eleanor Roosevelt, they are a sounding-board and a counsellor. In both *Hamlet* and *Julius Caesar*, ghosts make short and unexpected appearances in the second half of plays in which their main action (in *Julius Caesar*, quick, in *Hamlet* already dead) has been in part one. In both cases, their reprise is to remind not us but the characters they appear to of their message: they are not just revealing the past, but insisting on it. Similarly, the ghosts that appear outside Richard III's tent the night before his death tell him (and us) nothing new, except that the time for evasion and deceit is over.

Ghosts have one crucial characteristic as a theatrical device, which they share with all those *alter egos* and imaginary friends which are the contemporary drama's equivalent. We expect that they will not be seen by all the characters on the stage. Often, we share our sense of them with only one character; sometimes, as in *Hamlet*, there are a few. Like the soliloquy and the aside, the ghost gives us privileged access to the characters, sometimes to their consciences, sometimes to their demons.

In all these devices, it's possible to define the split between the person we see and the person the other characters see in a number of ways. Literally, we see the lie and the truth, spacially the outer and the inner. Psychologically, we are seeing the conscious and the unconscious mind (which is why the *alter ego* is more effective than the aside *or* the ghost in the post-Freudian world). Dramatically, I believe we are seeing the character's objective function set against her or his individual subjectivity. The other people get the role, we get the character.

The distinction between role and character arises out of drama's historic commitment to genre. From the young lovers, wily servants and deluded ancients of Plautine comedy to the brilliant detectives, loyal sidekicks and slow superiors of the whodunnit, drama's genres have presented the public with stock roles with whose plot function the audience will be familiar before the play begins. The skill of the dramatist has always been to invest these stock figures with originality, so that in the hands of a Shakespeare the boasting soldier becomes Falstaff, the revenger Hamlet, the pantaloon Polonius, the wicked sisters Goneril and Regan and the deceived father Shylock or King Lear.

The contrast between character and role is thus at the core of drama as a medium. It is also central to what the drama explores. Arthur Miller said that the skill of the theatre is to do the expected thing in the most unexpected way. The balance between expectation and surprise which is at the core of our experience in the playhouse is in large part the balance between the revolt of the original and unique character against his or her casting in an otherwise predictable role.

Casting and role playing are central both to psychiatry in general and to Mary Barnes's story in particular. In the book, the whole of the first section is devoted to Mary's life before she decided to 'go down' and submit to her own madness at Kingsley Hall. Having rejected Richard Nixon, I considered a prologue set in Mary's 'abnormally nice' and in fact literally maddening family, and then considered flashing back from her alternative family at Kingsley Hall to the original article (I may even have pondered the haunting appearance of a mother-ghost). But in fact the solution to representing Mary's backstory was contained in her 'present' behaviour: one could read her past family life off her casting of the residents of Kingsley Hall – and particularly Joe Berke – as her new and surrogate family, simultaneously purging but also parodying the behaviour of the old.

Indeed, the story of Mary's relationships could be seen as a gradual change from seeing others in roles relative to her (as surrogate mothers, fathers and brothers) to seeing them as individuals, with an independent life. A crucial turning point for Mary was the moment when she realised that a young psychiatrist was in distress and pain, while she herself was feeling cosy and content. This understanding that she could sympathise without inhabiting another person was for her the moment when she gained independence from her demons.

In the play, I placed this moment at the end of a sequence in which Mary had been engaged in role-play of a different kind. Mary's fervent Catholicism was expressed in the wild baroque grandeur of her religious paintings, which she would execute as dramas, with herself acting out the parts. It struck me that when painting the Crucifixion, Mary would have been dramatically engaged in crucifying herself. It was at the end of a scene in which Mary acted out the various parts in the Crucifixion while painting it that I placed her moment of resurrection, the moment when – through her understanding of the separateness of others – she stopped being The Errant Daughter, The Resident Lunatic and The House Problem and became herself.

The Resurrection is an escape story (it occurs, after all, when a man unexpectedly absents himself from a guarded cell). It is one of the ironies of Joe Berke's role with Mary that he was in a sense both her gaoler and her liberator, and her resurrection consisted of an escape both with and from the man who had been her only lifeline. After Mary Barnes, I adapted an escape story of a more literal kind, that of a white South African lawyer detained without trial for six months in South Africa in 1963 (Sachs 1966). Albie Sachs's experiences came back to me very forcefully when reading Brian Keenan's book about his experience as a captive in Lebanon, *An Evil Cradling* (Keenan 1992); as did a number of other prison books, including Alexander Solzhenitsyn's *Ivan Denisovich* and *The First Circle*, Vladimir Bukovksy's *To Build a Castle* and Vaclav Havel's *Letters to Olga*.

The Sachs/Keenan comparisons, however, went beyond the normal iconography of prison books. True, both emphasise the importance of small objects, the use of ferreted bits of rubbish for entertainment (making chess-sets and draught-boards), the centrality of shit, distress at moving, playing games with the Bible, contemplating suicide, bonding with guards by joke-telling, having problems with blankets, holding birthday parties, fearing release and becoming infantalised. But what can one make of the following common factors: yearning for a chair; the phrase 'this is it'; the prisoner looking at his face in both sides of a spoon; suffering from an ear infection; fantasising about swimming; and undergoing a mystical experience with an orange?

Brian Keenan is an extrovert Irishman of no political or religious alignment, arbitrarily selected for kidnap by left-wing religious fundamentalists for an an unspecified period in an unstructured prison system out of contact with the outside world. Albie Sachs is an introverted Jewish South African ANC member, chosen for incarceration in known places by right-wing political fundamentalists for a specified if repeatable period under a known system of state law. They were, however, both kept locked alone in closed rooms with very few facilities or possessions for long periods of time.

Clearly, in cases of extreme privation, one's circumstantial role becomes more important than one's character. What Sachs and Keenan share is neither their personality nor the political specifics of their situation but the role in which they are cast, the circumstances of a particular form of persecution.

For the observation that great characters transcend their role does not imply that they don't have one. Our lives are a dialectic between circumstance and character, and the more extreme the circumstances, the more pressing the exigencies of role. As George Eliot notes in *Middlemarch*, 'unwonted circumstances may make us all rather unlike ourselves' (1965: 675); as she puts it in *The Mill on the Floss*, character is part but not the whole of our destiny:

> Hamlet, Prince of Denmark, was speculative and irresolute, and we have a great tragedy in consequence. But if his father had lived to a good old age, and his uncle had died an early death, we can conceive Hamlet's having married Ophelia and got through life with a reputation of sanity notwithstanding many soliloquies, and some moody sarcasms towards the fair daughter of Polonius, to say nothing of the frankest incivility to his father-in-law.

(1979: 514)

The drama thus warns us against both determinism and voluntarism. In the period when liberal discourse was coloured by Marxist assumptions, too much attention may have been paid to circumstances. In the last two decades, the pendulum has swung the other way, and the individual is ascribed superhuman powers to overcome the most extreme social and psychological privations. Indeed, on occasions, the theories of a more collective age have flipped into reverse: those of us who were impressed by the contribution of psychoanalytic insights to politics in the 1960s are alarmed by the way those insights served the move to the right in the 1980s.

Thus, the insights of holistic medicine have been used to claim that all disease can be defeated by positive thinking. The idea that we are responsible for our own health has mutated into the notion that illness is proof of irresponsibility. The concept that madness is not a disease has led us back to the idea that the mad are bad, or at best lazy, and should shape up or be shipped out on to the streets or into the gaols. Because some left-wingers have strange family backgrounds, it's argued that all radicals are basically trying to kill their fathers or take revenge on their schoolmasters. The proposal that oppression has a psychological dimension leads to the assertion that oppression is a psychological concept, which doesn't exist outside the head of the person experiencing it.

Part of the problem is a kind of literalness of thinking: the language of causality easily mutates into the language of blame. However, there are certain kinds of metaphor that do contain truths about the relationship between the individual with the role in which they are cast. I am generally irked by the sloppy (and indeed syllogistic) use of metaphor on the both sides of the political divide: I try not to claim that unemployment (or bad housing) *is* violence, or that pornograpy *is* rape. However, one of the many things I learnt from Mary Barnes is that metaphor has real meaning even if used in this slippery way.

A man who thinks he's Christ because he experiences his life as being nailed to a tree. A young woman who calls herself Mrs Taylor because she experiences herself as a 'tailored maid' (Laing 1965: 192). A person who cannot understand why people treat them badly concludes they must be guilty of extensive crimes. A woman who feels frightened pretends that she has returned to the only place she ever felt safe. Taken together, these are all examples of the anti-psychiatrist David Cooper's great epigram: that one might define 'delusion' as a real idea a patient holds, but which a psychiatrist deludes himself into taking literally (Cooper 1970: 41).

The history of resistance to persecution is littered with ideas that shouldn't be taken literally. 'Black Power' and 'Wages for Housework' are two examples of what appear to be slogans but which are in fact metaphors (as, from the other side of spectrum, are 'The Right to Bear Arms' and 'There Ain't No Such Thing as a Free Lunch'). But if we are to discriminate between slogans and metaphors, if we are to learn not to apply literally those ideas that are meant to be visionary, then we must allow the presence of the visionary and the utopian in our lives.

The conservative revolution of the 1980s was in essence a revolution against utopia. In accepting existing circumstances, with their predictable functions and unalterable roles, it denied the importance or even the existence of the world beyond our immediate grasp, and the visionary individuals who in their words or acts hold it out to us. As part of this revolution, psychiatry seems to have veered from blaming everything on circumstance (persecution) to blaming everything on the individual (paranoia). Through its staid, ancient and sometimes seemingly mechanical distinction between role and character, the drama reminds those concerned with the workings of the human mind that this is a contradiction that can be exaggerated, and that even paranoids have enemies.

REFERENCES

Barnes, M. and Berke J. (1973). *Mary Barnes: Two Accounts of a Journey through Madness*, London: MacGibbon and Kee.

Cooper, D. (1970). *Psychiatry and Anti-Psychiatry*, London: Paladin.

Edgar, D. (1978). *Mary Barnes (based on Mary Barnes and Joseph Berke: Mary Barnes: Two Accounts of a Journey through Madness)*, London: Methuen.

Eliot, G. (1965). *Middlemarch*, London: Penguin.

—— (1979). *The Mill on the Floss*, London: Penguin.

Keenan, B. (1992). *An Evil Cradling*, London: Vintage.

Laing, R.D. (1965). *The Divided Self*, London: Penguin.

Sachs, A. (1966). *Jail Diary*, London: Sphere.

Sher, A. (1985). *Year of the King*, London: Methuen.

Styan, J.L. (1963). *The Elements of Drama*, Cambridge: Cambridge University Press.

Woodward, B. and Bernstein, C. (1976). *The Final Days*, London: Secker and Warburg.

Woodward, B. (1996). *The Choice*, New York: Simon and Schuster.

Part II

Social and institutional

Introduction

This part contains four chapters that relate to the social and institutional aspects of paranoia and persecution. The psychological component, described in some of its manifestations in Part I, provided us with interpretations of the meaning of the mental suffering that originates from either external or internal persecutors. In this part groups, institutions and bureaucracies are studied in order to expand our understanding of paranoia beyond the scope of the intrapsychic.

The four authors of this section include three psychiatrists, two of whom are also psychoanalysts, and a businessman/lawyer.

In 'Paranoid social developments as a consequence of ideological and bureaucratic regression', Otto Kernberg analyses from a theoretical perspective the psychoanalytic contributions to our understanding of paranoia-genesis in institutions and how severe persecutory and paranoid behaviour develops in groups and organizations. Kernberg first describes the paranoid and narcissistic pathologies of individuals with graphic explanations as to how and why one may develop persecutory and paranoid thoughts and behaviours. Then Kernberg moves on to the psychopathology of groups and organizations in order to fine-tune our understanding of how bureaucracies and ideology are the breeding-grounds for aggression, which is the root cause for severe narcissism and paranoia. Kernberg writes with specific reference to a group-analytic understanding of large-group dynamics. When social organizations tend to regress, they activate paranoid and/or narcissistic elements. Implications for pathological conditions for society-at-large are also described.

R.D. Hinshelwood, in 'Paranoia, groups and enquiry' examines groups within the social context in order to understand how a group identity is formed. Only by viewing the impact of persons upon each other can we truly understand their state of mind. Therefore, Hinshelwood believes that it is only within social groups that paranoia and persecution can exist. In small groups the destructive forces tend to take place within the grouping itself. In larger groups, however, destructiveness is directed outwards, towards another grouping. In addition, there is an inherent danger in joining a large group – the threat of losing one's identity. Often this fear of loss leads to an outward expression of anger; for this may be the only way one can defend one's inner self feelings and perceptions against potential annihilation. The anger may also be directed towards destroying the actual persecutor – the enemy. Hinshelwood utilizes the term 'enquiry' as a way of avoiding a drifting into a depersonalizing group mentality.

We all too often relate to groups and institutions as viable entities and almost take their presence for granted. Leonard Fagin, in 'Paranoia in institutional life: the death-throes of the asylum', describes a psychiatric hospital due to close down soon. Intrapsychic and group-dynamic forces are explored in order to see how misperception among staff and patients occurs in total institutions. These forces are exacerbated by the impending closure of the institution. The fears and paranoia are the result of anxieties of a persecutory nature that are split off and projected onto others as well as onto the institution itself. Fagin pursues the point that when an institution is forced to go through radical changes, which are likely to substantially affect the lives of its residents and staff, the chances of a full-blown paranoid explosion increase dramatically. If the institution is in its death-throes, and bureaucratic personnel are responsible for its closure, mistrust and suspicion can run rampant, foiling all attempts at therapeutic working through. The institution that Fagin analyses was often on the verge of a 'psychotic breakdown', where boundaries became blurred and reality parameters began to disappear in the midst of impending doom and frightening external attackers. Fagin contrasts the destructive with the constructive forces in some institutions, so that we can obtain a more balanced picture of what goes right as well as wrong.

John Jackson concludes this part with his chapter, 'Bureaucracies at work'. Jackson, a businessman and lawyer, feels that no study of persecution and paranoia could be complete without closely examining ways in which people behave in the world of organized work. Jackson describes the life and work of a bureaucrat and the development of a corporate personality. He traces tribal behaviour in social animals in order to understand what influences are likely to produce success or failure in the social world. Examining organized work in the western world and the influence of the industrial revolution, Jackson traces the movement from trade shops and merchants peddling their wares to the modern company with shareholders and professional management. Bureaucracies are not far behind in this historical and developmental view, and paranoia and persecution round out the work picture. Outside 'fresh blood' is rejected for employment – it is too threatening. The inside, 'company man' is preferred because that reduces the paranoid flavour of intrusion. This chapter is the bridge from the social and institutional world to the cultural and political, which will be explored in Part III.

Chapter 6

Paranoid social developments as a consequence of ideological and bureaucratic regression

Otto F. Kernberg

I would like to share with you an overview of the psychoanalytic contributions to our understanding of paranoia-genesis in institutions. This is related to the development of severe paranoia and persecutory behaviour throughout groups, organisations and social institutions.

I need to say, first of all, that as far as I can see, there is no integrated psychoanalytic theory in this area. But there are a number of significant contributions that I will try to bring together. Secondly, I think it is exaggerated and inappropriate to assume that psychoanalytic theory has an exclusive or comprehensive view about phenomena of social persecution, paranoia and violence. They also have to be analysed from other viewpoints: from sociological, political, cultural, economic viewpoints, and not only from a psychological and particularly psychoanalytical perspective. But having said that, I think that there is enough that we can contribute, from a psychoanalytic viewpoint, to make the effort worthwhile.

There are two types of psychopathology that are of interest to us, because we find them, again and again, at an individual level, at a group level, at an organisational level and at the social and political level. I refer to the pathology of the paranoid individual, or the paranoid personality disorder, and the narcissistic personality disorder. Let me remind you very briefly of the main characteristics of these severe personality disorders that we frequently find in clinical practice.

The paranoid individual is an individual who is significantly aggressive and provocative. Extensive rationalisation of this aggression goes together with a strong predominance of projective mechanisms, especially projective identification, as well as an attitude of alertness and vigilance towards the environment, of suspiciousness and self-reference, and 'justified indignation.' The latter is noticeable when a target for this aggression can be found that is easily rationalised. Moreover, we see self-righteousness and an attitude of grandiosity, and, in spite of this aggressive relation to most others, there can occur a split-off idealisation of some relationships, although these are unstable idealisations. Finally there is a tendency to carry out omnipotent and controlling behaviour towards others, in order to prevent potential enemies from gaining the upper hand.

This description, familiar to all of you, is in contrast to that of the narcissistic individual, who has in common with the paranoid pathology a sense of grandiosity, superiority and self-righteousness. But here the accent is less on the moral and ideological qualities of self-righteousness, and more of a child-like self-centredness, a grandiosity which has infantile qualities, showing exhibitionism, recklessness, entitlement, a grandiosity and self-aggrandisement accompanied by devaluation and depreciation of others, a tendency of exploitiveness and parasitic behaviour towards others. The dominant psychopathology is 'envy', both conscious and unconscious, directly expressed as well as defences against it, such as spoiling what others have or what he or she receives from others as part of the process of devaluation. In therapy these persons show the typical negative therapeutic reaction out of envy, not out of unconscious guilt. They evince a tendency towards greedy incorporation that contrasts with the spoiling of what is incorporated. The result is a sense of emptiness, the use of other people as 'lavatory' in the sense of dumping into them negative experiences, getting rid of such experiences by communicating them to others and then depreciating and leaving others aside. Such a narcissistic individual at best shows certain mild super-ego pathology, a tendency to regulate himself not by focused self-criticisms, but by mood swings and a tendency for a prevalence of infantile rather than adult values. He wishes to be appreciated for being wealthy, beautiful, having nice things, rather than for integrity, intelligence and commitment to values. This pathology can also present in a more severe form which is of particular interest to us, because it signifies a combination of narcissistic and paranoid features.

One, and that's the one from the clinical viewpoint that most concerns us, is the syndrome of malignant narcissism; a combination of the narcissistic personality as I described it, plus ego-syntonic aggression, in contrast to the mild, secure, self-assuredness and grandiosity of the ordinary narcissistic person. Here we see sadistic behaviour, ego-syntonic sadistic behaviour directed against others, and at times against the self. They also present severe paranoid features, similar to those of the paranoid personality, and anti-social behaviour, showing severe super-ego pathology, with an infiltration of the pathological grandiose self with aggression.

That syndrome of malignant narcissism – I repeat: narcissistic personality, plus ego-syntonic aggression, plus paranoid features, plus anti-social behaviour – can reach a quality that leads us into a next and fortunately rare pathology. I refer to the extreme of this type, namely the anti-social personality proper. Here is the 'psychopath' of the older literature, the person with total destruction of all super-ego, or unavailability of all super-ego functions, absence of capacity for guilt, concern, any non-exploitative commitment to others, and lack of absence of concern for the self. So the psychopath, or the anti-social personality proper, is the most virulent form of the narcissistic pathology that goes from the ordinary narcissistic personality to the syndrome of malignant narcissism to the anti-social personality. Now, what is interesting then is that we can recognise a polarity if you think of it, between a pure paranoid individual, and a purely narcissistic individual, and the potentiality of these two things coming together in a dangerous mixture that exaggerates the pathological potential of both.

We know from the studies of Melanie Klein that what we are dealing with are two basic aspects of the human response to the development of severe aggression as part of the personality (Klein 1957). Melanie Klein first pointed out how in the earliest stages of development internalised object relations of an all-good gratifying ideal type co-exist split off from all the painful, frustrating and aversive ones that constitute the early expression of object relations under the dominance of aggression (Klein 1946). Idealised and persecutory internalised object relations alternate without touching each other during the dominance of the so-called paranoid-schizoid position. This position, in her view, constitutes the earliest level of development, dominant in the first six months of life, and is gradually replaced by a later level of integration between such idealised and persecutory relationships in the depressive position. Then a more cohesive self develops from split-off idealised and all-bad segments of the self. In addition, the representations of significant others integrated into integrated object representations emerges out of the most primitive, split-off idealised and persecutory representations of objects.

As you noticed, I'm using a language which is not purely Kleinian, but signifies a combination of Kleinian and ego-psychological object-relations theory. But I think that the semantics are less important than the essential concept that our earliest way of dealing with aggression is to split it off from our ideal relationships, to protect the good and ideal relationships. From that viewpoint the paranoid personality is a pathological fixation of an early stage of development, usually due to a dominance of aggression, of the aggressive investments, the dominance of aggression over love, to such an extent that integration cannot be tolerated. The paranoid individual identifies himself with an idealised version of self, while projecting onto the outside the aggressive aspects of the self together with aggressive object representations. He then perceives himself in an idealised self-state that attempts to relate to idealised individuals while all the bad persecutory ones are projected. These have to be controlled omnipotently so that projective identification, denial of aggression, idealisation and omnipotent control are the dominant features of the paranoid personality.

In contrast, in the case of the narcissistic personality, there is a further complication – namely, the setting-up of an idealised self-structure that does not only incorporate ideal aspects of the self, but that incorporates the idealised segments of the early super-ego. In this way the pathological grandiose self eats into what would become the ideals of the super-ego, and absorbs them into the self. This process leaves the super-ego weakened and only constituted by its persecutory precursors, which, in turn, are projected outside. Consequently the narcissistic individual, in addition to a sense of grandiosity, suffers from a weakening of the normal super-ego functions. This brings about the dangerous deterioration or absence of super-ego functions, leading to the extremes that I have described in the syndrome of malignant narcissism and psychopathy.

Obviously this is a gross simplification of complex psychopathology, but I want to point to the essence of the relationship between these two pathological individual structures, their connection clinically, and their causal connection in terms of the failure of dealing with severe internal aggression.

SMALL-GROUP AND LARGE-GROUP PROCESSES

Now, let's shift our perspective and go from the psychopathology of individuals to the observations that have been carried out from the psychoanalytic viewpoint of small groups, large groups and masses. These studies started out with Freud's description of mass psychology, the psychology of the horde, of the mass movement, in which an idealised leader represents the projected super-ego of all the participants of the large mass (Freud 1921). There is a mutual identification of all the members of the large mass, giving them a sense of power, strength and belonging. They present a loss of their individualised super-ego functions, which is projected onto the leader, with the freeing up of primitive impulses, particularly destructive impulses, and a free, powerful and joyful expression of violence. This increases the sense of closeness and belonging within the mob, justified by the leader's commands, and that coincides with the gratification of the total dependency on the idealised leader.

Historically Freud linked this development with the Oedipus complex. However, what interests us here is the descriptive quality of 'masses'. That first description by Freud was complemented by Bion's now classical studies of groups, his observations that small unstructured groups whose task is not clear, and who are not integrated in terms of a task relating them to the environment, tend to regress into what he called 'basic assumption groups'. These are dominant emotional states which Bion classified into three types, and which now have become generally known, accepted and integrated into clinical practice (Bion 1959).

One of the basic assumption groups is that of 'dependency', in which there is a tendency of the primitive idealisation of the group leader, selected by the regressed group, who is imbued with capacities of omnipotence, while all the other members of that dependent group experience themselves as needy, as incompetent, greedily trying to extract knowledge and guidance from that leader. In case of the leader's failure to gratify the dependent longings of that incompetent group, the devaluation of the leader leads to his replacement by an alternative one. In other words, the dependent group has a quality of idealisation, neediness, greedy incorporation, that reflects an infantile narcissistic tendency, while the kind of leader they select very often has the quality of a narcissistic personality. In fact, such dependently regressed groups typically select the most narcissistic, self-assured individual leader to gratify these needs.

In contrast to the dependency group, the basic assumptions group of 'fight/flight' described by Bion is one in which the atmosphere of the group is suspicious; there is a search for an external enemy. If such an enemy cannot be found, a division of the group between in-group and out-group occurs, with mutual projection of hostility, as well as the development of an *ad hoc* ideology of the subgroups justifying their aggression against outgroups or the other subgroup. The leader of such subgroups is typically a paranoid personality. The fight/flight group selects as leaders paranoid personalities corresponding to their emotional needs, in contrast to the narcissistic leader of the dependency group.

As a defence against both these primitive regressive groups, Bion described the 'pairing group' in which a couple, usually heterosexual but not necessarily so, is selected as an idealised leadership with the potential promise of a better future. The group at that point acquires Oedipal characteristics, and one might say that this pairing group is really a defence against the more primitive, pre-Oedipal dependent and flight/fight groups.

This psychology of the small group was complemented by Pierre Turquet's study of the psychology of the large group, in my view, the most important contribution to group psychology in general. His work provides the clues to both the small groups that Bion described and Freud's description of masses (Turquet 1975).

Large groups are groups of between 30 and 150 individuals. They are characterised by the fact that they can still hear each other, there is still individual communication, but there is really no possibility of a clear, defined relationship within that group, as it is much too large for that. It differs, therefore, from the small group in that mutual projections become ineffective, and it is no longer possible to see the effect of one's actions. There is a general atmosphere of uncertainty, and yet there is still enough communication to explain the generalised involvement in an intense emotional atmosphere, in contrast to the mass movement, where the relationship is simply of the mass to the leader.

What happens to individuals in large groups? Large-group situations are those in which such large numbers are together in a limited space without a specific task relating them to the environment. Again, absence of a clear-cut task and task structure brings about regression, the same as in a small group.

Any large audience can be transformed into a large group in five minutes by simply giving everyone the instruction to look at each other. Moreover, everybody could feel free to say whatever comes to his or her mind. Our task is only to observe and reflect about what is going on, say for an hour and a half. I assure you that pandemonium would develop within a few minutes, confirming the observations that have been made very frequently in therapeutic settings: that sometimes very sick patients in a group that has a realistic task and task structure behave very normally. Clearly, crazy patients can behave normally in a group, while therapists and well-analysed mental health professionals, in a regressed group situation may behave totally psychotically. This is a very powerful contribution to our clinical observations and I'm going to suggest, to our theoretical understanding. What the individuals experience in the large group is a loss of identity and a painful sense of impotence, they typically present fear of violence, fear of aggression, and there is a tendency to rapid development of irrationality, mutual distrust. Subgroups develop that are unstable; anybody who speaks up and represents rationality, individuality and autonomy – that is to say, who does not seem to be submerged in the informal mess of the group – is rejected and shouted down. It is as if the large group experiences envy of autonomy, of individuality, of rationality, and, on the contrary, there is a search for escape from this uncertainty by the search for a reassuring, soothing leadership that does not challenge anybody's envy. In other words, the narcissistic, cliché-ridden mediocrity becomes the ideal leader, and the group calms itself in a narcissistic, static situation that is quite similar to that of what Canetti described, as the 'feast crowd'. The participants experience a kind of relaxed sense that the world is safe, that they have a slightly ridiculous but reassuring and stable, self-assured leader (Canetti 1962).

The calming effect of the narcissistic leader is the counterpart to another potential development of the large group, namely the emergence of the paranoid leader who transforms the large group into the mass movement, develops an *ad hoc* ideology that permits the projection of aggression outside the group, and unifies the group around the leader. He takes over the super-ego function, and the violence against the outgroup becomes a relieving, unifying principle. So that there are two solutions for the large-group situation: a narcissistic regression, selection of narcissistic leadership in a passive, static, narcissistic group, or a paranoid regression, with characteristics of the mass movement described by Freud.

But there is another resolution, namely the organisation of the group in terms of rituals and principles of interactions that regulate all behaviours, to the extent that individuals are safe. I refer specifically to 'bureaucratisation' of the relationships within the large group. This avoids the regression into either narcissistic or paranoid structures, with the corresponding development of narcissistic or paranoid ideologies. Bureau-cratisations are ways to escape the large-group situation, in addition to supporting actual task performance.

Psychoanalytic studies of what is causing all these processes include the formulations of Bion himself, who proposed that in such small-group situations, primitive, internalised object relations tend to come to the fore. In other words, the paranoid-schizoid level of development described by Melanie Klein is reached in such informal group situations, implying that the normal development throughout the depressive position is particularly geared to ordinary role/status situations, to dyadic or triadic relation-ships, in which we interact with others in terms of socially well-defined roles and statuses. But if those roles and statuses disappear, the under-lying potential for regression, in Bion's term, the psychotic aspects of the personality emerge and create the situations that I have summarised. In other words, the emergence of primitive paranoid-schizoid object relations and defensive operations become dominant ways of interaction. Turquet described the same phenomena at the level of the large group, using Bion's formulations. Didier Anzieu suggested that what happens in such large-group regression is a regression in the super-ego that returns to the most primitive level of the primitive ego-ideal so that the group replaces the most primitive ego-ideal (Anzieu 1984). The group functions as an ideal, primitive mother who nourishes everybody as long as they are part of the group.

The narcissistically regressed small and large group would represent the fantasy of being submerged in an ideal relation with a giving mother, a dependent relationship that eliminates awareness of Oedipal con-flicts, differences between sexes and generations. This would explain the fact that under such conditions the fear of leaving the group, or the resentment of anybody leaving the group, would be like the resentment of abandoning the idealised relation between an infant and an ideal mother.

I have suggested in an earlier work that there are two basic levels of internalised object relations that are part of the normal personality as well as being reflected in the pathology of personality disorders. There is a basic level, in which the relationships are multiple, split up into idealised and persecutory ones, reflecting the state of development that Melanie Klein considered the paranoid-schizoid position. In Edith Jacobson's (1964) and Margaret Mahler *et al.*'s (1975) formulations this is represented by the stage of separation–individuation, in which there is a clear differ-entiation between representations of self and object, but an absolute split between idealised and persecutory ones. In contrast, there exists a second level of organisation of internalised object relations, when total object relations are reached. This is the the stage of object constancy in Mahler's and Anna Freud's terms, with an integrated representation of self and of others, the achievement of ambivalence, and integration of love and hatred under the domination of love (Freud 1952).

The large group, in my view, is the basic group situation that activates the more primitive of these two levels of relationship. Small-group processes, as well as the mass psychology described by Bion and Freud, are defences against large-group situations that threaten the emergence of the aggression that is part of the split-off aggression of early development, as part of an inbuilt structure of all human beings.

The large-group process is the basic group situation which reflects the enactment of primitive object relations against which small groups and masses are defensive structures. Similarly, we can also view the development of ideology, regressions into a paranoid or narcissistic dimension, or bureaucratisations in this light. Consequently, there exists a basic reality of threats of irrationality, eruption of aggression, envy of autonomy, of creativity, of intelligence, built into our basic functions in the group processes that are informal social settings. This then illustrates how individual dynamics, the dynamics of the paranoid and the narcissistic personality are repeated, so to speak, at a higher level, in the group situation, oscillating in the group's stabilisation efforts between narcissistic and paranoid developments.

ORGANISATIONS AND PATHOLOGICAL FUNCTIONING

Now, I would like to shift from talking about individuals in groups to a few words about organisations. Pathological group processes tend to be submerged in social organisations, namely those that have a specific task and specific boundaries to carry these tasks out. I refer to areas such as education, health, industry, the military or the church: organisations with organised leadership, organisational boundaries and which are task-oriented as long as tasks are performed and the leadership is capable and adequate to such task performance. When, however, such task performance suffers, the group processes that I mentioned, immediately emerge and tend to bring about organisational regression. This is what is ordinarily called 'loss of morale', and concerns the precise activation of narcissistic and paranoid group formation.

The causes for such regression are multiple. Nowadays we know that one, perhaps the most important, cause is the failure in the functional organisation of the institution. In other words the structure is inadequate to the task that is to be performed, or else the tasks can no longer be performed because of lack of resources or excessive constraints. Or, there is a poor leadership, incapable of defining the tasks, the constraints, and of setting up a rational and functional task organisation.

In all organisations that fail, where morale goes down the drain, leadership first appears as responsible, then bad leaders seem to be the cause. Organisational analysis shows that this is like the temperature, it's a symptom, in that often it is faulty organisation of task performance, excessive constraints, lack of clarity of the task, which are the causes of organisations malfunctioning. But at times – although not always – it is also a feature of leadership. And what brings about faulty leadership may be in part bad organisation.

One has to differentiate between functional authority and authoritarianism. Authoritarianism is the condition under which excessive authority is carried out by the leadership, creating dictatorial and oppressive conditions, activating both Oedipal submission, rebellion and conflicts in the organisation, and tending to bring about regression in the group processes, of the type I mentioned. The contrast to authoritarianism is chaos, where there's inadequate, insufficient authority or, if you want, insufficient power in the leadership to carry out functional authority. Power that corresponds to functional authority is rational and reasonable. Excessive power brings about authoritarianism; inadequate power, chaos.

But while excessive use of power on the part of the leadership is an important aspect of faulty leadership and of regression in institutions, very often the excessive use of power on the part of authority is unconsciously fostered by the entire organisation, in which non-recognised dissociated aggression is projected onto those in power, or both leaders and 'guardians at the gate'. Some degree of aggression is subtly expressed, for example, in the selection processes of organisations, in the promotion processes of organisations, in the tendency to select leadership with severely narcissistic or paranoid features. Excessive activation of power may reflect the regression in the functioning of the group, in that the aggression activated in large-group processes is concentrated as the primitive power activated in a mass movement, stimulating the exercise of irrational power on the part of the paranoid leadership, as well as reflecting the aggression of paranoid personalities in leadership positions. Sometimes the combination of organisational defensive functions, such as paranoid leadership and excessive bureaucratisation, amplify the exercise of pathological power. A paranoid leader finds a perfect bureaucratic organisation that brings about a despotic regime throughout the organisation, without any basic change in its preexisting structure or bureaucratic functioning.

This brings us to the origin of aggression and excessive power in the leader himself, and the qualities that are needed for good leadership and the danger of bad leadership.

In essence – and I'm summarising here a great number of studies, with a particular reference to Elliott Jaques's very important studies (1955), throughout his professional life, of the qualities of leadership – it is important that leaders of organisations combine high intelligence with a sufficient emotional maturity that gives them the capacity for evaluating themselves and others in depth and therefore select good intermediate leadership around them. Also important is a certain degree of paranoid potential, as opposed to a dangerous naivety (in other words a 'motivated innocence') that would prevent the leader from becoming aware of the constant risk of the activation of aggression in the organisation. A certain degree of narcissism is warranted in the leader, in the sense of the self-assuredness that protects the leader against the regressive pull in the organisation, against the aggression that is usually directed at leadership as part of the expression of both Oedipal and pre-Oedipal individual psychopathology. And finally, the leader needs sufficient development of super-ego functions to resist the corruptive temptations of power that are very concretely present in all organisations in which decisions have to be made regarding levels of personnel or staff or subordinates that go beyond personal levels of contact; and where important social resources are to be distributed. I repeat, a combination of high intelligence, capacity for object relations in depth, a certain degree of paranoid potential, narcissistic potential, and incorruptibility seem to be essential qualities for good leadership.

But as you see, I have already included here two dangerous leadership characteristics. Namely, I refer to a certain degree of narcissistic and paranoid potential as protective features that may easily get out of hand. This particularly happens when regression in the group processes of the organisation tend to seduce the leader or suck the leader into the narcissistic or paranoid function respectively needed by the narcissistically regressed or the paranoidly regressed group.

So, under the worst circumstances, you may have a situation in which ordinary corrective and protective functions against group regression tempt the leadership into narcissistic and paranoid stances that may bring to the fore leadership with severe narcissistic and paranoid features – in a worst-case scenario, leaders with malignant narcissism who then may trigger a reign of terror in the organisation.

So far I've talked about organisations. When it goes to a broader social spectrum, when we talk about society at large, we can no longer apply organisational theory, because society is too large, has an infinite number of boundaries, and a leadership at that point can no longer be defined in functional terms; when a political dimension takes over, this presents a new complication to this picture. New complications arise in that the political process may either veer toward a dictatorial, authoritarian, or totalitarian regime in which control of decision-making is totally centralised and relatively independent from the political process. This carries the danger of authoritarianism and severe regression in leadership. Alternatively, the political process may be democratic, which implies collective decision-making. This protects against despotism, against authoritarianism and against totalitarian regimes, but may activate large-group processes. Such an activation develops because in the political process of democratic elections, for example, the leader depends on everybody in the large group and in the crowd, and everybody's dependency in an electional process on an anonymous large mass tends to activate the primal fears and fantasies characteristic of the individual, in the large group. So that the political process tends to activate paranoid and narcissistic regressions, and paranoid and narcissistic behaviours in leadership as well as in its followers, that creates an ongoing stress and danger to the social and group processes operating in an open community.

At the politically desirable, democratic stage of development, we have risks of the development of regressive ideologies that may foster primitive regression and aggression. The risk of regression in ideologies takes two extreme forms. On one hand, in relatively stable social conditions, a superficial narcissistically gratifying ideology, a reassuring and soothing triviality can occur. At the other extreme a severe paranoid ideology can develop that usually shows characteristics that are quite similar to that of the paranoid-schizoid level of development. These are ideologies that search for a utopian solution of absolute happiness, and promise that if they acquire control, happiness will reign on the Earth. Moreover, the ideology forces absolute submission, doesn't tolerate outsiders or non-believers. These have to be fought off – in a worst-case scenario, outsiders are de-humanised and thus justify the brutal attack on them. Finally, such ideologies tend to have an anti-sexual, anti-couple, anti-privacy, anti-individualistic quality. In other words, they express the envy, in the deepest sense, of the Oedipal couple. And they stress the obligation of each individual to the mass, to the collectivity, to the State. In between those extreme ideologies we have an intermediate, humanistic, more functional one that provides a belief system that relates to overall tasks, tradition and history of a certain social group or entity.

The same ideological thinking may operate at all these levels. For example, if you look at terrorist Marxist movements in South America or the Middle East, it's the paranoid narcissistic extreme of Marxism. On the other hand you have the banal and reassuring clichéd communist statements in Soviet Russia during the last ten years of its existence. Thus you have those two extremes within the same ideology, and you might say that the Marxism with a human face developed in Western Europe during that same time and represents the intermediate humanistic, deeper level of that same type of ideology.

What I'm saying is that it's not that certain ideologies belong necessarily to one or the other pole, but they may extend according to group regression and social situations, to any of these three levels. By the same token, the individual's entrance into an ideology depends on the individual's levels of development, from normal super-ego development and individuation, abstraction, de-personification of the super-ego at optimum level, to the more primitive all-black, all-white, split-off rigid infantile nature of the infantile super-ego. Then there is a tendency to enter into an ideology at one or the other extreme or the middle zone.

So, ideology as a defence against regression can miscarry and bring about a regression into severe aggression, fostering brutality as ideological commitment. Bureaucracy as a defence against aggression may be used by dictatorial leadership for regressive and oppressive purposes. There are inbuilt limits to the corrective functions of democracy, and inbuilt limits to the possibility of task-orientedness when it comes to leadership of social institutions and political institutions with an infinite number of boundaries.

In conclusion, I think that what we have observed in totalitarian regimes is the extreme combination of all the regressive factors that I have mentioned, that potentially are available at all times everywhere, in various ingredients, but hopefully or luckily don't always come together at the same time. But in a worst-case scenario, you have a combination of severe social upheaval or a revolution with breakdown of ordinary social structures, severe regression into primitive large-group processes, a revolutionary movement with a leader who combines a primitive regressive ideology with qualities of the leader that express malignant narcissism. By the way, these latter qualities correspond very exactly to the personal psychology, for example, of Hitler and Stalin. If you have a highly effective bureaucracy, the combination of such terrible leader characteristics, a centralised, primitive ideology, a mass movement, and the modern possibility of complete control over information, mass media, the economy and social organisation, then you have the condition for a totalitarian, in contrast to an authoritarian, regime; in other words, a regime that combines a paranoid and narcissistic structure. If you have a purely paranoid structure you only have an authoritarian regime – you only have to obey and submit and you can survive. But if you have a totalitarian structure, you have a combination of the paranoid and the narcissistic, you don't only have to obey: you have to love your leader, your ideology, your religion, whatever it is, and that goes into the deepest depths of the individual, of the family, of the social structure. Then you have the kind of conditions under which mass murder on the grand scale – such as, for example, was carried out in the Soviet Union or Nazi Germany, or can be carried out by still-existing totalitarian regimes in the world – becomes natural and unavoidable.

REFERENCES

Anzieu, D. (1984). *The Group and the Unconscious*, London: Routledge and Kegan Paul.
Bion, W.R. (1959). *Experiences in Groups*, New York: Basic Books.

Canetti, E. (1962). *Crowds and Power*, New York: Viking.

Freud, A. (1952) 'The Mutual Influences in the Development of the Ego and the Id,' in *The Writings of Anna Freud*, Vol 4, New York: International Universities Press, 1968.

Freud, S. (1921). 'Group Psychology and the Analysis of the Ego', *S.E.* Vol. 18, London: Hogarth Press.

Jacobson, E. (1964). *The Self and the Object World*, New York: International Universities Press.

Jaques, E. (1955). 'Social Systems as a Defence against Persecutory and Depressive Anxiety', in Klein, M., Heimann, P. and Money-Kyrle, R. (eds) *New Directions in Psycho-Analysis*, London : Maresfield, 1977.

Klein, M. (1946). 'Notes on Some Schizoid Mechanisms', in *Envy and Gratitude and other Works 1946–1963*, London: Hogarth Press 1975.

—— (1957) 'Envy and Gratitude', in *Envy and Gratitude and other Works 1946–1963*, London: Hogarth Press 1975.

Mahler, M., Pine, F. and Berman, A. (1975) *The Psychological Birth of the Human Infant*, New York: Basic Books.

Turquet, P. (1975) 'Threats to Identity in the Large Group', in Kreeger, L. (ed.) *The Large Group*, London: Karnac.

Chapter 7

Paranoia, groups and enquiry

Robert D. Hinshelwood

We tend to think that in the course of evolution the enlargement of the human brain has given rise to a comparable enlargement of the capacity to reason and to understand reality. However, there is, it seems to me, evidence that the same enlargement must also be responsible for a vast enlargement in the capacity for impulses and intensity of feelings. No animal is more sexual; none more destructive. Only human beings are afflicted by serious mental illness in epidemic proportions. The irrational or so-called animal side of our nature is, in reality, as hypertrophied as the cognitive, rational side.

There is another size factor in human life. Whereas sexuality tends to be found focused into the smallest of all social groups, the couple, destructiveness increases with the size of the group. It is with this hypertrophied destructiveness, that we will begin. In smaller groups, destructiveness tends to take place *within* the grouping. The couple that comprises a torturer and his victim is devoted to the destruction of one of that group; or we might recall that a large majority of murders occur within a love affair, a marriage or the family.

However, only small increases in size result in the tendency reversing – in larger groups, destructiveness turns outwards, towards another group. Then we really see destructiveness getting going.

The intensity of a group's destructiveness increases seemingly in proportion to its size. This is mitigated, to a degree, only by spontaneous divisions of the group into separate, smaller and mutually hostile factions. At the extreme – in a group of one – self-destructiveness is not unknown. But it is deemed highly abnormal. Being infrequent as well as abnormal, we might wonder if self-destructiveness only occurs when the person is sufficiently abnormal to think of himself as a group, as a number of separate (and independent) parts.

The other side of the coin to destructiveness is a fear, i.e. an expectation of being the victim of someone's destructiveness. That frequently entails fighting back from a position of weakness, though not always. Inviting being treated as a victim can have considerable advantages –

mostly moral (which may in many circumstances, confer a degree of powerfulness). Alternatively the heroism of escape and rescue may be accomplished. Being a victim has various shades of feelings. Suffering a victimisation is called 'persecution'. But when the source of the victimisation is only identified in one's own imagination, that is 'paranoia'. Sometimes these 'others' who are believed to be responsible, are not actually real – but they *are* real to the victim, and they do make him suffer. And perhaps it is only within social groups (imagined or real) that paranoia and persecution can exist. Probably only within a real social context can they become fully-fledged, and that is because of a peculiar and important plasticity in social groups which we will now consider.

THE INDIVIDUAL IS LOST IN THE GROUP MIND

The features of a group's mentality are remarkably changeable. A particular state of feeling can sweep across the members, even in very large and unorganised groups, or crowds. Consider: the terrified rout of a defeated army, the rebellious feelings of a ship's crew at the moment of mutiny, the anger in a railway carriage full of people at the announcement of a delay, or the sudden surge in a football crowd that discovers fans from the opposing team. These are all moments when something afflicts large numbers of people almost simultaneously. They do not have to be people who know each other; in fact an instantaneous *bonhomie* or comradeship seems to occur at the same time across the group, all feeling in the same plight. Individuals – as they were before the moment of panic or rage – become lost in a corporate urge that identifies them all together in one emotional moment. The natural variation of responses between people vanishes spontaneously and immediately. Those who do not join in are neglected, may even be trampled underfoot. It is as if the individual relinquishes his individuality, and succumbs to a group essence or being. An identity spawned within the group is instantly spread across all the individuals of the group.

Gustav LeBon[1], a French sociologist of the nineteenth century, called this phenomenon 'contagion'. It is as if an agent, like a flu virus, sweeps through the crowd. It is an emotional epidemic. He had in mind the crowd disturbances that happened all through the century following the French Revolution. Contagion is a cohesive process, and it can happen with barely a word spoken, although commonly it is enhanced by inarticulate noises and shouting. At times it may be channelled or harnessed by political oratory. In fact politicians owe their success to being able to tap this collective energy, especially by directing it at specific enemies. Police trained in riot control attempt to subdue it – by containing it within itself through delimiting the physical space in which the crowd can operate.

Let us be clear what is happening. One person's state of mind is being affected by that of the person standing next to him – and in a myriad repetitions around and around. The effect is to bring the adjacent persons into a like-mindedness. They become mentally one, emotionally identical, for that moment. Rage and fear seem to be such basic responses that they can be absorbed through the skin as it were. Ultimately the individuals barely exist, or exist in a mindless state. Their own minds have been super-seded by a group mind.

Now, consider a group of people gathering, perhaps many hundreds, many dressed expensively and immaculately, obviously for the occasion. They enter a large building in a controlled orderly way, as if sens-ing each other and moving carefully not to harm, intrude or interfere with each other. Most are in smaller groups, often twos, and look after each other. In a continual orderly activity they take allotted seats in a vast space, perhaps with several tiers. They all face one end of the building where there is a stage, screened away by vast curtains. Many people have quietly and efficiently organised this crowd with tickets, programme-selling and a myriad of unseen activities and functions. Having come together, at this appointed time, the lights dim, the curtains part and a dramatised action ensues over the course of a couple of hours, often violent, suffering or tragic. During this time the audience behave much the same, seated, calm and with a riveted attention on the figures enacting human relation-ships and human dilemmas on the stage. Whilst externally each member of the audience appears inactive though attentive, that attention betrays a complex and intense internal activity within themselves. It is a form of identifying. The person in the audience opens himself to imagining the experiences of a figure on the stage. That figure explicitly conveys in gesture, grimace and above all words, the nature of the experience for the persons in the audience to identify with. Those observing persons actually have an experience of the displayed relationships, dilemmas, humour, etc. Their emotional states are co-ordinated by the action of the play; tragedy brings out sadness across the audience, humour brings out laughter, and so on.

Of course there must be some individual variation between people, but the striking quality is the identicalness of their behaviour and their internal reactions. And afterwards the persons are left with an enduring state of mind, emotional states. They also work over intelligently the experiences and emotions they have been led through.

Once again, like the destructive mobs, people have voluntarily given up a degree of their individuality and entered a collective experience, knowingly and obviously with great anticipation, often with the feeling of being in the presence of something magnificent, something quite out of the ordinary. It may take a while for people to regain themselves after-wards, to disengage from feeling for the figures on the stage, to return to their own pre-occupations, to the dramas and dilemmas of their own relationships which they live out in reality.

The orderliness, calmness, the dimmed lights, the comfortable surroundings, the architected ambience and so on, are all cultivated features that allow for the intensity of group behaviour and emotions to be orchestrated in a controlled way. The violent explosiveness of crowd outbursts is tamed in these ways, like the taming of a nuclear reaction in a power station; dangerous, but imposing and exciting when under control. For a time, during the performance and until he recovers himself, the person has not quite been himself. Who, then, has he been? Perhaps he is the author of the play who has directed the sequence of experiences the person suffered; perhaps the character(s) in the play, for whom the person felt, during and after the performance. But is it possible to answer the question at all in this way? Looking in from outside, he is part of a group mentality. Though he may be aware of himself having the experiences, the person does suspend his awareness of himself; and no longer has his *own* pre-occupations. He gives them up in favour of having the pre-occupations that all the assembled crowd have. His identity is, in an important sense, therefore, the group itself, the crowd he sits down with.

Consider now, being in a restaurant, near to a table with a number of people; perhaps sitting right next to them, but not part of them. They are strangers. They are however animated and merry, and with a great deal of lively talk and humour. You may overhear some of the jokes, and listen to the guffaws of uncontrollable laughter at the table. You might see the joke, know it is funny, even smile to yourself and remember to tell it the next time you are in a party – like the one you are next to. But you don't guffaw with the people at the next table. You have to make overtures, smile at them, ask them a question or two, before you can find yourself invited in, and only then infected with their spirit of good humour and laughter. Only then may you suffer the contagion of their emotion, and feel it as they do. However, until that moment of entry to their group, there is a boundary to the emotional infection. The laughter comes right up to you and bounces back from the edge of the group so that outsiders are hardly moved themselves – they can only recognise that humour is happening, and cannot be a part of it. And outside of the boundary there can be great feelings of exclusion, often hard to bear.

In these ordinary experiences we can see how individuals are drawn to submersion in the group, cradled in a merger with something vaster than themselves. An individual's boundaries are precarious. It can be a severe problem to remain a person that is not defined by the group, either by total inclusion or by exclusion. The individual must balance the urge to sink into the life of a group against remaining an individual. Both are compelling.

The urge to 'lose oneself' is enticing in Bill Buford's experience. Being on the football terraces with gangs of thugs feels like a liberating life; 'with numbers there are no laws' (Buford 1991: 64).[2]

However, the personal urge to leave self behind for the balmy comforts of group life is not uncomplicated. Immersion demolishes the self. Pierre Turquet[3] described sessions of unstructured large groups conducted for research purposes. There the individual is beset by

> the dislocation every conference member experiences as he takes himself into a world which transcends the usual parameters of his own individuality ... Any one session of a large group is in itself so kaleidoscopic, however, that any equilibrium appears transitory ... [The member] seeks to make something of the situation, to give it a meaning, to make a construct of it ... but often it seems to express not only the singleton's destructive feelings, but also ... his own experience of being threatened with annihilation as he interacts with the large group and its members.
>
> (Turquet 1975: 94–5)

The underlying experience in joining a large group, or crowd, is highly threatening in the way it can strip off the sense of being an individual altogether. Such a sense of demolition has to be understood somehow by the individual.

There are other demolishing circumstances too. At times the urge to join in a group is coupled with a severe and threatening pressure from the group itself. Join in – or else ... And in line with this, in some countries systematic oppression and torture are standard methods to get a person to leave their own mind and to take residence in a prescribed set of attitudes and beliefs.

So, not only a carrot but a stick too can push people into the swirling movement of the group mentality.

With all these pressures, from within the self or from without (i.e. from the group) how is it possible to keep coherence and independence of mind?

THE INDIVIDUAL FINDS PROTECTION

Brian Keenan was kidnapped and held hostage by Shi-ite militia in Beirut for nearly four and a half years. He then wrote a book describing his familiarity with these threats and terrors. In the book, *An Evil Cradling*, he described moments *in extremis* when 'I needed anger to pull me back from these moments of madness' (Keenan 1992: 75). It is commonly reported that cultivating anger maintains a sense of being a person when it is about to collapse. Brian Keenan described times when the rescuing quality of anger may be completely conscious and striven for as an act of will. The effort is to sustain personal boundaries against the encroachment of a demolishing force from the torturer or his group. A psychoanalyst working in Argentina during the time of the Galtieri dictatorship was familiar with the experience of torture victims through that of one survivor who was in a psychoanalytic treatment: '[Torture] seeks to provoke breaches in the identity, i.e. in the sense of internal cohesion and continuity ... the torturer's aim is to destroy thought and identity' (Amati 1987: 112).

So, one desperate way that personal identity and the sense of self can be supported is in the cultivation of an enemy who we can hate and attack in angry ways. It creates a specific identity through being separate from the enemy. Anger deters or destroys an actual persecutor, but also, in the event of being helpless in the hands of a persecutor, it can also shore up a demolished structure of the self through the exaggerated separation from the torturer.

This is all very well when there is real coercion and the threat to the self is in the form of an actual torturer. But what do we make of the instances when the person is not obviously coerced and tortured – in a crowd, at a political rally, going with a lynching mob, paying for a seat at the theatre? That voluntary urge towards the mind-blowing plunge into the group emotion also demolishes the person. That wish relinquishes personal boundaries, gives up being separate. It is both deliciously compelling and personally reducing.

The exciting enticements of relinquishing oneself to the group may be an internal urge but it carries the dangers of an external coercion. It can stretch the person too far. Even though internal, it is felt as real coercion. And therefore as real danger.[4]

Harry Guntrip made a special study over the whole of his lifelong practice of these problems of 'getting in' and the panic of 'getting out' again: '[A]n agoraphobic patient who is "safe inside" and afraid to be born may alternate with the claustrophobic patient who feels smothered inside and is in such a hurry to be born that he repudiates all dependencies whatsoever' (Guntrip 1961: 316). Being so far 'inside' that it feels dangerous is called claustrophobia. Guntrip described these oscillations between feeling outside and excluded and feeling inside and dangerously cramped, and studied them within the relationship of a psychoanalysis. It also occurs in the relationship to a group: '[F]irstly, people object often to remarks which are said to depersonalise everyone by talking about "the group"; and secondly remarks to individuals are often criticised as "individual psychotherapy in public" ' (Hinshelwood 1982: 88). These are twin complaints: either the individual is depersonalised by the group mentality, or the person is separated out in a terrifying exposure. These examples are experienced most pointedly in therapeutic situations (psychoanalytic or group), but there, shown up in high relief, are representations of the ordinary problems that ordinary people suffer in an ordinary day.

When the threat comes from inside, it is very different from that of an actual 'external' persecutor who is doing you harm. It may be perceived, however, in a similar way – as the threat of a 'persecution' from the person or group that is longed for. That group is persecuting because it will swallow you up – even though you want it. Such 'imaginary' persecution, or paranoia is therefore a group event. It emerges from relationships with others. Wanting to be in the group can be so strong that identity and personhood are sacrificed, so that the group, from which exclusion is too painful, does really become a threat to the self. This is a serious distortion: what is desired becomes a threat. Such urges from inside a person arise from a deep positive longing, and create a persecutor out of one who is needed and loved!

This is a contrived enmity. It comes to the rescue, just like the torture victim cultivating his anger. But it is an enmity that will startle the 'other' who is longed for and needed. That 'other' is perversely written down as a persecutor, when he/she is in fact desired. This is close to Freud's recognition that paranoia is a cover for a love that feels as though it is so intense it is beyond tolerable limits.[5] We might revise it in the following way: a love that is felt to be inappropriately intense in *any* way can threaten a person's boundaries, as surely as actual torture. If that is so then that person's loved one can appear distorted as an actual persecutor, an invader of boundaries. Even though ordinary enough, this paranoid reaction is rarely recognised. But it is a serious one. It turns loving forces into destructiveness.

FREEDOM COMES FROM THOUGHT

We want to know if there is any other mode of operating against this internal paranoiogenic factor.

Can we take recourse to that striking feature of our evolution, our hypertrophied brain? Though I have been at pains to demonstrate how its hypertrophy has intensified our animal nature, can we make a virtue of its equally fabulous expansion of our reasoning? Can it protect a robustly separate sense of self? Can it protect a person from being swamped, and achieve that protection in a different way from a contrived anger and paranoia?

To follow this line entails a brief examination of the place of thinking in groups and institutions. I shall base this on Tom Main's descriptions of how reason and thought succumb in mental hospitals. He investigated how the culture of a hospital could encroach upon the minds of its staff and patients.[6]

All staff and patients, he said, together become caught up in systems of behaviour which were called therapeutic, but which in many hospitals in the course of time had long since lost any real meaning. He described the freedom from having to do any thinking. This, he claimed, is the advantage to be gained from immersion in the group and its rituals. Focusing on the fate of thinking itself, he described the 'danger of becoming culture-bound, of being enmeshed unthinkingly in moral beliefs and beloved practices that were once reality-oriented ideas and techniques' (Main 1967: 65). These are group solutions to problems, in the form of carefully observed rituals which once had been sensible practices. An idea starts as being realistic within a certain context arising from pressing problems, but it changes to become a morally charged instruction, a tablet of stone or an invocation – 'a captor of the self and the thinking processes' (Main 1967: 71).

Now consider for a moment the solemnity of occasion during a Spanish *feria* when the vast portals of the cathedral open and the procession of the image of the Virgin slides through towards the surrounding and venerating throng of its worshippers. It is the public epitome of the elevation of the ordinary to the sublime – the 'hierarchical promotion' of the idea of motherhood to become divinity.

The history of the Western world in the last few hundred years has been to regenerate the ordinary – exemplified in the evidence of one's own eyes in simply seeing through a telescope as Galileo pioneered. The clash between enquiry and divine ritual has never been sharper than in Galileo's fate. Nevertheless, the achievement of a position of doubt and ignorance is possibly the greatest achievement of those hypertrophied hemispheres. Whatever the cost, being stretched upon the rack of not-knowing is the antidote to being dissolved in the group. In our historical context, we have used our over-large brains to reason and enquire against prejudice and ritual.

Let us return from this power of reason and observation, to the illustrations in this chapter. Whilst advancing through them we have come across different stages of group mentality. We can see three situations: 'crowd, 'ritual' and 'theatre'. In each case a contagion infects the group mentality of the individuals forming them. But what distinguishes them is the quality of insight and enquiry that is possible within them.

The triplet – crowd, ritual and theatre – form a string drawn across a dimension we might call thought. The law of thought is missing altogether in a crowd. But it is not quite missing in ritual. There, many participants can be perfectly aware that immense theological thought adheres to the ritual. Participants may not be able to recite the theological debates, interests and rivalries that comprise the background to the ritual, and which forms its meaning, but they know of the existence and importance of meaning and thought to the ritual itself.

When it comes to the theatre, for many in the audience, enquiry and thought are required in the performance, and in the audience. Thought has a potential existence in the theatre; its potentiality may eventually be realised. Perhaps thought gets going really after the performance is over (or in the intervals), when the persons have regained something of themselves again. Then the individual may give thought to what he has experienced, its meaning to him and to human life in general, and to the particular experience of that play with those actors and actresses, and that specific performance that they gave for him.

If enquiry and the pursuit of thought is contrasted with immersion in the group mentality, typically in the crowd, then there are certain conclusions we must draw. The group mentality contributes profoundly as a cause of paranoia. An investigation of paranoia requires an investigation of the group. In any particular case, we need to know what is the group mentality. Are members sucked into especially unthinking forms of experience, and out of their mode of thinking? Is there particular coercion to immerse in the group and lose boundaries as a result of invasion?

If the thinking hemispheres on top of our heads are any use, they need to find ways in which the group can enquire of itself and reflect on its state, rather than simply drive mindlessly onwards in controlled or uncontrolled form. For instance important modern experiments in the theatre have attempted to encourage reflective participation in hitherto depersonalised audiences.

Thought, being the counterpart to the sweeping contagion of emotion, may lead to another problem. It is not so much a direct conflict between reason and emotion. Indeed that would be sliding out of the real problem of integrating them into a thoughtful enquiry into passion. Ideas that are 'disembodied' become hard task-masters. The history of our present century gives us many disastrous examples. Ideas became dislocated from their personal context, to rule over persons – in the Soviet Union it was an economic idea, in Nazi Germany the notion of racial purity.[7]

Thought divorced from its human passions is sterile and dangerous. We need a necessary enquiry *of* emotional states and commitments. We need to track the promotional hierarchy of ideas into unthinking practices and attitudes. And we need to do these at the group level.

Though enquiry and thought increase with the size of brain, they decline as groups enlarge. The enlargement of the human brain is a mixed blessing. The crucial point of balance, as the total size of the human group around the world approaches and passes five billion, is whether our brains can tip the balance in favour of the hypertrophied intelligence in groups, or remain in favour of hypertrophied passions and paranoia.

NOTES

1 Gustav LeBon's book *Psychologie des foules* was originally published in France in 1895. The French Revolution had left the ruling classes very nervous throughout the nineteenth century; the increasingly wealthy and powerful middle classes throughout Europe were equally jittery that their heads would be at risk. Therefore the behaviour of crowds was anxiously studied, and on the whole believed then to be the manifestations of the uneducated (and ineducable) classes. LeBon's meticulous study was very influential. It had the benefit of astute observation and was not merely a rehearsal of contemporary prejudices about the poor. In recent times the fascination has transferred to the book itself – see Nye (1975) and Moscovici (1981).

2 Bill Buford is an American journalist who spent eight years travelling with a football supporters' club to matches in this country and abroad. The outcome was his book *Among the Thugs* describing his shock at the crowd violence he witnessed but was also a part of. His book is a remarkable attempt to review in hindsight the loss of his individuality and judgement when in the midst of the crowd.

3 Pierre Turquet was a psychoanalyst who also worked in experiential groups and wrote movingly about the experiences and sense of threat in rather large groups. His classic description is published as 'Threats to identity in the large group' in Kreeger (1975).

4 This conflict reaches intense proportions in people with severely disordered personalities, and we meet those in a psychoanalytic practice.

5 Freud's theory of paranoia in its completeness, was that homosexual love lay beneath the hatred of paranoia. See Freud (1911).

6 Tom Main was an innovative psychiatrist and psychoanalyst, the inventor of the name 'therapeutic community', and one of the originators of the idea. The Arbours Association itself is one prominent example of a therapeutic community, as well as the Cassel Hospital in which Tom Main developed his ideas between 1946 and 1976. He wrote about the corruption of thought in groups and organisations in Main (1967).

7 I have explored recently how groups possess ideas and the ensuing political implications, in a chapter in Kennard and Small (1996).

REFERENCES

Amati, Sylvia (1987) 'Some thoughts on torture'. *Free Associations* 8: 94–114.

Buford, Bill (1991) *Among the Thugs*. London: Secker and Warburg.

Freud, Sigmund (1911) 'Psycho-Analytic Notes on an Autobiographical Account of a Case of Paranoia'. In *Standard Edition of the Complete Psychological Works of Sigmund Freud*, 14: 9–82.

Guntrip, Harry (1961) *Personality Structure and Human Adaptation*. London: Hogarth.

Hinshelwood, R.D. (1982) Complaints about the community meeting. *International Journal of Therapeutic Communities* 3: 88–94.

—— (1996) 'I have an idea . . .' In Kennard and Small (1996).

Keenan, Brian (1992) *An Evil Cradling*. London: Hutchinson.

Kennard, David and Small, Neil (1996) (eds) *Living Together*. London: Quartet.

Kreeger, Lionel (ed.) (1975) *The Large Group*. London: Constable.

LeBon, Gustav (1895) *Psychologie des foules*. Paris: Alcan. Republished in English as *The Crowd* (1995) Brunswick: Transaction.

Main, T.F. (1967) 'Knowledge, Learning and Freedom from Thought'. *Psychoanalytic Psychotherapy* 5: 59–78 (1990).

Moscovici, Serge (1981) *L'age des foules*. Paris: Fayard. Published in English as *The Age of the Crowd* (1985) Cambridge: Cambridge University Press.

Nye, Robert (1975) *The Origins of Crowd Psychology*. London: Sage.

Turquet, Pierre (1975) 'Threats to identity in the large group'. In Lionel Kreeger (ed.) *The Large Group*.

Chapter 8

Paranoia in institutional life
The death-throes of the asylum

Leonard Fagin

Governments in the United Kingdom have been pursuing a policy to replace large psychiatric hospitals with smaller community units. Whilst this has been a policy which has responded to the concerns about life and treatment in these old asylums, it has not always been welcome, particularly amongst patients, their relatives and staff, who have not been confident that community care arrangements adequately provide for the needs of those suffering from severe mental illness, with its associated handicaps and disabilities.

As particular examples of closed, or total organizations, psychiatric institutions present ample opportunities for misperceptions amongst staff and patients. When the institution is forced to go through radical changes, it is likely to substantially affect the lives of the residents and those that work there. During the process of change, rumours and gossip tend to be given more credence than official announcements from management. In these circumstances opportunities for fully blown paranoid ideas multiply exponentially as bacteria proliferate actively in a suitably enriched medium. If the institution is in its death-throes, and the driving force to close it is felt to be in the hands of distant managers and paymasters, mistrust and suspicion can become rife, impregnating and poisoning all attempts at therapeutic activities. In this chapter I will explore the potential danger to staff relationships, as well as to clinical activities, which I believe threaten large psychiatric hospitals when they close down. This phenomenon is not only likely to cause detriment to the life of patients and staff during this process of closure, but can, I believe, also leave behind a trail of negative experiences which can affect the services that replace the old institution.

The move to close down psychiatric institutions started in the early 1960s, and the process has accelerated as we reach the end of the millennium. In the USA, the movement of de-institutionalization was heralded by President J.F. Kennedy's 1961 call for a closure programme in which hospitals would be replaced by a network of community mental health centres, providing out-patient services, partial hospitalization regimes, emergency services and staff bases for domiciliary support services (Fagin 1985). Changes followed rapidly, with a massive growth of out-patient services replacing hospital-based care. In 1955, 27 per cent of mental health care was provided as out-patient services, 70 per cent as in-patient care. By 1975, the situation was almost completely reversed: 70 per cent was out-patient, 3 per cent day care, 27 per cent in-patient care. These changes were mirrored by parallel moves in the United Kingdom, although the transition to alternative services has been more protracted. The movement for a closure programme followed a tide of optimism which was prompted by a paper by Tooth and Brooke (1961) predicting that the long-stay population in hospitals in 1954 would be run down by 1975. This prediction proved to be largely erroneous, partly because the community care programme failed to offer a range of 'active treatments' which would prevent the rise of a new long-stay population, and also because it did not take into account powerful societal forces mediated by fluctuating economic cycles, unemployment, rising crime and immigration. Despite this, many large Victorian asylums have closed down or are in the process of closing down, due to be replaced by smaller units in district general hospitals or as small acute facilities attached to the rapidly developing number of community mental health centres.

I worked for many years in a large Victorian asylum in the outskirts of London which closed down at the end of 1996. Claybury Hospital was commissioned at the end of the nineteenth century, opening its doors in 1893 to patients 'of all classes', serving a scattered population of 680,000 in East London, Middlesex, Hertfordshire and Essex as the first London County Council Asylum. In 1948 it was taken over by the National Health Service, with no private beds. It was arranged in what was then a novel architectural design. A network of two-floored 'villas' was interconnected by long corridors, designed to allow residents and staff to socialise and communicate outside their residences and protect them from the inclement weather. Like many other institutions, the hospital practically functioned as an independent community. It had its own administrative departments, farm, gardens and nurseries, maintenance departments, workshops and builders' yards, laundry, needle room, kitchens, chapels, recreation hall, library and residential facilities for staff. At its peak of occupancy, in 1916, the hospital offered accommodation for over 2,700 patients, in 53 single-sex wards or units, in a distinctly hierarchical social structure. It was headed by a medical superintendent and nursing matrons, supervising just over 400 nursing staff (Pryor 1993). With the advent of the open-door policy, out-patient care and psychopharmacological treatments the numbers of patients started to decrease. During this time Claybury started to develop a unique experiment, transforming the hospital into a 'therapeutic community', under the leadership of Denis Martin. The aim was to provide in our hospitals an atmosphere in which the patient feels free to express himself and, at the same time, learn how to develop good human relationships.

(Martin 1974: 42)

Martin and his colleagues had become acutely aware of the effects of institutionalization on his patients.

Perhaps the most important realisation, brought home to us by our study of the old system and by information from our patients, was that in the past we have been treating people as things, or, at best, as interesting diseases. Somehow we had lost our way in giving pride of place to the inherent value of persons. When this happens, the end begins to justify the means and many measures were used in order to control the disturbed behaviour of mental illness, much of it produced by the system itself which denied the fundamental importance of recognising our patients as people with rights, opinions and feelings that we should respect.

(Martin 1974: 43)

The new social experiment was mediated by ward meetings, where free discussion took place. Staff were trained not to press their own opinions, adopt a listening stance, creating an atmosphere of acceptance and increased permissiveness. They were also encouraged to explore their own feelings in staff meetings as a way to better understand their patients' predicaments. For the first time in this previously traditional Victorian asylum, patients from the opposite sex were encouraged to mix as much as possible. In groups, patients slowly began to realize they had a say in the running of their ward, were allowed and encouraged to express their views on how disturbance should be managed, on how administrative tasks on staff could be made lighter, or state their views on when one of them should be allowed to leave hospital. These changes were met with considerable suspicion, not only by patients, but perhaps more so by staff who had become accustomed to a much more regimented and authoritarian structure. Nurses were particularly threatened when two patients, no doubt inspired by these changes, started campaigning against alleged acts of cruelty on the parts of nursing staff. 'The patients will be running the hospital soon', was an often-quoted remark. It was during this time that scapegoating and paranoid accusations were levelled at those who were instigating change. Much of this process is discussed in Martin's book, and I will not refer to it here. But it is interesting to note, in the light of future developments, that this was an early episode of transition which prompted paranoid projections. They often split the staff and threatened the smooth therapeutic running of the institution. Despite these initial reservations and problems, 'therapeutic community' principles were soon applied across the hospital, and Claybury developed a national and international reputation as one of the most enlightened institutions of its time.

When I arrived at Claybury in 1978, much of the 'therapeutic community' fervour had declined, but many wards continued to work under the same principles, and some still did until its closure. During my initial years at the hospital I devoted much of my attention to the establishment of community facilities. I felt that Claybury, like other psychiatric institutions, had become too inward-looking and had neglected mental health work which was aware of people's social circumstances. I was also concerned at the possible stigmatizing role of an admission to a psychiatric hospital, and interested in a therapeutic approach which could prevent it by early intervention and family work. We set out plans to see patients and their families at home, established our out-patient services in non-hospital environments, started to talk more to other agencies, statutory and non-statutory, to develop a multidisciplinary network, and finally planted ourselves in the middle of our catchment area in a community mental health centre which opened in 1983.

In that same year a new threat to the hospital emerged. The Regional Health Authority decided to close two hospitals in its catchment area, Friern and Claybury, both in north London, and a ten-year programme of closure was agreed. This was met with a mixture of dismay and excitement, particularly when the Region originally promised to replace the hospital with adequate and comprehensive community facilities, well resourced and funded, and the chance of developing novel approaches to mental health care with the active participation of clinicians, community agencies, voluntary bodies and patient representatives. During the protracted programme of closure, however, many of the promises were not kept, creating a feeling of uncertainty and impotence in both staff and patients. At one point, the Claybury plan was frozen, when the Region realized that it could not afford the closure of two psychiatric hospitals, investing all their efforts and money on Friern. Later, when the plan resurfaced, Claybury's closure was put on 'fast-track'. At the same time, the Health Service began a major restructuring exercise, separating those that provided the service, the clinical teams, from Health Authorities, who purchased it. More and more of the planning activities were passed on to a succession of managers rather than clinicians, often more conscious of financial rather than clinical considerations. Many staff started to leave the hospital in the wake of these uncertainties, looking for safer pastures elsewhere, particularly as management did not offer guarantee of employment in the new services to its existing staff. Closure therefore not only meant a definite change of conditions and environments for patient and staff, but it also threatened the latter with the loss of livelihood. Patients also began to worry about their future, whether long-term residents or habitual users of acute services. In many therapeutic groups, veteran patients would often ask what, if anything, was going to replace the old institution. Where would they turn to in the future if they felt out of control and needed some protection? Staff were often as much in the dark about the future as their patients, only able to give vague promises that alternatives had been planned, even though it was unclear where or how these would materialize. The plans had changed so frequently in the course of the planning process, that some even wondered, or perhaps hoped, that they would be aborted. Rumours began to spread wildly in the corridors of the hospital, particularly as the deadline grew closer and no definite jobs were being offered to existing staff. Soon, the reality of the closure began to sink in, accompanied by the knowledge that not everyone would have a place in the new service. Staff had either to move to areas far away from their homes, or take on responsibilities they had little experience of, or even compete for their own jobs, being told, perhaps for the first time in their experience, that some of them were likely to be made redundant. There was an obvious growing discontent and distrust in the management of the hospital and in the Health Authority, which often manifested itself in the clinical arena. Morale was low, and patients were quick to pick this up. It is perhaps not surprising that during this time many of the wards, which had previously prided themselves on an open-door policy and a psychodynamic understanding of their patients, had to lock the doors and implement much tougher regimes in order to respond to increasing incidents of acting-out behaviour in patients. Staff who had dedicated their lives to the service and to their patients felt let down and that their commitment and past efforts were not taken into account in the scramble to get the closure plan completed. Despite the fact that society at large had become accustomed to the idea of massive redundancies in the commercial and private sector, NHS clinical staff had always considered their jobs to be safe, practically for life. They were therefore unprepared for the idea of having to sign on the dole and seek jobs in an increasingly competitive health market, where so many large hospitals were being downsized, except, that is, in the numbers of management staff which steadily increased over this period.

I often wonder how we were able to survive and continue to offer treatment to acutely ill patients during that stressful period. There had been many instances when the hospital was on the verge of what I can only describe as a 'psychotic breakdown', where reality parameters began to disappear in the mist of impending doom and frightening external attackers. The enemies were experienced as vicious, callous and inhuman pillagers, called Regional Managers, who carried out their destructive activities at the behest and on behalf of a Mechanical Dictator, the Thatcher, whose main ambition was to destroy the jewel and envy of the rest of the world, the National Health Service, and inherent to this, the omniscient power of the medical and nursing establishments.

The attacks, coming wave after wave, were sometimes couched in calming rhetoric and humane language, inviting the most suspicious to read continually between the lines of policy. It is my belief that we were able to overcome this dark period mainly because the hospital had a foundation of relationships based on our earlier experience working as a therapeutic community, and we were able to support each other and talk about events openly and honestly, accepting at the same time that we had to live through hard times and adapt to inevitable changes. But the experience has permanently altered many staff attitudes, and one perceives how vocational commitment is being eroded and replaced gradually by notions that 'a job is a job', that it is dangerous to put all one's energy and hopes and convictions in the work at hand, as it is always possible that someone may decide to 'pull the carpet under one's legs' with no notice.

One of the obvious antecedents to paranoigenicity is the threat of unwanted change. The origin of this change often lies outside the institution, or it may be located in just one or two prominent but influential figures within. It often is presented as a much-needed, well-supported and modern shift in emphasis, with phrases such as 'bringing psychiatric care into the 21st century', 'community care' or 'consumer or client satisfaction'. The 'enemy' makes her first visit dressed in angelic attire, haloed with good intentions, for the 'common good'. Paranoia begins to emerge almost simultaneously. In an institution under attack you can never trust a smile or a pleasing turn of phrase, they are here to make your life miserable, to make you do things you don't want to do, to undermine your safe space and render you helpless and fragmented. There are usually two assumptions which are heavily disguised when this angelic arrival makes itself known: the first is that all institutions are bad, pernicious organizations, which harm rather than help those in emotional distress. The second is that mental illness does not exist, and that those so labelled are misunderstood. They are indicators of splitting and projective forces. The institutional staff are seen inherently as bad, patients as victims of staff attitudes and oppression.

In the first assumption, it is believed that those involved in the organization are so concerned about their own needs, so bogged down by their own institutional norms, that they have lost touch with the primary objective of offering a therapeutic milieu to those in need. The institution has become an end in itself, not a means to convey care. This view is often fuelled by reports of institutional negligence, sometimes communicated by the prying eye of the press, inevitably ending in internal or external processes of inquiry. This can become a lengthy procedure which in turn creates a paranoid melting-pot of rumour and mutual accusations, as those most likely to have fingers pointed at them are seen hurriedly to adopt holier-than-thou policies and cover the unpleasant odour of inefficiency or neglect with the false perfume of bureaucratic statements, agreed policies or responsibilities that lie somewhere else. Institutional literature, pioneered by the sociologist Goffman in his book *Asylums* (1961), attests to the manoeuvres, ceremonies and rituals which inmates and staff of total organizations adhere to or are forced to comply with. Part of these procedures are geared to ensure personal accountability, which in turn determines an objectification of the personal work at hand, and an emphasis on defensive practices. Take this passage from his book:

> mismanagement of either animate or inanimate objects may leave tell-tale marks for supervisors to see. And just as an article being processed through an industrial plant must be followed by a paper shadow showing what has been done and by whom, what is to be done, and who had last responsibility for it, so a human object, moving, say, through a mental hospital system, must be followed by a chain of informative receipts detailing what has been done to and by the patient and who had most recent responsibility for him.

(Goffman 1961: 73)

This bureaucratization of care, rooted heavily in paranoia, is prevalent in any health organization today, and even more so in psychiatric units. Nurses, particularly, are asked to spend over half of their clinical time filling out, amongst many others, 'nursing processes', accident forms, cash-withdrawal forms, special observation forms, Care Programme Approach forms, diet sheets, budget proforma, as well as inputting questionably confidential computable personal data into information networks. The main purpose of all this activity is often experienced by staff as having one main objective: to prove to the inquisitor, often feared and powerful, that tasks have been completed according to pre-set standards. The fear is that if there is no written proof, no objective means of answering probing questions, responsibility will fall back on that member of staff, and their livelihood, career and peer-esteem will be threatened.

Institutions cater for basic human needs, such as lodging, warmth, nourishment, social interactions, establishment of routines and so forth, but in so doing they also instil a dependency culture which will be threatened if that institution is under attack. It is often said that total organizations attract particular types of individuals: those who are not self-reliant when dealing with the pressures of ordinary social life. Organizations such as the army, the police, the civil and prison service, provide for the total needs of individuals, and some suggest that they lure individuals who need this type of protection. This applies to a lesser or greater extent at all levels of institutional hierarchies. Those in powerful positions within institutions often create a world over which they have total, if not despotic, control; they are big fish in small ponds. One can often detect hidden fears of what would occur if these fish were suddenly to be released to the rigours of the wide, open sea. They are not authentic leaders. The literary example is William Blake's Urizen, who needed to control, limit and structure his life and that of others to avoid the terror of freedom of possibilities. Those in subservient or less influential posts barter offers of security and permanent employment for a say in the way in which they conduct their lives, feeling that this is a reasonable trade-off for this protective assurance. This institutional symbiosis is usually homeostatic, resisting any attempts at change.

In the late 1960s, anti-psychiatrists seriously challenged this state of affairs. None more dramatically than the late David Cooper, who gave a vivid account of his battles in his book *Psychiatry and Anti-Psychiatry* (1967), when he tried to change radically the institutional structures from within at Villa 21, a ward for young schizophrenics in Shenley Hospital. His attempts included letting go of staff–patient boundaries, reducing the use of tranquillizers, allowing psychotic patients to dictate their timetables and schedules of activity or inactivity, and a refusal to stick to institutional norms of cleanliness and order. He used the term *institutional irrationality* when referring to the needs of staff to defend themselves from the madness which they were supposed to contain. I propose that this term be extended to include the defences staff use in institutional environments which are under threat of change. To our own modern eyes and with reflection, his attempts at producing change in such a revolutionary way may seem injudicious and worryingly self-destructive, as if he wanted to prove that change was not possible in institutions. He concludes:

> The mental hospital as a social system defines itself by certain limits within which change is possible, but beyond which one cannot venture without threatening the stability of the whole structure. This structure as it has developed has acquired institutional sclerosis. This fact is proved repeatedly by the experience of the incipient disintegration in the whole institutional world of relationship and non-relationship [sic] when one pushes rather hard against the limits of the structure.
>
> (Cooper 1967: 112)

Other, more gentle, reformations took place in British hospitals with the advent of the therapeutic community and the work of Maxwell Jones at Belmont and Dingleton Hospitals (Jones 1968). Denis Martin, at Claybury, was inspired by these and other early experiments (Martin 1974: 111–18). He particularly focused on the role of the psychiatric or, as they were then called, the mental nurses in the process of change, especially as they seemed to be most resistant and vulnerable. Nurses are often at the forefront of any hospital reorganization, but are not usually the instigators. They have direct contact with the patient, more so than any other mental health professional, and yet they are the working class of the psychiatric social structure, and have to respond to edicts from their superiors without much say or influence. Many have likened nursing to the military professions. Adherence to rules and deference to superiors are deeply entrenched in the nursing psyche. When change occurs, as in the break-up of old asylum systems to the open and flatter hierarchical structures of therapeutic communities, some of these military structures are put under strain. So happened between the ward-based nurses, who were active participants in the therapeutic community principles, and their superiors, the assistant matrons and the chief nursing officers, who saw these modifications as threats to their authority and control. The changes were then imbued with features of the 'bad object', intensely persecutory and frightening. Martin recognized that one of the limitations of change was that it was often hampered by unconscious processes, which required 'a living experience of psychodynamics, especially group dynamics'. David Clark, in *Social Therapy in Psychiatry* (1974) described the turmoil produced by therapeutic communities in traditional psychiatric hospitals:

> Most live in a state of constant tension with the parent organisation – usually the psychiatric hospital – with threats of enquiry and closures, and pressures for conformity from the organization, and dreams of independence within the community. The major organization, however, pays the salaries of the doctors and the nurses and acts as a buffer, however unwillingly, between the pioneering unit and the pressures of the outside world. It may be that a truly permissive therapeutic community cannot survive without a buffer of some sort.
>
> (Clark 1974: 88)

In his book, *General Theory of Bureaucracy* (1976) Elliot Jaques, a Kleinian analyst, formulated characteristics of organizations which fostered positive relationships between employees and employers, as well as enhanced opportunities for personal achievement and self-worth. He called these organizations *requisite*. An *anti-requisite* organization, by contrast, raised obstacles to normal relationships and took on 'paranoia-genic' features, by creating envy, hostile rivalry and anxiety. This in turn was likely to make such an organization ineffective: persecutory anxiety, by inhibiting 'normal' human relationships, interfered with this process. He emphasized the importance of the interaction between the internal persecutory anxiety of individuals and interpersonal relationships. A basic way in which individuals dealt with internal persecutors was by projection, a defence prevalent in anti-requisite organizations. Personal defences, according to Jaques (1955), affected structures of organizations, and institutions were thus used to reinforce individual mechanisms of defence against anxiety.

In this sense, individuals may be thought as externalising those impulses and internal objects that would otherwise give rise to psychotic anxiety and pooling them in the life of the social institutions in which they associate.

(Jaques 1955: 479)

By splitting and projective mechanisms, particular individuals or groups within organizations are selected as the main depositors of this paranoid anxiety, thus becoming the focus of feelings of hatred and fear (see also Miller and Gwynne 1972). This may be further projected onto external sources, who then become the enemy of the institution, allowing coalescing forces within the organization to patch up differences in their fight against the common, external enemy. For clinicians, for example, managers in charge of administration and budgeting were, in the days preceding current health reforms, the focus of this paranoid anxiety, and often scapegoated for the wrongs of the institution as a whole. It is interesting to observe how, with the changes leading towards the purchaser/provider split – and here there is no pun intended – the purchasers, now external to the institution, have currently become the source of 'split-off' fear and hatred. Institutions and health organizations are now life-dependent on decisions made beyond the confines of their own management.

Isabel Menzies (1970), another Kleinian analyst, illustrated Jaques's theories in her studies of student nurses in a large teaching hospital. She identified the nursing role as the psychological vessel into which patients' and relatives' gratitude, dependency and envious hostility is deposited. These are identified as persecutory anxieties generated by the nature of the nurse's work. Difficulties arise when these anxieties have particular relevance to the nurse's personal development, and in these situations work, rather than contain this anxiety, might raise it and cause nurses to regress. Fantasy anxiety situations are projected onto the work, in an attempt to master the objective environment as a representation of this inner world. If the nurse, however, is unable to master the work situation, or if work becomes indistinguishable from this inner fantasy, the task becomes the source of anxiety rather than the means to develop skills to deal with it. Social defence systems are then resorted to, for example, by rigidly adhering to ritual proforma or stated guidelines when discretion would be more appropriate at times when decisions have to be made. If responsibility is too much to bear, a powerful internal conflict ensues, between that part of the nurse which wishes to take responsibility, and that part that wishes to act out irresponsibly, and avoid it. This is the part that is often split off, denied and then projected onto others, usually those in subordinate positions. The sterner disciplinarian self is in turn projected onto superiors, who then are feared for their monitoring and punitive potential. All this is done with great use of psychic energy. It is obvious that not much is left for the patient, in terms of a meaningful attachment.

Menzies Lyth (1988) bleakly concludes that nursing structures in hospital settings prevent nurses from directly dealing with the source of anxiety, creating paranoid forces and structures which are passed on to younger generations of professionals.

I have so far dealt with the assumption that institutions are evil. In the context of this chapter, I only want to mention the second assumption, which leads us to believe that so-called mentally ill people can be liberated by an apostolic mission to release them from their chains. The ravages of mental illness are denied in this process, and those suffering from it are seen as martyrs of misunderstanding and suspicion. I will not delve into this aspect of projective identification, epitomized by the writings of Laing and Esterson (1964) and Cooper (1971), in which the psychotic experience, or those suffering from it, were beatified, or seen to be the possible hidden messiahs or purveyors of a political message. This assumption has had a powerful impact on the language used by those who try to change mental health policy, and has been largely influential in the moves to close down psychiatric institutions.

I would now like to return to the start of my presentation in an attempt to integrate some of these ideas into a more coherent picture. Psychoanalytic writers, in my view, have understandably given the intrapsychic forces pre-eminence when addressing the problem of paranoid institutional forces. They have not incorporated historical, social and political dimensions which clearly affect institutional processes into which individual psyches are framed and contained. Perhaps we can illustrate this by a flying look at the pendular swings in the care of the mentally ill over the past century. When asylums were created, they were built in response to the neglect of the mentally ill which had become obvious in pre-Victorian Britain. Deranged and demented people wandered aimlessly along squalid streets in slum areas of great cities, raising concerns and anxieties in society at large, not only over their welfare, but also over their potential dangerousness. In a humanitarian mood, it was felt that by housing these people in large confined institutions, which could remain on the fringe and totally disconnected from the rest of society, their lives could be enhanced and society in turn be protected from their intrusion and their emotional presence. Inevitably, over the years, this warehousing of human beings eventually brought its detractors when questions were raised over the conditions in which they were living, their objectification and institutionalization, with reports of brutal attacks by staff at their worst or serious neglect at their best. Institutions and the psychiatric profession were then seen as oppressors, curtailing human life, especially of its undesirable or politically uncomfortable aspects. The opening of locked wards, and the advent of therapeutic communities were not enough to stem this growing discomfort with asylums as symbolic representations of all that was bad, and moves were then set afoot to close them. Liberal views then took over: the mentally ill could be 'normalized' if only they were allowed to integrate back into society, and in turn be returned to a community that cared. Rapid plans, spurred on by the illusory hope of cheaper services in the community, were implemented to close down these large institutions. Unfortunately, it was soon discovered that the community didn't really seem to care and that it certainly couldn't afford what proved to be a more expensive option. Deranged and demented people started to be seen on the streets of inner cities . . .

This cycle of policies is determined, to a great extent in my view, by powerful paranoid societal forces. Mentally ill people, or those involved in their care, become the vessels into which, at different times, projections of good and bad split-off feelings are deposited. When they are associated with danger and mystique, mentally ill people are diabolized, and all that is bad must therefore be excised and extirpated away into a foggy limbo. Guilt and reparatory gestures are evident by the humanitarian language and semantics used to explain away and justify these actions. When the mentally ill are seen as victims, the negative projections are then switched on to those in charge of their care, who are then seen as evil, self-seeking and pernicious, gaining gratification by pseudo-powerful positions. The full force of these paranoid projections has an immediate impact on staff. This is particularly true when government edicts seem to confirm this view, by suggesting that all staff are guilty of mismanagement, neglect and shoddy practices. Let us give an example: the creation of supervision registers.

The Christopher Clunis incident (Ritchie, Dick and Lingham 1994), in which a schizophrenic patient unpredictably attacked and killed an innocent bystander at an underground station, sparked off an explosion of outrage against government policies for the mentally ill. For some years, organizations such as MIND, the National Schizophrenia Fellowship and SANE (Schizophrenia A National Emergency) had criticized the government on its Community Care plans for renegation of its responsibilities, by not endowing the 'community' with enough resources to ensure the welfare of the mentally ill outside institutional care. The subsequent enquiry into the incident culminated in the Clunis Report, which primarily placed the blame, not on pressure of demands on services or scarcity of government resourcing, absence of guidance or clarity of responsibilities, but on the lack of clinical coordination of care. This in turn led the Secretary of State to issue guidelines, which is government-speak for directives, to have in place by the beginning of October 1994 supervision registers for patients deemed to be vulnerable or dangerous. No extra money was provided for these measures, and they were placed as extra responsibilities on local trusts and mental health providers already overburdened, especially in inner cities, where prioritization of scanty facilities meant that many deserving and very ill patients remained untreated or uncared for. Psychiatrists, not slow to comprehend that a poisoned chalice had been offered to them, immediately and publicly highlighted that not only would the names of vulnerable or dangerous patients be on the register, but that their own names would be placed on it as well. The aptly named Responsible Medical Officers would, in the eyes of the public, the media and the courts, have to give an account of his/her actions in the case of a tragedy, and explain why he or she had not taken measures to prevent it. The government, in the meantime, could sit quietly in the background leaving a scapegoat to pick up the flack. If the clinicians were able to convince the enquiry, the coroner or criminal court that they had done everything possible within the means at their disposal, then the focus of blame could be with the providers, the curiously named Trusts. If in turn, Trusts were able to show that this was due to a shortfall of money allocated to mental health, the accusing finger would then be pointed at the purchasers, in this case the Health Authority or, soon, the GP fund-holders. Only when this last port of call of blame-seeking was exhausted would enquiries be made of central government, who would then be dependent on the electors for survival. This circle of blame-search, passing bucks of guilt and responsibility, has characterized mental health provision for centuries, and in my view underlies the pendular swings of policies for the mentally ill, between humanitarian but paternalistic and restrictive patterns of care, to an insistence on human rights and freedoms. At its roots, it reflects perverse paranoid defences, the splitting off of anxieties of a persecutory nature prompted by fears of madness and rejection. At the end of the day it alienates those suffering from disturbances of the mind from those who think that they do not suffer from them. It makes the experience of madness a solitary one, and serves as the foundation of stigmatization and ghettoization of the mentally ill. Only by owning madness, by containing the anxiety it creates, both for those that are and those that are not in the throes of madness, can a serious attempt be made to tackle a vicious and perverse cycle which characterizes western society today.

REFERENCES

Clark, D.H. (1974) *Social Therapy in Psychiatry*. Harmondsworth, Penguin.
Cooper, D. (1967) *Psychiatry and Anti-Psychiatry*. London, Tavistock Publications.
—— (1971) *The Death of the Family*. Harmondsworth, Penguin.
Fagin, L. (1985) 'Deinstitutionalisation in the USA', *Bulletin of the Royal College of Psychiatrists*, 9: 112–14.
Goffman, E. (1961) *Asylums. Essays on the Social Situation of Mental Patients and Other Inmates*. London, Pelican.
Jaques, E. (1955) 'Social Systems as a Defence against Persecutory and Depressive Anxiety'. In Klein, M., Heimann, P. and Money-Kyrle, R. (eds) *New Directions in Psychoanalysis*. London, Tavistock Publications.

—— (1976) *General Theory of Bureaucracy*. London, Heinemann.

Jones, M. (1968) *Beyond the Therapeutic Community*. Boston, Yale University Press.

Laing, R.D. and Esterson, A. (1964) *Sanity, Madness and the Family*. London, Penguin.

Martin, D. (1974) *Adventure in Psychiatry*. London, Cassirer (second edition).

Menzies, I.E.P. (1970) *The Functioning of Social Systems as a Defence against Anxiety*. Centre for Applied Social Research. London, Tavistock Institute of Human Relations.

Menzies Lyth, I. (1988) *Containing Anxiety in Institutions*. Selected Essays. London, Free Association Books.

Miller, E.J. and Gwynne, G.V. (1972) *A Life Apart*. London, Tavistock Publications.

Pryor, E. (1993) *Claybury. A Century of Caring*. London, Mental Health Care Group, Forest Healthcare Trust.

Ritchie, J.H., Dick, D. and Lingham, R. (1994) *The Report of the Inquiry into the Care and Treatment of Christopher Clunis*. London, HMSO.

Tooth, G.C. and Brooke, E.M. (1961) 'Trends in the mental hospital population and their effect on future planning', *The Lancet*, I: 710–13.

Chapter 9

Bureaucracies at work

John Jackson

THE WORLD OF WORK AND THE ROLE OF BUREAUCRACIES: PERSECUTORY POTENTIAL

> Work is central to human life – as fundamental as the family to individual experience. From 16 to 60 most adults in Britain will spend a third of their waking hours working – usually for someone else – or, if they are unemployed, aspiring to do so. Most will spend less time with their partners and their children. The quality of that working experience is, therefore, vital to the quality of life of every citizen.

These are the opening words of a report titled 'Changing Work' published by the Fabian Society in London in July 1996. The situation they describe exists to an important extent in all industrialised societies and increasingly, with the spread of industrialisation, in the population of the entire world. Work (being in work) is so closely linked with real or perceived survival that the potential for persecution and paranoia is obvious. How and why bureaucracies play a pivotal role in relation to that potential is less obvious.

Organised work in societies using complex wealth-creating systems is a relatively modern phenomenon, probably no more than ten thousand years old. Its development has been influenced heavily by accelerating technological change (the wheel, iron, new products, new methods of production, particularly more effective means of communication) and, more recently, by the emergence of frameworks within which providers of capital and providers of labour have found new ways of working together. Capital represents accumulated – and transferable – wealth. As between capital and labour (labour in this context being a collective description of those who work for those who have capital), capital has always been the commodity in shorter supply and those who have had it have been able to play a dominant role. Recently, the concept of limited liability, a privilege which was designed to create a relationship between risk (limited) and reward (unlimited) attractive to those dominant owners of capital, has influenced strongly the structure of the frameworks and the new ways for capital and labour to work together.

An early concomitant of the privilege of limited liability was the emergence of corporate personality. Corporate personality, the notion of a corporation as a being with separate recognised and enforceable rights, duties and obligations was developed originally as a legal doctrine but has become increasingly a matter of social and economic reality. Lawyers talk of the corporate veil, an unpierceable conceptual membrane which separates the corporation from those who own shares in it. Those share owners cannot be 'got at' for the activities of the corporation. They are the activities of 'another' person. This has become more than an expression of limited financial liability: it now goes much further than that. The broomsticks have acquired a life of their own which is separate from that of their creators and that of those others who give them continuing vitality: employees, creditors, customers and, in some senses, interested communities, local, national and international. Moreover those broomsticks not only have interests of their own which can be pursued by agents purportedly acting on their behalf but interests which are usually conceived of, if not in perpetuity then certainly within time-frames longer than those applicable to the interests of shareholders, employees and customers.

The emergence of the separate personality of corporations links with the development within corporations of bureaucracies specific to those corporations. A simple definition of a bureaucracy is an authority (official, working formally or unofficial, working informally) at the centre of a social or economic system which administers (and sometimes makes) the rules for the structure and governance of, the behaviour within and the membership of that system. This definition is very different from that proposed by Weber (and generally accepted) because it admits unofficial bureaucracy and informality. By inference that admission challenges Weber's view of the evolution of human societies.

Within corporations bureaucracies are not only the necessary official organs of administrative control – parts of corporations' internal management structures. They are also, and often more importantly, unofficial aggregations of people who viewed separately as individuals have little influence but collectively have considerable influence. The members of these powerful unofficial bureaucracies are mainly, but not exclusively, drawn from the official bureaucracies. They are inner circles and people may move in and out of them. These bureaucracies work informally. They create climates of opinion. They determine the internal culture of the corporation. They establish the unwritten rules of conduct desired to be observed by everyone within the corporation. They have their own (sometimes self-serving) view of the interests of the corporation and they suggest the criteria to be applied in pursuance of those interests. The alignment with the interests of the corporation which are seen as separate and 'confidential' because of the opacity of the corporate veil which endows these unofficial bureaucracies with significant power. And particularly because the corporations they reside in are employers (providers of work) that power carries with it the potential for persecution and fear, rational or irrational, of that potential.

N.V. Philips, a famous Dutch company trading globally and dominated for many years by its founding family, was a great enterprise which became highly bureaucratic, both officially and unofficially, and in which the expressions 'a Philips Man' and 'the interests of the Concern' were important items in the company phrase book. What a 'Philips Man' was – something in which the founding family took great pride – and what 'the interests of the Concern' were deemed to be, evolved over time and were never written down – rather like the British constitution. But the bureaucracy which was their guardian created in continuity the climate of opinion which determined what they were. For those who aspired either to be 'Philips men' (knowing they might thereby gain both an embracing security and the possibility of preferment) or to comprehend 'the interests of the Concern', they were highly respected, but threatening, concepts. They were defined by the admonitory utterances of some unseen higher authority the precise meanings of which were changing and uncertain. What was certain was that they were internal to Philips and expressed a way of thinking which saw shareholders as a whole (and their interests), employees as a whole (and their interests) and, indeed, the community, as external and, in a sense, subordinate to the enterprise itself. Another certainty was that those who refused to surrender their individuality and made it clear that they did not aspire to be 'Philips Men' and that they wished to think out 'the interests of the Concern' for themselves did not thrive. Moreover it was particularly difficult for newcomers to enter Philips other than as 'infants' (apprentices, trainees and other holders of their first job): that is at the least threatening level. This, whilst not necessarily 'bad' for the individuals or for Philips, exemplified one of the main characteristics of bureaucracies: they control 'membership' by controlling processes of acceptance and rejection. And in this way they play a key role in giving expression to persecutory potential particularly if, as inferred above, acceptance or rejection equates to being in or out of work.

The example provided by the history of Philips also illustrates that other important feature of bureaucracies: they exist, define their purpose and establish their power base by reference to the 'interests' of external authorities – external, that is, to the bureaucracies themselves. The pharaohs and the bureaucracies within their courts provide another and colourful example from earlier human history. In the case of Philips that external authority was 'the Concern': interestingly not the founding family. Even they were the other side of the veil. Historical evidence also tends to emphasise that the most powerful authorities (and thence the powerful bureaucracies associated with them) are threatening both because of what they can cause to happen and because of their remoteness from those they affect. This remoteness makes them mysterious: what their interests are and how they will be pursued are not obvious. The combination of power and uncertainty generates apprehension which lends potency to the bureaucracy using it, affects the way in which that bureaucracy is itself likely to be perceived and frequently reflects a subtle form of persecution not always clearly perceived as such by the persecuted.

Perhaps the authority which has given rise most prolifically to such bureaucracies is God, certainly as perceived by Catholic Christians. The power base of God cannot easily be challenged by earthly means. God enjoys an awesome authority at the edge of human comprehension. God moves in mysterious and fearful ways. God has 'children'. What more nourishing broth for bureaucracies to breed in could there be? Catholic priesthoods are the most powerful, long-lasting bureaucracies the human world has yet seen. The power and longevity flow largely from the self-assumed right to declare the will of God. Through the ages there have been challenges. Some have asserted that there is no such declaratory right: some that there is no will to declare because there is no God. Both have engendered debate. In relation to the existence of God, the debate has been fruitless. It is, by definition, not a topic lending itself to rational discussion in temporal terms. Why then has its consideration absorbed so much human time? It may reflect humankind's yearning to find its spiritual home. It may reflect a powerful instinctual drive to belong. Arguably there is little difference between the two standpoints – they may simply be different ways of delineating what Sartre called a God-shaped hole in the human consciousness. This is directly relevant to a discussion of bureaucracies, their origins and workings.

THE ORIGIN OF BUREAUCRACIES AND THE INSTINCTUAL NEED OF HUMANS TO BEHAVE AS SOCIAL ANIMALS

Plainly bureaucracies both official and unofficial are phenomena in human societies older than corporations endowed with the modern characteristics of personality. Their origins might lie in the most important behavioural feature that, so far as is presently known, distinguishes humankind from the whole of the rest of the living world. This is not the ability to apply intelligence but a highly developed ability to communicate by speech very complex, even abstract, results of that application. Bureaucracies in human societies (like corporations) reflect sophisticated means of organisation which would not be achieved easily in a verbally uncommunicative world. This would suggest a recent origin. On the other hand, bureaucracies, particularly in their unofficial form, might have an older and more basic origin. To pursue this possibility, why would humankind so readily create, or permit the creation of, bureaucracies?

Is there something deep in human nature – some instinctual drive – which makes humans do so and underpins bureaucratic behaviour? Instinctual drives, which determine some behaviours in a pre-programmed way, have a genetic origin. The more distant that genetic origin the more ingrained and 'basic' the instinct is likely to be. It has stood the test of time. However it is difficult to identify with certainty behaviours which are 'original' and of ancient genetic origin.

Firstly, there is a great shortage of direct evidence. It is not possible to 'know' what the 'original', natural behaviour of the modern human (*Homo sapiens*) was. At best it can only be deduced. Modern molecular biology helps. It suggests (Sibley and Ahlquist 1984, 1987) that genetically *Homo sapiens* is more than 98 per cent the same as the smaller of the two known species of chimpanzee. It also suggests that chimpanzees are humans' closest relatives. The anatomical differences between humans and chimpanzees relate mainly to brain size, posture and reproduction. As to behaviour, if humans behaved in the same manner as the smaller chimpanzee they would be omnivorous, territorial individuals which live and chatter together in tribes, both sexes of which are promiscuously heterosexual and homosexual and which are xenophobic, murderous and careless of their environment. Humans are not like that, are they?

Secondly, although instinctual behaviour of ancient origin should be readily identifiable (because it gives, in Darwinian terms, obvious competitive advantage) it is not easily disentangled from the totality of observable modern behaviour. This is because it may be masked or modified by emotional and intelligent behaviours which, whilst arising from inherited capacities, are not themselves genetically pre-programmed. Many expressions of creativity – highly individual activities resulting from the application of intelligence and emotion – and, indeed, many other similar aspects of what humans call civilisation – do not fit easily with evolutionary theory. They do not seem to give advantage to the individual in Darwinian terms. Consider the making of music. The lone human whistling as he walked home through a primordial wood probably got to be eaten as a consequence of advertising his presence to predators. This example points up the problem. When did it pay to be a whistler? Historical evidence suggests that the answer lies in the accelerating emergence of accumulated capital – transferable wealth. It seems likely that as humans found a way of living which both resulted in and used the accumulation of capital, it became possible, even enjoyable, for them to behave in ways which were not competitive in evolutionary terms but did not have Darwinian consequences. However, there is no certainty whatever either that there were not successful whistlers from the 'beginning' or, if there were not, of when humans did start to whistle for reasons of personal creative satisfaction. Moreover, human tinkering with the laws of evolution, the protection and encouragement of the creatively talented and of the 'weak' could itself produce genetic consequences. The individuals which survive will not be only those who are successfully selfish in the observable manner of other living creatures. All living creatures evolve, continuously or sporadically: humans may have been evolving in an 'unusual' way for a long time and much 'original' instinctual behaviour may have been obliterated or extensively modified.

However, despite all the uncertainties, it seems likely that humans have always been social (not solitary) animals of some kind. And it is reasonable to suppose that, in some respects, they have always been genetically programmed to behave in ways similar to their nearest relatives, chimpanzees. If an animal is social and congregates with others of its kind, in a tribe, it is because it has inherited the instinctual knowledge that it will be more successful as an individual (and have more descendants) as a result of doing so. This is a powerful and fundamental drive which might evidence itself in different ways. Indeed, in the case of humans, the need to belong to a tribe may explain Sartre's God-shaped hole. Perhaps the word 'God' describes the 'great tribe in the sky' to which all humans, as individuals, feel they may (should) belong. In immediate, earthly terms each individual in a tribe is necessarily closely attuned to signals within the tribe and behaves in a way expected to give that individual the best chance of competitive success. This includes giving the tribe of which he or she is a competitive member the best chance of success also both during the lifetime of that individual and the infancy of its progeny. It follows that there will be mechanisms which determine, mainly in a re-active way (re-active both to changes within the tribe and to a changing hostile environment), what tribal behaviour is likely to produce success, what individual behaviour should be 'permitted' to members of the tribe and what the tribal reaction to non-conformers should be.

The most successful members of the tribe are most likely to be either those that most strongly influence tribal behaviour to their own selfish advantage or those that are most skilful in turning the prevailing norms of tribal behaviour to their own advantage. The first are rudimentary bureaucrats (not mere politicians because they 'organise' as well as invite assent) who define the boundaries, character and membership of the tribe. The second are rudimentary manipulative, but compliant, beneficiaries of bureaucracy – the majority of the tribes' members. It would be purely conjectural to say that this is a snapshot of original human behaviour. But it feels right and suggests that the phenomenon of bureaucracies in human societies is underpinned by and has its origins in humans' ancient, fundamental and instinctual drive to band together in tribes and behave as social animals. It follows that persecution which, in its most elemental form, involves exclusion or ejection from the tribe and fear, rational or irrational, of such persecution owes much to the instinctually social nature of humans and, particularly, its bureaucratic consequences.

THE CONFLICT BETWEEN BUREAUCRACIES AND THE INDIVIDUAL: FORMS OF PERSECUTION

How is all this relevant to the world of work? What is the world of work? And what happens in it? It is an environment in which most people spend much of their time and in which they are in close physical proximity to and close communication with others. Work is a means of support, usually the only means, and, moreover, it is provided by a (frequently corporate) person which fights for its existence in competition with other similar persons in a generally hostile environment. That person is in many respects like a tribe of chimpanzees hoping, perhaps needing, to get to the best jungle fruits before another tribe. A particular characteristic of the world of work in modern human society is that those in work are likely to be more closely knit than the community as a whole, particularly if that community is industrialised, diffused, multi-ethnic and practising elective democracy. They have a common interest in the success of 'their' tribe. They also secure their own identity by reference to membership of 'their' tribe. Being a member of a tribe is reassuring for most, essential for some, for more than economic reasons. Being a 'Philips man' was of great personal importance to many employees of Philips. Although some forms of trade unionism run counter to this, reflecting the possibility of belonging to alternative tribes or even, simultaneously, to more than one tribe, the world of work provides modern humans with many – perhaps most – of their opportunities to behave socially – tribally – in the same manner as their genetic forebears did. It calls up powerful instinctual urges from deep within.

Those instinctual urges are primitive and can give rise to primitive behaviour. This can be very marked in the case of bureaucratic reaction to highly individualistic behaviour. The difficulty of determining the 'original' nature of humans has already been discussed. It is no easier to determine the 'modern' nature of humans. Ultimately it is a matter of assertion. One assertion could be that it is in human nature to seek to be a successful member of a successful tribe, another that it is to seek to give maximum expression to personal creativity. The first is the instinctual pursuit of individual success by being strongly social. The second is strongly individual behaviour which whilst not necessarily anti-social is (probably) not instinctual in itself and may or may not give competitive advantage to the individual or the tribe. The two are extremes and do not fit well together. Bureaucracies, which are a social phenomenon, do not easily accommodate the strong expression of creative individuality either within themselves or within the system they control. Ironically, the more modern societies become 'civilised' and protect and encourage the individual the greater the difficulties that will arise from the clash (with all its possibilities of persecution) between individualism and socialism.

This partly explains the vigour and violence of Mao's Cultural Revolution – an attempt by humans behaving socially to suppress, even eradicate, humans behaving individually. The walking whistler presents problems for the bureaucrat. This is as true in the world of work as anywhere. Many individuals express distaste of bureaucracies on the one hand, because of the sensed hostility to their creative individuality, whilst seeking personal reassurance and personal identity by responding to an urge to relate to other individuals (socially) in a way which inevitably gives rise to bureaucracies. This internal conflict in individuals, which, *qua* individual, is likely to be there for the bureaucrat also, results in a continuous behavioural paradox. Most individuals attempt to resolve the paradox by compromise.

The popular image of a bureaucrat is that of a tight-mouthed clerk in a grey suit who works to the clock and, on going home at the end of the day, runs his finger along the tops of the picture frames and shows the dust to his wife. This is a prejudiced caricature of bureaucrats, even of those who are invisible members of official bureaucracies. Bureaucrats, both unofficial bureaucrats and those attracted to working in official bureaucracies, are widely varied individuals who as a common characteristic express an instinctual drive to try to advance themselves as individuals by wielding power and influence over others in their community (their tribe) by capturing the right to define the needs and interests of that community. Individual bureaucrats may not realise that this is what they are doing. They may well think of this behaviour as a 'public' service for the 'public' good. And, viewed from the perspective of the 'public', it may well be.

Of course, such individuals can be dangerous when working together collectively. They can behave in a manner similar to that of uniformed soldiers where the anonymity of the uniform provides the opportunity for 'uncivilised', primitive, instinctual and, sometimes, self-interested 'group' behaviour. The significance of anonymity (no risk of being identified – being found out, being able to 'hide' behind the interests of a superior authority) is that it permits – perhaps encourages – the blocking off of intelligence and emotion, the capacities which might otherwise, for better or worse and in an individual way, moderate the instinctual behaviour. Moreover any system based on the power of some over others lends itself to the possibility of persecution. Within a corporation individuals who do not 'fit' can easily become subject to persecution. This can take the form of making their lives miserable – a form of torture – or causing them to 'leave' – a form of murder. Such persecution frequently results from the conflict between the social 'animal' (the bureaucracy and the bureaucratised) and the individual expressing strongly personal creativity. In those cases the individual is classified as a stranger and thereby becomes available as a 'victim'. Such persecution can have other origins: an individual may be neither strongly and successfully social, nor be capable of strong expression of personal creativity. Such 'weak' (not useful) individuals may become the victims of bullying even if the energy expended on that bullying could instead have been expended on helping the individual to become 'stronger'. Sadly, in the world of work, as elsewhere, bureaucracies latch onto, even welcome, opportunities to unite the tribe by igniting the social human's inherent distrust of and conflict with the individual. This was the theme of Golding's *Lord of the Flies*, a theme familiar to observers of school playgrounds. The weaker the individual available for bullying (torture) the better: the less the risk of retribution by the individual and the easier the task of persuading the whole tribe to join in the fun. Bureaucracies like to be 'popular' and to 'rabble rouse' by plucking sympathetic chords: successful bureaucrats (or the authorities to which bureaucracies relate) can be brilliant demagogues. Demagogy feeds off tribal instinct.

This persecutory characteristic can become pronounced and potent if it has a xenophobic taint extending to a class of individuals. It will serve not only to prevent or inhibit the entry of new kinds of members but, if it links with xenophobia originating outside the corporation, can result in the importation of, and infection by, more general social (tribal) prejudice. Silent anti-semitism and other forms of ethnic discrimination within corporations are examples of this. Sexual discrimination is another. This institutionalisation of prejudice within corporations can also affect the official behaviour of the corporation itself, particularly if its function requires a high level of bureaucratic activity. Well before the emergence of the AIDS epidemic, examination of the questionnaires of some life assurance companies raised the suspicion that within those companies there was inbuilt unconscious prejudice against (persecution of) homosexuals.

Generally, of course, the activities of bureaucracies are intended, and are likely, to have benign results. Reverting to the example of Philips, that corporation which at one time employed over 300,000 people on excellent conditions, traded in most parts of the world, serviced its capital extremely well and behaved as a responsible member of the communities in which it traded, undoubtedly maintained its coherence because of its bureaucracy based in Holland. There was a substantial official bureaucracy policing the application of Philips's accounting policies and other internal disciplines and that played an important role. But of greater importance was the powerful unofficial bureaucracy and the ability of that bureaucracy to influence informally others – particularly Dutch nationals – working for Philips outside Holland. The notions of the 'Philips Man' and the 'interests of the Concern' provided a powerful glue which kept the whole stuck together. However, the innate conservatism and resistance to change which is a feature of bureaucracies – tribes should not change too much and too often because that destabilises the bureaucracies within the tribes (or change may make it more difficult to raise infants, an especially female point of view) – finally endangered Philips. Like any organism – and as if it were itself a real living thing – it had to evolve if it was to survive in a changing environment which became hostile in a new way. Philips had to subject itself to violent change both in organisation and behaviour and with that change came a new bureaucracy: the old went and the 'new' Philips Man was invented.

Bureaucracies can also operate to protect their corporations – their tribes – from the activities of an over-strong, inconsistent or impetuous leader. The business leader who says with brutal candour 'I am this firm and will have within it those whom I want to have within it' is expressing more egocentricity (as opposed to 'firmcentricity') than is likely to be tolerated. Such leaders, frequently highly creative individuals, incapable of distinguishing themselves from the firm, are likely to be thwarted by the silent evolution of unofficial bureaucracies intent on protecting the firm – the tribe – from the consequences of such autocratic – and probably insensitive – behaviour. This tendency of bureaucracies (often in the name of moderation) to prevent excesses of individual power usually prolongs the successful life of a corporation. And the failure of bureaucracies to prevent excesses can have serious consequences. The fate of companies controlled by Robert Maxwell exemplifies this. Maxwell was a pharaoh with a substantial court: but that court did not contain, or encourage the emergence of, a bureaucracy. Much of the recent drive for better corporate governance in public companies stems from the refusal of investing institutions to rely on the existence or operation of such internal self-regulating systems. Policeable sets of official rules which are imposed from outside are seen as preferable. But internal bureaucracies can also result in a corporation becoming endangered or unsuccessful. If the environment changes in such a way that quick entrepreneurial action is needed either to take an opportunity or to prevent disaster it is unlikely that the impulse for this will come from a bureaucracy. As already remarked, bureaucracies are inherently conservative and a tussle is likely to develop between an individual who sees a need for change and the resident bureaucracy. If there is no such individual or if the bureaucracy prevails failure may result.

A variation on this theme emerges from what appeared to outside observers to have happened in the period leading to the tragic and highly publicised collapse of Barings – the London merchant bank. This was a case of a corporation with two long histories (it collapsed – and was rescued – once before) of strong domination by a ruling family. That family set an example of 'civilised' business behaviour which was generally admired within and outside the corporation. Barings had a clearly identifiable culture. It was perceived as very 'gentlemanly'. A relatively short time before the second collapse the family 'withdrew' in the sense that it entrusted the running of the business far more to professional managers with considerable discretion as to how they did so. The continuing unofficial bureaucracy maintained its belief in and loyalty to the long-standing and honoured culture. It is plain that it failed to assist the official bureaucracy to control sufficiently, perhaps even to comprehend, the activities of strong-willed individuals within the corporation, who wished Barings to behave in a new way which they believed was necessary for its successful survival in a rapidly changing business environment. Those individuals who were provided with large financial incentives to do well as individuals, to be 'stars', were not necessarily wrong but the consequences of the clash between those who held to old values and those who were frustrated by resistance to change (and acted accordingly) were catastrophic. Friendly outside observers expressed a general feeling of unease, based in part on fear that the potential damage was not seen (perhaps voluntarily at the subconscious level) by those who could have done something about it, well before the finale. The form that finale took, gross deception by a rogue trader, was arguably a disaster waiting to happen, partly because of official bureaucratic failure and partly because of a clash between an unofficial, apparently complacent and blind, bureaucracy and emerging, impatient, individuality.

Bureaucracies are more frequently found (or, to be accurate, are more easily identified and observed) in larger corporations. Smaller corporations, if successful, frequently depend on the (unconservative) nimbleness and fleetness of foot which goes with smallness for that success. In those cases the whole of the firm, like an infant emerging tribe, determines the rules and is, in a sense, the bureaucracy. It may have a single leader accepted as the rule proposer or it may be a form of collective organisation: both are possible. Almost certainly it will take pride in not being bureaucratic. It will probably have been founded by and mainly employ people who attach high value to individuality and its creative expression. They will have concealed from themselves the bureaucratic component latent in infant tribal behaviour. Self-deception can be used in different ways: sometimes it helps because it looks like constructive single-mindedness. But sometimes that single-mindedness leads to disaster.

This comes close to what is frequently described in the world of work as the size problem: the situation which arises when a small enterprise is so successful that it grows out of its ability to behave as small. It can either sub-divide itself into a number of small units (to recapture smallness – an approach well understood by Richard Branson, the founder of Virgin) or it can decide to adopt officially bureaucratic methods of organisation. If it takes the latter path a recognisable unofficial bureaucracy is likely to emerge also. If most modern humans struggle to compromise by balancing social behaviour and individual behaviour, where that balance is struck will often determine the course of action chosen in such circumstances. Those who value their individuality, 'feel' that they are more likely to be successful in small tribes and dislike bureaucracies will gravitate towards the small company, despite the risks of smallness. Those, on the other hand, who are more social and 'feel' that they will be more successful in large tribes – probably the majority – will favour the larger company.

Sometimes a bureaucracy becomes tyrannical or overtly self-perpetuating. It would be nice to think that in those circumstances, it is overthrown by the rest of the tribe – as in the final stages of Orwell's *Animal Farm*. In the corporate world this rarely happens. Clearly this reflects the instinctual tendency to compliant acceptance by the majority. Such bureaucracies are usually only turned out as a result of external intervention and then only if the corporation is plainly not prospering. This external intervention is usually financial takeover or the threat of such takeover, frequently by a corporation led by a powerful individual. There are many well-known examples of this. The fact that such activity is politically controversial is a striking illustration of the inherent conflict between individuality (and its champions) and social behaviour (and its champions). The politicians themselves are probably unaware of why they have these strong 'gut' feelings or that they are treading in the footprints of Freud and Marx, the great prophets of individualism and of socialism.

What of the relationship between members of a bureaucracy? A bureaucracy within a corporation behaves in some ways as a tribe within a tribe. It also consists of individuals in (potentially intense) competition with one another who have banded together. These individuals are likely to be the equivalent of dominant males and dominant females in nature. Whilst making common cause they may not have an overriding sense of 'togetherness'. From time to time they will fight with one another. There will be winners and losers. Ejection from a bureaucracy is a particularly unpleasant fate. The relationship between unofficial bureaucracies and the other members of their community is based on respect for, or fear of, uncertainty and authority. In a sense, a former member of an unofficial bureaucracy is a stranger to the rest of the tribe. Those who have wielded power will not easily be accepted into the rest of the tribe. Indeed, if the tribe has been encouraged to bully, particularly by that individual, a readily available new victim may well be gleefully seized on. It is observable in the world of work that those who have the greatest possibility of persecuting (that is, members of the bureaucracy), and particularly those who use that possibility, are frequently both the most anxious about the way they are perceived by others as well as the most likely to have irrational (paranoid) fears about the motivation of the perceivers. That is not surprising: they know that ejection from the bureaucracy would have extremely painful consequences. The combination of fear and imagination can start devils stalking in any human mind. It is also observable that those who come from a category of people which traditionally suffer from oppression are frequently the most clever and imaginative (cruellest) oppressors.

Finally what about those in modern industrialised societies who are not in organised work? Those who would like to be so – most of the officially unemployed – are to some extent in the same state as captive social animals; they are artificially sustained, kept solitarily in cages – away from the tribe. They may be there because they cannot enter the world of work, often because there is no work for them to do. Or they may have been ejected from the world of work, not necessarily because of bureaucratic activity. There are also those whose genetic programming is such that they are not strongly social animals under any circumstances: they are so strongly individualistic that they do not wish to enter the world of organised work or to join any other kind of tribe. Arguably, one attribute of a society which has become civilised should be that it tolerates, even embraces and helps, those who depart from the norm or who cannot conform to the norm. It should eschew rejection and bullying – murder and torture. Sadly, the reality is that exclusion, or self-exclusion, from work is seen all too frequently by society as 'strange' – as unsocial individual behaviour. The predictable consequence is 'strange' or unsocial behaviour by the individual. This unsocial behaviour may be the human equivalent of crib-biting and wind-sucking – the psychotic activities of some stabled horses. They are expressions of frustration by social animals denied the chance of being social. Or there may be attempts to find a surrogate tribe. 'Down and outs' tend to congregate (roost) together at 'bedtime'. On the other hand, the unsociability may lie in the perception of others. It may be the behaviour of an animal not strongly genetically programmed to be social behaving oddly in the eyes of others which are so programmed. Stress caused by unemployment, or the fear of it, and the problems of those regarded as socially inadequate in a work sense owe something to a tribal bureaucratic rule – the notion of a duty (not a right) to work, the work ethic. Arguably the maintenance of such an ethic by a community which does not also guarantee employment to all its members is, itself, a form of persecution. The place (and nature) of a work ethic in a civilised society is an important topic for debate and needs to be debated.

The thread of argument running through this chapter has been that the creation of bureaucracies official or unofficial is a part of a human's instinctual social behaviour – because the bureaucracies define the tribe to which the individual needs to belong – and that the modern world of organised work provides ample opportunity for those instincts, with all their consequences (particularly those of rejection and ejection) to prevail. On the other hand what humans call civilisation largely reflects highly individualistic behaviour involving the moderation of instinctual behaviour by intelligent and emotional behaviour which may have been liberated by the use of accumulated wealth – capital. It is frequently argued that the greatest danger for humankind is that this moderation will not be sufficiently pronounced and that the instinctual pursuit of competitive success will result, in the fairly short term, in such rapid environmental and other change that the human species will extinguish itself. Neither by the accidental consequence of evolution nor by the application of intelligence will it adapt in time to the consequences of the changes it has wrought.

However, that case can be argued the other way round. If over a sufficient period the increasing majority of humans were those whose basic instincts to survive selfishly and breed in tribes were most strongly suppressed, the likely evolutionary consequence would be an important change in the genetic make-up of humankind. This might result eventually in a highly 'civilised', non-tribal, non-bureaucratic society as a new state of instinctual nature for humans emerged – a world of whistling walkers knowing neither persecution nor the fear of it. But such a happy state might well be unsustainable. Rapidly active and violent external causes could change the environment to such an extent that only highly selfish and competitive individuals could survive long enough to produce sufficient progeny. If there were not enough of them, extinction could come that way also.

Either way, organised work, as it is known and valued in human society today – 'as fundamental as the family to individual experience' – and the forms of bureaucracy (with all their attributes) which support it and flourish in it would have been relatively short-lived phenomena.

REFERENCES

Sibley, C.G. and Ahlquist, J.E. (1984) 'The Phylogeny of the Hominoid Primates, as Indicated by DNA-DNA Hybridization', *Journal of Molecular Evolution* 20: 2–15, New York: Springer-Verlag.
—— (1987) 'DNA Hybridization Evidence of Hominoid Phylogeny: Results from an Expanded Data Set', *Journal of Molecular Evolution* 26: 99–121, New York: Springer-Verlag.

Part III

Cultural and political

Introduction

The five chapters in this concluding part consider large-scale cultural and political forces which may induce paranoia or directly embody danger. The section begins with Joseph Berke's 'Reefer madness', a discussion of the problem of illegal psychoactive drugs. Berke demystifies a wealth of disinformation by looking at the history of drug use in Western countries, and by reviewing the cultural, political and legal context of their current usage. This background includes the puritanical wave which countered the 'counter-culture' of the 1960s, and the 'war on drugs' initiated by the former American President Richard Nixon.

Berke points out that the most dangerous feature of proscribed drugs is their illegality. This means that users fall victim both to the legal system that is supposed to protect them and the illegal drug industry which is supposed to supply them. And, if this were not enough, Berke traces how and why the fear of drugs and drug users have an increasingly noxious effect on non-users. It appears that both users and non-users inhabit complementary persecutory worlds, for as Berke demonstrates, when it comes to drugs, because of the clash between a huge criminal industry and a powerful legal machine, one cannot be paranoid enough.

Calvin Hernton was brought up in the American 'deep South' during a time when racism was particularly virulent. In his chapter, 'Between history and me', he traces the development of his fear of the 'white' police from the point when he first becomes aware of their cruising his neighbourhood in Chattanooga, Tennessee; to his being 'arrested' at the age of eight for talking to a white (female) child on the way home from school; to his being accused of burglary and rape; and, ultimately, to his being set up by the police to become a drug informer.

In Hernton's personal experience, the white police have existed and continue to exist to persecute people for being black. He cites the pervasive image of the 'criminogenic' black man as rapist, thief, drug user and dealer, murderer and all out 'nogoodnik,' and muses that the police act to protect white civilisation from 'spoiling' blacks.

Throughout his life Hernton has managed to mediate the boundaries between 'paranoia', and an acute sensitivity to the dangers of the predominant cultures in which he has lived. Despite, or perhaps because of all this, Hernton has retained a fascination with the white world and has managed to maintain close friendships and productive partnerships with white men and women in many countries.

Following Hernton's delineation of the mechanics of colour, Stella Pierides sees 'the machine', a non-human 'transforming device' or tool, as the central metaphor of our age, a metaphor which helps to construct reality itself. On one hand, machines do our drudge work as well as entertain us, transport us and help us to think. They embody ideas of power, regularity, objectivity, strength and wisdom. On the other hand, machines imprison and torture us with an alienating mastery and control. Everyday expressions denote the extent to which machines convey negative, lifeless and repetitive states. Not uncommonly people are said to walk mechanically, talk like an automaton or behave like a robot.

Machines are not simply transforming devices, but controlling devices. In Berke's chapter we see how the machinery of the state can be used to prevent socially unacceptable behaviour and experience. The latter has become an increasing target. Thus, mandatory biochemical tests have been increasingly used to detect drugs and drug-altered states, while devices like lie detectors have also been used for decades to discover false or discordant thoughts and intentions.

In 'Machine phenomena', Pierides goes on to show how people can use the capacity to identify with machines and become like machines to control their own subjectivity, especially when they hate and fear their own thoughts and feelings. She describes how one of her patients turned himself into a 'bionic humanoid', while a second became a 'tear machine'. Invariably such 'machine phenomena' denote psychotic states of unreality and are last-ditch defences against intolerable intrapsychic and interpersonal realities. Paradoxically, when this happens, these persons may be treated with medicines which are far more toxic than 'illegal drugs'. These psychotropic agents complete the process of transforming individuals into robotic machines, which is what many chronic institutionalised 'schizophrenics' look like.

Hisako Watanabe extends the idea of 'machine phenomena' to the central institutions of Japanese society. In her chapter, 'Paranoia and persecution in modern Japanese life', she points out that the whole educational, vocational and military edifice has served to grind people down in order to fit them as cogs into a well oiled, super-efficient engine. This is the Japan Inc., a state which maintains a sophisticated tightly knit system of control over its citizens. During the Edo period (1603–1867) any dissident would be decapitated on the spot. Now Japan maintains a gloss of democracy, although conformity and compliance remain the rule. Any deviance from the 'norm' is punished by shaming and ostracism.

Many Japanese have tried to step out of their highly regimented oppressive society by joining one of hundreds of religious and semi-religious cults which have sprung up since the end of the Second World War. Watanabe argues that these cults represent frantic attempts to overcome the main problem in Japanese life since the war, that is, how to acclimatise a society to Western thought and practice while retaining a great nostalgia for prewar values.

All of the persecutory phenomena that Berke, Hernton, Pierides, Watanabe and others have described share a common cause. They involve metaphors which have moved from realms of symbolic meaning to concrete or literal expression. Thus, Berke shows how opium became demonised during the Opium Wars after Britain and China began to equate the drug with the way the two antagonists saw each other. Similarly, Hernton demonstrates how, for many American whites, black equals bad. Then Pierides explains how patients transform machine metaphors into actuality and Watanabe traces how the Aum cult, once the symbol of the 'Priest Ultimate Enlightenment' became the embodiment of malicious destructiveness. As David Edgar considered earlier in the book, all too often literal thinking results in paranoid ideation, if not concrete persecution.

War and peace bring these issues into sharper focus. In the concluding chapter, 'Peace and paranoia', Stanley Schneider explores the dynamics of personal conflict projected onto a national and transnational tableau. By taking as his primary example the 'peace process' between Israel and the Palestinians, Schneider shows that war can be a way of resolving or attempting to resolve paranoid fears. By the same token peace, a peace forced upon a population unready or unwilling to accept it can arouse severe persecutory fears and exacerbate the very hostilities that the peace was supposed to overcome.

Whoever or whatever outside adversaries may do or be, Schneider points out that the enemy without is invariably less dangerous than the enemy within. He ponders how people are able to overcome long legacies of internal hate and persecution, a question which was also posed in the preceding chapter by Hisako Watanabe. Both thinkers seek to reconcile and resolve the problems of paranoia and persecution by encouraging those who may be the subject or object of persecution to see the reality of their situation as profoundly as possible. For Watanabe this means a willingness to perceive external events, no matter how disturbing or painful. For Schneider this means a willingness to grapple with inner demons: to acknowledge them, to contain them, and to refuse to project them outwards. Only in this manner, he argues, can we begin to overcome paranoid thoughts and persecutory experiences in ourselves, and others.

Chapter 10

Reefer madness
Social fears and self-fulfilling prophecies

Joseph H. Berke

Reefer Madness is a drug education film produced by the US Federal Bureau of Narcotics. It describes the personal and social disintegration of a young man who goes berserk after smoking marijuana. One puff is all that is needed to hurl him down the slippery slope of violence, perversion and financial ruin.

Released in 1937, the accompanying advertising is appropriately lurid. A typical poster displays a large lit cigarette with 'MADNESS' written alongside. It is held aloft by an alluring woman whose loose bosom, wry smile and wide eyes all announce 'Drug Crazed Abandon.'

The upper-right part of the picture shows the head of a sinister-looking man, a bit like Dracula, with the caption, 'The Sweet "Pill" that Makes Life Bitter!' Although marijuana (the diced leaves of the cannabis plant) is never taken as a pill, this image implies a close connection between the cigarette and 'pills,' meaning other drugs.

Between the man at the top, and the 'loose' woman at the bottom, the word 'REEFER' appears, crowned by the caption 'Women cry for it – Men die for it!' The clear warning is, addiction.

And as if all this were not enough, there is a further insert at the lower right-hand corner, a photo of a man lighting up a cigarette for a young woman. Here the caption declares, 'SEE youthful marijuana victims. What actually happens.' The key word is 'victim.' It signifies the impending corruption of a decent couple. No doubt, he will become demented and she will become dissolute, like the figures on the other side of the poster.

Reefer Madness is a prime example of a wide genre of disinformation spread primarily by agencies of the American government. The purpose has been to prevent the use of narcotic, stimulant, psychoactive and psychedelic drugs by instilling fear in whomever might use them. Generally these fears have to do with going mad, becoming violent or turning evil. The cumulative effect has been to induce a state of paranoia in drug users and non-users alike, about their health, mind, social relations, place in society and, indeed, their very existence.

Are these fears justified? Or are they artifacts, drug-exaggerated delusions of a fragile personality? Are they essentially the products of internal processes? Or do they reflect actual events, the specific action of social forces mediated by external persons? In other words, are we dealing with 'paranoia,' or 'persecution'?

There are many similarities between these two states. Experientially both feel real. Both feel threatening. And both can lead the affected persons to respond psychologically and socially in peculiar ways. In the first place, there may be emotional withdrawal and inner fragmentation. These phenomena tend to be followed by desperate bursts of psychic evacuation, in order to get rid of the unwanted contents of a terrified mind. The projected fragments can be directed to influence the outside world, people and things, either to make them better or, paradoxically, to make them worse. Making worse comes under the category of a 'self-fulfilling prophecy.' You act to bring about what you fear so you can say, 'I always knew the danger was there. I'm not mad.'

'Paranoia' and 'persecution' are not the same phenomenon. Quite the contrary. 'Paranoia' denotes a state of mind, while 'persecution' denotes the fact of being threatened. In common usage, 'paranoia' refers to a state of suspicion and fear generated from within the mind: false beliefs and fantasies and other realms of the unreal. On the other hand, 'persecution' has to do with fear and terror aroused by outside persons, forces or events: tangible threats and verifiable risks.

In practice the terms 'paranoia' and 'persecution' are often synonymous. Persecution is persecution, whether by outside forces or inner demons. But 'paranoia' may not be imaginary. Rather it may reflect confused and confusing attempts to grapple with the malign effects of political policies and social processes.

The drug scene provides a good opportunity to explore these issues. Paranoiac fears and fantasies are rife. And there are obvious reasons for this, ranging from the personalities of the users, to the drugs used, to the context in which this use takes place. But perhaps the most potent instigator of fear is the illegality of certain drugs, and the consequences that follow from such illegality. I shall discuss these fears in more detail shortly.

Interestingly there is another set of fears, more like panic states, that need to be considered. I refer to the feelings that many non-users harbour towards drugs and drug users. If anything, the feelings of non-users can be more irrational, more intense, indeed, more dangerous than the mental state of the users. I say dangerous because non-users have the political power to delegitimise and criminalise and stigmatise the lives of users, and do so to the point where their very lives may be at risk.

In fact, users and non-users inhabit complementary persecutory conditions. Each acts to make the life of the other miserable. I will try to show who does what to whom, and in so doing, I shall demonstrate the complex interconnections between paranoid states, persecution and persecutors. Suffice to say, one person's paranoia leads to another's persecution.

In this chapter I shall concentrate on three specific mind- and mood-altering drugs: marijuana, heroin and cocaine. Collectively they comprise the vast majority of illegal psychedelic, narcotic and stimulant drugs currently in use. Obviously, there are many more kindred drugs, like LSD or opium or amphetamine, that could and should be mentioned. But to do so would take me beyond the scope of this chapter. Suffice to say, the problems engendered by marijuana, heroin and cocaine, and their users, typify the problems of all prohibited mind- and mood-altering substances.

Let me begin with marijuana, the subject of *Reefer Madness*. A 'reefer' is a cannabis cigarette. As I mentioned before, marijuana (cannabis) consists of the diced leaves (and flowery tops and small stems) of the plant. This is usually smoked or sprinkled over food. The term marijuana can also encompass other sources of tetrahydrocannabinol, the major psychoactive ingredient, including the dark resin, called hashish.

There exists recorded evidence that marijuana has been employed as a medicinal and intoxicant for thousands of years. European and American intellectuals including François Rabelais, Charles Baudelaire, Oscar Wilde, Fetish Ludlow and Havelock Ellis began to explore and expound its mood-altering properties from the nineteenth century.

Professor Stephen Duke and Albert Gross, in their extensive study, *America's Longest War* (1993), point out that in America large-scale use of marijuana for pleasure did not begin until the First World War. Soon afterwards the State of California enacted legislation against it. Then state after state followed suit until 1937, when federal prohibitions became law.

Marijuana had effectively been driven underground. Why? Because no sooner did it begin to become popular, than a flood of sensationalist propaganda began to flow from newspapers, magazines and books alleging that marijuana turned people into violent maniacs.

Thus when Harry Anslinger, the director of the US Federal Bureau of Narcotics, testified before Congress in support of the marijuana Tax Act, he asserted that marijuana was worse than opium. Referring to the story of Dr Jekyll and Mr Hyde, he concluded:

> Opium has all the good of Dr. Jekyll and all the evil of Mr. Hyde. This drug [marijuana] is entirely the monster Mr. Hyde.
>
> (Conti 1932: 146)

Note how 'monster' is deployed to anthropomorphise and demonise part of a plant.

Perhaps Anslinger had read *Dope*, a book published a few years earlier that claimed:

(The) man under the influence of hashish catches up his knife and runs
through the streets hacking and killing everyone he meets.

(Conti 1932: 141)

More likely than not, the author was regurgitating material about the
'Assassins,' a secret sect of fanatical Muslims who terrorised the Middle
East with political assassinations from the eleventh to the thirteenth
centuries. The connection with hashish may have come about because the
spelling of 'hashish ins' (hashish users) is similar to 'Assassins.' I know
no conclusive proof that they killed while 'high' on hash. However, Marco
Polo did provide a secondhand account of the way that one of their leaders
drew his followers into a trance-like state with hashish. And ever since
his travelogue was published, the association has stuck (Polo 1875).

According to Duke and Gross, almost all newspaper and magazine articles in the 1930s asserted that marijuana created 'maniacal frenzies' during
which time the intoxicant could commit 'unspeakable crimes.' Similar
ideas continue to circulate today about proscribed substances like
cannabis, opiates and cocaine, while prestigious people, like the former
first lady Nancy Reagan, who warned that even if a person is a casual
user, he or she is *an accomplice to murder* (*Chicago Tribune*, 6 March
1988).

Changing social mores have focused on substances like cannabis, heroin,
and cocaine in order to create the idea of 'drug-crazed killers.' Yet, there
exists little evidence that these drugs, in themselves, lead to violent
abandon on the part of the user. On the contrary, marijuana, heroin and
other narcotics induce a relaxed, floating, pleasurable state of mind, that
militates against aggression.

Nor are these drugs, contrary to public perception, intrinsically dangerous to health. Consider the opiates. Study after study has concluded
that, when properly used, the user is medically a 'well' person. For
example, in the late 1950s a blue ribbon report on narcotics drugs by a
Joint Committee of the American Bar Association (ABA) and the
American Medical Association (AMA) concluded that:

The facts (are) ... that the use of drugs like heroin and morphine is
consistent both with a reasonable state of health and with a reasonable
degree of efficiency on the part of the individual user.

(1963: 46)

Similarly, many comprehensive studies of cannabis including the *La
Guardia Report* (New York, 1938), the *Wootton Report* (Britain, 1969)
and the *Le Dain Commission* (Canada, 1972) have confirmed that
cannabis has no adverse effects on physical health and that any psychological effects are 'slight' and have 'little clinical significance.' Moreover,
in contrast to many narcotics or stimulants, or widely used recreational

drugs like tobacco or alcohol, or medicaments like aspirin, it is impossible to overdose on cannabis. No known instance of intentional or accidental death from cannabis has ever been proven. Quite the reverse is true. Cannabis is an effective clinical agent against many symptoms and illnesses. Currently it is being used to counter glaucoma, as an antiemetic (to counter nausea) in chemotherapy, to relieve chronic pain and to control the spasms of multiple sclerosis.[1]

Yet, baseless pronouncements by a wide variety a governmental and institutional officials predominate in the media. Typically the former British MP, Mr Tim Rathbone, in a letter to *The Times* asserted that cannabis has 'known bad effects on the brain and body' including 'paranoia, epilepsy, malfunctioning of the reproductive organs, lost motivation and hallucinations' (24 July 1992: 13).

Perhaps Mr Rathbone is confusing cannabis with other substances, like cocaine. Although most users suffer no serious physical or psychological difficulties, people who abuse it, that is who persistently take large amounts of cocaine over short periods of time can indeed get into serious trouble. Aside from lack of sleep, loss of appetite and runny nose when smoked, chronic use can lead to nasal septal rupture, paranoid psychosis, hypertension and related conditions.

Addiction is a further issue that has contributed to the notoriety of marijuana, heroin and cocaine. One puff, one shot (injection), one snort – all are capable of turning the user into a 'dope fiend.' But what do we mean by addiction? The primary definition involves three considerations: tolerance, withdrawal symptoms and craving. Tolerance means the body needs more and more of the drug to maintain the same level of intoxication. Withdrawal symptoms refer to the physical ill-effects that occur when the drug is not available. Craving is a strong emotional need or desire for the drug and may be called psychological dependency.

When cannabis, the opiates and cocaine came to public attention they were all said to be highly addictive. Hence the term 'dope fiend,' someone with a fixed stare who will do anything to get a puff. Then even the most implacable opponents of these drugs began to realise that cannabis and cocaine are not addictive, and that even narcotic drugs are incompletely addictive. What happens is relative to set and setting, that is, to the personality of the user and the context in which the drugs are used.[2] Even frequent users may not become addicted, unless they have severe emotional problems in the first place. These are expressions of mental pain which the opiates serve to relieve. Thus the Joint Committee of the ABA and AMA back in the 1950s observed:

> There are many persons, particularly in the slum areas of our large cities, who have the drug habit – who use drugs more or less regularly, but who have not become addicted.
>
> (1963: 25)

Addiction is not an elusive concept. It is straightforward to demonstrate. But it cannot be attributed to most users, because they do not demonstrate one or more of the three basic criteria. Therefore, during the past couple of decades, 'addiction' has been superseded by the concept of psychological dependency. This term is much more elusive and easier to apply. At any given point, most users want the drugs they are taking, so they are said to be 'afflicted' with psychological dependency and to suffer the 'sick' or 'evil' consequences of such an affliction.

Since this 'affliction' involves cravings, and cravings are escalating and escalated desires, drug experts have asserted that the use of one drug invariably leads to the use of others. This is the escalation effect often portrayed in the following way: 'Soft Drugs (marijuana) opens the gate to Hard Drugs (heroin and cocaine).' 'Soft' and 'hard' are relatively recent ideas which attempt to distinguish between degrees of addiction and harmfulness.

This theory, that cannabis is a 'gateway drug,' is based on anecdotal evidence. But anecdotal evidence is not a proof. No one has been able to show that the eating, smoking, injecting or sniffing of one drug leads to the same with another.

In the 1970s I conducted a major study of cannabis users in London together with the American sociologist, Calvin Hernton. During the course of investigating the experiences of 522 users, we queried both their use of cannabis and other drugs. We were not able to find any statistically significant correlation between the use of cannabis and other substances including heroin, cocaine, amphetamines, barbiturates, LSD, alcohol, tobacco and other medicinals (Berke and Hernton 1974).

In this survey, many respondents did report that they had some experience of other drugs. However, to prove escalation, one has to demonstrate a causal connection, not just a contiguous connection. The latter can and has been used to show a relationship between cannabis and narcotics. But contiguity can also be used to show an even closer relationship between cannabis and milk, since all cannabis users have drunk milk. In as much as we live in a multi-drug-taking culture, guilt by association is not sufficient to prove drug escalation.

I have just referred to a very small part of the immense literature on cannabis, heroin and cocaine in order to reflect on the evidence that these substances in themselves are not inherently harmful, nor necessarily addictive, nor invariably lead from one to the other.

Given the views of governmental agencies across America and the rest of the world, as well as a barrage of pictures and articles about drugs, drug users, drug dealers and drug damage that dominate our television screens, newspapers and magazines, how is it possible for 'facts' to be so contrary? And if these drugs are not so bad, why are America's prisons filled with hundreds of thousands of people, roughly a third of the entire prison population, for drug dealing or possession, offences which did not exist prior to the First World War?

DRUG HISTORY AND CULTURE AND THE POLITICISATION OF FEAR

Every culture has its favoured substances to alter states of consciousness, both for ritual and recreational purposes. Often the introduction of a new substance is met with suspicion and vehement rejection. In the seventeenth century, for example, when tobacco became popular in the New World, it was banned in many parts of Europe and Asia. Draconian penalties accrued to anyone who sold or smoked it. Thus the Sultan of Constantinople called tobacco an unhealthy 'infidel weed,' and demanded death for users. Similarly, in Russia, smokers attracted 'nostril slitting,' the bastinado (foot beating), or execution, while in Japan, the Emperor imprisoned both buyers and sellers, and confiscated their property.

In contrast, opium and its derivatives, morphine, Demerol, heroin, Codeine, used to be entirely legal both in the Old World, and the New. It was grown everywhere and has been nature's principle painkiller and relaxant. Indeed, not long ago, generations of babies were given a tincture of opium, called laudanum, to quiet their crying.

The demonisation of opium began in the nineteenth century when Great Britain decided to expand the Indian economy by growing opium and forcing it on China, thereby creating a huge market for the drug, and many other products as well. Two opium wars were fought over this issue, China trying to prohibit opium, and Britain trying to push it. This clash between two imperial powers led each to portray the other in lurid terms, all part of a propaganda war that coincided with diplomatic and military efforts to overcome the other.

The reciprocal projections each country directed to the other spilled over on to the point of contention between them, that is, opium. So from the Chinese point of view, it wasn't just Britain that was evil, but opium. And from the British point of view, it wasn't just the Chinese who were lazy, corrupt and corrupting, dangerous, no good and so on, but opium itself. Then as invariably happens in these propaganda exchanges, the protagonists forgot that 'the demon opium' was only a symbol for how they saw each other. They began to equate the symbol with the real thing, so instead of representing a spectre, it embodied a 'monster.' By means of an interpersonal transaction and a perceptual transformation, opium actually became the demon England, or the demon China.

The same process holds true for the demonisation of all drugs: the drugs become the outcomes that their antagonists allege, as well as the fantasies that their users fear.

But let me continue with the story of opium, because it exemplifies these processes again and again. The rapid spread of opium in China came at a time of social upheaval and personal demoralisation. Meanwhile, across the Pacific, many thousands of coolies were imported by contract bosses to build the railways. These labourers, far from home, in an alien environment, and without family or friends, naturally brought their habit with them. In itself this was not significant, for opium was taken throughout the States in a wide array of patent medicines. But when the Chinese workers took other jobs, and preferred to remain in the country, rather than return to China, the labour unions became alarmed they would take the place of American workers at a lower rate of pay. Now it was the turn of the union leaders to decry the 'yellow peril.' Within a couple of decades this yellow peril, the dirty conditions in which they had to live, the gauntlet of hate which they had to run, their strange customs and endemic diseases, all became equal to the opium to which the Chinese immigrants turned for consolation.

The consequent mixture of economic conflict, racism, anti-colonialism and political gamesmanship, as well as yellow journalism in the service of moral fervour, led the US to initiate curbs on the opium trade (the Shanghai Commission, 1909) and prohibitory regulations (The Hague Convention, 1912).

In Britain similar factors fed a clamour to ban cocaine during the First World War. At this time Germany was the leading producer and distributor of cocaine. The authorities became alarmed when they noticed that servicemen were using it. They worried that this would cause a collapse of morale at the front. Even worse, many saw cocaine as a 'Hunnish plot to undermine the British Empire.' This view is not unlike contemporary fears that Colombian coke dealers are out to 'undermine the moral fabric of America.'

As for marijuana, racism, economics and politics again provided the basis for prohibitory legislation in the United States. In this case the issue was 'drug-crazed' lower-class Mexican workers and blacks, who roamed the American Southwest during the 1920s and 30s. The general perception was that most smoked dope, lived by crime and were dangerous and violent men. So society was threatened, both by these people themselves, and by their proximity to middle-class youth who would learn to smoke dope from them, and then become like them. Although there was little evidence that this actually happened, lurid rumours and press reports whipped up the public's imagination.

It will now be useful to explore in greater detail the intense fears that many non-users carry towards users, and to consider who or what is responsible for them. The resultant issues are intimately concerned with the question of paranoia and persecution, and the connections between them. I intend to demonstrate that the fears of non-users (madness) generate actions (social policies) which frighten users. In turn the fears of users (lack of supply) generate actions (crime) that frighten the non-users. All this can cause reciprocal cycles of fear and response with devastating personal and social consequences.

It is hard to pick a good place to start, for as we have seen, almost every drug scare has an antecedent scare, which may or may not be related to the drug in question or, for that matter, any drug. There was a flurry of propaganda in the 1920s and 30s when Harry Anslinger intimidated America with the help of the *Readers Digest* and the *Saturday Evening Post*. Then drug use and abuse lost the limelight until resurrected by Richard Nixon during his presidential campaign in the late 1960s as the 'War on Drugs.'

This 'War on Drugs' began the contemporary era of drug propaganda and enforcement. Nixon exclaimed two months before his election:

> Drugs are among the modern curse of the youth, just like the plagues and epidemics of former years. And they are decimating a generation of Americans.
>
> [My administration] will accelerate the development of tools and weapons ... to fight illegal drugs: a tripled Customs Service, more federal drug agents, massive assistance to local police, and antidrug operations abroad.
>
> (Baum 1966: 12)

As part of this 'war', the Nixon administration targeted, 'the incendiary black militant and the welfare mother, the hedonistic hippie and the campus revolutionary.'

Later, Bob Haldeman, Nixon's Chief of Staff, noted in his diaries that no matter what evidence could be mustered in favour of marijuana, Nixon was determined to keep it illegal. He fired Bertram Brown, the director of the National Institute of Mental Health because he said marijuana offences should be treated like parking tickets. And he stripped HEW (Health Education and Welfare) of responsibility for drugs and gave it to the Justice Department because he believed everyone at HEW *'was on drugs anyway.'* Nixon wanted a statement on marijuana that was really strong, one that *'tears the ass out of them.'*

Nixon felt that everyone was against him. Haldeman recorded that Nixon especially wanted to know: 'why all the Jews seem to be the the ones that are for liberalising the regulations on marijuana' (Haldeman 1994: 292). Nixon ploughed on with his war on drugs. By 1970 he noted that 23 per cent of all Americans believed that drugs were the country's number one problem. He claimed heroin addicts alone stole over $2 billion worth of property. Yet in 1971, the estimated total value of all property stolen in the United States was $1.3 billion.

Furthermore, Nixon believed that violence was on the increase. *Time* magazine reported the dawn of 'drug violence,' with almost two dealers a week being killed. Yet in the same year, 1971, that drug deaths were a major issue, the number of Americans who died from all drugs, legal or illegal was 2,313. In contrast, during the same year, 2,227 Americans choked to death on food, and 2,360 died in gun accidents (Baum 1996: 66).

Nixon could not have maintained this war without the support of many prominent Americans such as Supreme Court Justice Hugo Black. The year before, Black confidently stated:

> Commercial traffic in deadly mind-soul-and-body destroying drugs is beyond a doubt one of the greatest evils of our time. It cripples intellects, dwarfs bodies, paralyses the progress of a substantial segment of our society, and frequently makes hopeless and sometimes violent and murderous criminals of persons of all ages who become its victims. Such consequences call for the most vigorous laws to suppress the traffic as the most powerful efforts to put these vigorous laws into effect.[3]
>
> (Baum 1996: 29)

The drug war slowed a bit under President Carter, but picked up steam during the Reagan era. It was as much about culture as it was against drugs. Marijuana was closely associated with hard-rock music, torn jeans, sexual promiscuity and 'the counter-culture.' It was about the stubborn refusal to conform to prevailing social values. For middle America, frightened of long hair, black beards and loose bosoms, Reagan played the clichés of non-conformity for a cavalcade of votes. He said all drugs, hard, soft or otherwise, were bad. And he was going after them.

In June 1982, while standing in the rose garden of the White House, President Reagan declared his War on Drugs.

> We can put drug abuse on the run through stronger law enforcement. [This country] ... must mobilize to let kids know the truth, to erase the false glamour that surrounds drugs, and to brand drugs such as marijuana exactly for what they are – dangerous.
>
> We're taking down the surrender flag ... and running up the battle flag.
>
> (Reagan 1982: 813)

These themes of wars, battles, crusades and campaigns occur and reoccur over the ensuing years. Thus, Army Lt. Gun. Thomas W. Kelly compared drug users to a ruthless enemy, as ruthless as the Nazis, or the Japanese, while William von Saab, former head of the Customs Service called for a *'war of action'* (*USA Today*, 6 September 1989: 8a).

This 'war' took a new twist after George Bush was elected President in 1988. He appointed the former Education Secretary, William Bennett, to be the czar (chief official with absolute power) of the Office of Drug Control Policy. Bennett immediately proclaimed that the big problem with drugs was that they were 'immoral,' not just a menace to life and limb: '[illegal drugs] obliterate morals, value, character, our relations with each other, and our relation with God' (Baum 1996: 266). Bennett argued that marijuana, heroin and cocaine should be illegal because they are immoral. But he also believed that drugs are immoral because they are illegal. So compliance to the law, not health, became the primary focus.

Less than eighteen months after becoming czar, and against all evidence to the contrary, William Bennett declared that the 'war' was won, and resigned. However, his boss, George Bush, did not give up. He continued the public relations battle with slogans such as, 'Just say no,' and unsuccessful projects such as, 'Weed and Seed' (Baum 1996: 322). Following Bush, Bill Clinton has tempered the propaganda, but has continued in the same vein, perhaps because of the political pressure that followed the revelation that he 'had smoked but not inhaled.'

As we have seen, marijuana, heroin and cocaine have been considered public enemy number one by a wide cross-section of people in the United States and Europe. Why? Because these and other illegal drugs which they represent have been deemed a 'curse,' 'a plague,' 'an epidemic,' 'soul destroying,' 'intellect crippling,' 'murderous making,' 'criminogenic,' 'dangerous,' 'bad' and 'immoral.' The list could go on and on.

The effect on non-users, in the face of incessant disinformation by political, religious and social leaders whom they should be able to trust, and without direct evidence to the contrary, can be devastating. At best, a constant state of vague apprehension is aroused, and at worse, terror.

One could well query whether the political leaders, writers, opinion makers, the ones who propagate the propaganda, believe what they propagate. Did Nixon really believe that drugs were decimating America? Or was this view a convenient way to redirect widespread fears of communism once the war in Vietnam had subsided and his administration had normalised relations with China? Did Nancy Reagan really think that druggies were degenerates and murderers, or did she mostly fear blacks, hippies and welfare mothers?[4] And was William Bennett really convinced that illegal drugs obliterated our relation with God? Or was he using 'drugs' to excuse his own lack of faith?

POLITICAL, BUREAUCRATIC AND FINANCIAL EXPEDIENCY LEADING TO THE PERSECUTION OF DRUG USERS

It is difficult to know whether leaders in the fight against drugs believe what they say without being privy to their innermost thoughts. However, it is likely that political expediency has enabled government officials to pursue personal ambitions and policies that would otherwise be unpopular. For example, there is some evidence that agents of the American government have themselves dealt in drugs in order to obtain funds to further covert activities in Central America and elsewhere. Various reports, subsequently denied by the CIA, suggest that the agency funnelled huge amounts of cocaine into black and Hispanic neighbourhoods of Los Angeles during the 1980s in order to fund counter-insurgency in Nicaragua (*International Herald Tribune*, 18 November 1996: 3).[5]

Bureaucratic expediency is another factor. In the United States, in particular, there has been an enormous expansion of drug-related agencies and ancillary personnel. This would not have been possible to sustain without the existence of a perceived 'drug menace.'

Thirdly, financial expediency must be considered. By 1996 the production and distribution of illegal drugs had become the second largest industry in the entire world (after the military). It is currently estimated that between $150 and $250 billion accrues to this industry per year, and it clearly has the power to subvert and bring down governments that refuse to accede to it. While I have not come across evidence, or even reports, that the illegal drug industry supports anti-drug propaganda, it is interesting to speculate that this may take place, because the industry would collapse if drugs were not illegal.

I have been discussing the rational reasons that permeate the fear of drugs. However, non-rational, mostly unconscious factors, are even more pervasive and persuasive. I refer to the dread of foreign influences (Russian, Asian, Mexican, extra Galactic creatures) and anti-social values (long-haired revolutionaries). These unexpected experiences tend to be associated with the alien forces that many people believe are taking over the world. The popularity of films like *Invasion of the Body Snatchers* illustrates such states of mind.

When comparable thoughts are equated with drugs, the results are drug-fuelled fears of mind-snatchers and madness. Anti-drug books such as *Dope: The Story of the Living Dead* (1928) are the direct antecedent of psychiatric diagnoses such as the amotivational syndrome. Indeed, all the illegal drugs have been called, 'alien invaders,' in many different contexts. Perhaps that is why former President Nixon referred to drugs as a 'plague.' He, or at least his speech writers, seem to have identified them with hostile bacteria.

These underlying non-rational fears, which are paranoiac to the extent that they are not based on fact, have in turn incited a massive social overreaction, akin to a hysterical outbreak of wild uncontrolled feelings about marijuana, heroin, cocaine and kindred substances. And, after exploding in the United States, similar frenzies have occurred in a host of other countries.

Hysterical episodes have happened many times in American history, and inevitably have to do with feared invasions of alien forces, values or persons. One of the first of these had to do with the dread of witches in New England in the 1600s. This has been graphically described by Arthur Miller in his play *The Crucible* and has to do with the fear of being bewitched or taken over, not unlike current fears about drugs.

More recently there have been mass panics about illegal immigrants, anarchists, Japanese citizens (during the Second World War), alcohol (Prohibition, 1920–33), communists (reds under the bed) and the missile gap. All were based on a major misreading and misperception of reality. In the same vein, it is likely that Nixon, Reagan, Bennett and other key figures in the upper echelons of the government came to believe, and continue to believe, the anti-drug propaganda that they have propagated, because they have wanted to believe it, and because their political positions demand it. As Bob Haldeman observed, no amount of evidence to the contrary could shift Richard Nixon's public position.

Whether motivated by expediency, or by unconscious dread, or both, the resultant policies have brought about the very situation that they were supposed to combat. The use of drugs is escalating. An illegal industry is getting bigger. The social, political and economic fabric of the United States, in addition to that of many other countries, has been damaged. And the lives of ordinary citizens, non-users as well as users, have been adversely affected.

In this respect it is noteworthy that there exists a word in the English language, paranoia, that denotes a mental state when a person thinks he is in danger, but actually isn't. But there is no word in the English language to denote a far more common situation – when a person is actually in danger, but doesn't realise it.

I refer to the direct danger of the effects of illegality. This means that drugs are impure, their dosage cannot be guaranteed and that their delivery systems are unsafe. Moreover, in recent years, highly toxic 'designer drugs,' have been developed and sold in order to circumvent the drug laws. By adding or subtracting atoms from a particular molecule, chemists have been able to make substances which mimic the effects of psychedelics or opiates, but whose possession and use are legal until specifically banned. All too often, however, the harmful effects of many of these designer drugs or their impurities do not become evident until users become sick. One such compound MPTP (1-Methyl-4-phenyl-1,23,6-tetrahydropyridine) turned out to be a severe neurotoxin which causes irreversible advanced Parkinsonism (Langston and Palfreman: 1996).

But there is a more pervasive problem, which effects non-users as well as users. Because of 'the war on drugs,' civil liberties which citizens in Western countries should be able to take for granted, have been undermined. In considering the issue, I shall focus on the erosion of liberties in the United States, because that country has a most clearly defined charter, the Bill of Rights (the first ten amendments to the Constitution which guarantee civil liberties). Abuses which happen there tend to trickle down to other countries.

The Fourth Amendment of the Constitution guarantees citizens against 'unreasonable searches and seizures,' and prohibits arrest, seizure or search warrants without 'probable cause.' Because of continuing pressure from the government agencies to interdict drug users, the administration of the law has been *de facto* changed from 'probable cause' to 'reasonable suspicion.' In practice this means that the police have *carte blanche* to break into houses, stop cars, interfere with travellers and violate people's bodies.

The courts have upheld close helicopter surveillance of homes and gardens, as well as piece by piece searches of personal garbage. Travellers may be strip searched, X-rayed and or ordered to defecate into waste baskets under the gaze of police because they fit a police profile of a drug courier. But this profile may be inconsistent from state to state, agency to agency, or week to week. Thus, in Tennessee an officer testified that he was suspicious of a man because he '*walked quickly through the airport.*' At a later date the same officer stated that he was concerned about a man because he '*walked with intentional slowness after getting off a bus*' (Duke and Gross 1993: 125–6).

The airport in Buffalo, New York, provides another not untypical example. In 1989, a large number of people were stopped but few arrested. Federal Circuit Court Judge, George Pratt commented:

> It appears that [the police] have sacrificed the Fourth Amendment by detaining 590 innocent people in order to arrest 10 who are not – all in the name of the 'war on drugs.' When pray tell, will it end? Where are we going?
>
> (Pratt 1991: 500)

'Reasonable suspicion' also provides the basis for an escalating invasion of privacy. Students and workers have been subject to compulsory urine and blood tests. Refusal to agree leads to a presumption of guilt and loss of status and livelihood. Thus, for fear of drug abuse, the Governor of Virginia, Douglas Wilder, proposed that all college students in the state submit to mandatory drug testing. Many large corporations have followed suit (Duke and Gross 1993: 127).

The Sixth Amendment has also been severely curtailed. Among other things, it guarantees the right of counsel in case of criminal prosecution. But to an increasing extent, lawyers are being harassed, even prosecuted, for defending drug users. And if this were not enough, the government is limiting the ability of clients to pay for counsel. Not only is it difficult for a lawyer to accept fees from such a client, but through greatly expanding the statutes on forfeiture, the government is making it impossible for anyone suspected of drug involvement to hold property or financial instruments of any kind.[6]

This attack on property reflects the attitude of even the most liberal Supreme Court Justices. In 1987 Thurgood Marshall, well known for his strong defence of the Bill of Rights, was interviewed in *Life* magazine: 'If it's a dope case, I won't even read the petition. I ain't giving no break to no dope dealer' ('Justice Revealed,' *Life*: 105). It is very hard to reconcile this statement with a commitment to defend the Constitution. Certainly it demonstrates the extent to which the government is able to intimidate its highest officials for the sake of 'the war on drugs.'

The problem is that the Fifth Amendment absolutely guarantees the right to private property. This used to hold even for convicted criminals. The first Continental Congress made only one exception, to allow the navy to seize slave ships, even if the owner wasn't aboard or known. This position remained until 1970 when the government decided that the only way really to hurt criminal organisations was to take away its money. So a new category of the forfeiture law was invented, criminal forfeiture. This meant that assets arising from a criminal venture could be confiscated. Originally there were safeguards. The government had to prove 'beyond reasonable doubt' that people who were losing assets had been guilty of a crime. But within a short time, the safeguards were whittled down. 'Organisation' was redefined to include a single person. 'Guilty' did not mean committing a crime, but merely knowing about it, or simply intending to do it. So an anti-crime bill that began an attack on racketeering soon became a major instrument to attack drug dealers and large-scale users (Baum 1996: 35–8).

But dealers are not the only ones to suffer. The public at large has been affected too. People have lost their homes for growing a few marijuana plants for personal use, or because their children stored a bit of marijuana in them, even without their knowledge.

No word can describe the nightmare that hovers over thousands of citizens without their being aware of what might happen to them. In 1974 this was made all the more imminent when the Supreme Court declared that the innocence of the property owner was immaterial. Not long afterwards the Customs Service and Coast Guard, under the policy of 'zero tolerance,' escalated the seizure of cars, yachts, boats and airplanes, aside from buildings, whenever the smallest detectable amount of drug could be found. Not untypically, the oceanographic research vessel *Atlantis* was confiscated because the tail end of a marijuana cigarette had been found in the crew quarters. Congressman Gerry Studs, whose district includes the home port of the vessel denounced the seizure as 'lunacy,' but to no avail (Duke and Gross 1993: 140).

Not surprisingly, criminal forfeiture has not only hurt guilty and innocent parties alike, but, as a number of spectacular cases has shown, the law has tended to corrupt the lawyers and police charged with executing it. Nicholas Bissell, a New Jersey prosecutor, for example, became known as the 'forfeiture king,' due to his flamboyant drug busts and property seizures. However, he himself was indicted after it was discovered that he had engaged in a large-scale extortion of businessmen, after threatening to plant drugs on their premises.[7]

Political expediency, it appears, leads directly to criminal expediency. But a further question can well be asked: if political expediency has redirected the fear of communism and communist regimes towards drugs, can such expediency be used to bring about an authoritarian, even demagogic regime in the United States? While such thinking might seem paranoiac, it is worth considering that the President of the United States, Bill Clinton, supports legislation even more draconian than that of his predecessors. During his campaign he advocated that all sixteen- and seventeen-year-olds should be tested for drugs before getting a driver's licence. And his get-tough measures include wider use of the death penalty for drug dealers as well as cutting welfare from mothers who fail drug tests. Meanwhile the anti-drug budget increased from $4.7 billion in 1988 to $15.1 billion in 1996.[8]

It would appear that the laws against marijuana, hashish and cocaine, are more dangerous to non-users than users. The latter tend to become an underclass that exists outside the political system. But non-users pay for the drug war through diminished political liberties and increased taxation (to pay for the war) aside from being caught in the crossfire between users, dealers and the authorities. Moreover, many people are deprived of effective medical care for a variety of conditions because of the government's anti-drug policies. This leads to the absurd and tragic situation whereby terminal cancer patients are deprived of adequate pain relief because of the fear that they might become addicted to narcotics.

Clearly an initial panic has provoked policies which have led to greater perils. In this instance, paranoia has generated persecution, not in the imagination, but in actuality. It is worth considering whether the damage that accrues from the use of marijuana, heroin or cocaine comes from the drug itself, or whether it stems from the psychic processes of non-users, inner events which emerge in our culture as prohibitory laws and policies. Ironically, drugs which are not illegal are far more harmful than those which are. I not only refer to tobacco and alcohol, but to widely available, but highly toxic tranquillisers, anti-depressants and sleeping pills. To put matters into a proper perspective, recent data in the United States shows that tobacco has a death rate of 650 per 100,000 users per year; alcohol: 150; heroin: 80; cocaine: 4 and cannabis: 0 (Duke and Gross 1993: 77).

Since the mid 1990s, a growing chorus of newspaper and journal articles and books, especially in the United States, has begun to query this conundrum. Even the prestigious magazine, *The Atlantic*, in an extensive review of the drug laws, 'More Reefer Madness,' has headlined the situation whereby in the States a murderer may only serve six years in gaol, but a person may be sentenced to life imprisonment without parole for possessing a single joint. The author, Eric Schlosser, concludes that the country 'is in the grip of a deep psychosis' (April 1997: 90).

Psychosis or not, the West is a drug-taking culture. Drugs wake you up and put you to sleep. They pick you up and calm you down. Terrible diseases succumb to a handful of tablets while others carry the promise of transcendent pleasure and longer life. In this context it is not surprising that people in emotional pain and social turmoil will be tantalised by a multitude of leaves, pills and powders, and will react with rage if these substances are withheld from them.

Negative policies effect a negative set and setting. This is especially pertinent with psychoactive drugs. There may be an initial excitement at doing something illicit, but these activities invariably lead to tension and apprehension. These feelings amplify the underlying distress of the user who invariably tries to overcome the primary and secondary states of mind – that is, the direct effects of drug on the mind, and the influence of social and political context – by turning to more drugs. More drugs lead to greater conflict with the law. And so on. This is a further example of how paranoia (fears of the non-user) lead to persecution (the war on drugs) which lead to paranoia (frightened response of users) or justified apprehension (awareness of social risks).

Users are no angels. Many will exploit the situation to make money, or to simply assure a steady supply. In the latter case, small numbers of users will commit an extraordinary number of crimes, usually of a predatory, but non-violent nature. In one study of 356 heroin users in Miami, Florida, it was found that they committed nearly 120,000 crimes including burglary, shoplifting, fraud and drug dealing. This amounted to 332 per person in one year. Comparable figures were found in other cities (Duke and Gross 1993: 108–9). These are huge numbers. But one has to consider that in every theft, there were one, two, or more people who were deprived of valuable property, hurt, shocked and severely scared. This demonstrates the power of users to arouse paranoia or, one might say, appropriate apprehension in the lives of non-users. They become preoccupied with fearful crimes which need not happen, if drugs were legal.

Such predatory crimes for personal need then lead to a huge illegal industry to manufacture and supply drugs to users. Most violent incidents are connected with this side of the business: personal rivalries, turf wars and contractual killings. Again many of the victims are innocent bystanders who happened to get in the way of shoot-outs. Indeed, in some

American inner cities, parents put their children to bed in the bathtub to protect them from stray bullets.

The further implications of crimes for supply and crimes for profit are terrifying. There has been a proliferation of deadly weapons in the schools. It is almost unbelievable that over 400,000 American children carry guns to school, aside from knives and flak jackets ('Straight talk,' *New York Times*, 30 March 1992).

The huge amounts of drug money about are able to corrupt all branches of the criminal justice system: police, judges, lawyers and congressmen. This should not be news. It is a repeat of what happened during Prohibition, with many officers going into business for themselves (Duke and Gross 1993: 113–18).

Social deterioration is perhaps the penultimate result of drug-related crime. Vandalism is pervasive, shops are abandoned and amenities disappear. The fabric of communal life falls prey to fear. People barricade themselves in their homes while the streets are left to the underworld, which is the only provider of jobs and money.

Here paranoia and persecution achieve complete expression. The fears of non-users engender negative policies which frighten users who turn to crime which frighten and persecute non-users who engender calls for more 'wars.' Or is it the other way around? At this point it is confusing about who is threatening whom, and over what. Is the issue drugs, or power, or wealth, or sheer perversity?

It is necessary to remind oneself that upwards of 50 per cent of all crimes in the United States are drug-related. In some inner cities the percentage is higher. Does it matter? Are drugs a plague? Or are they red herrings, the inevitable result of social demoralisation, communal deterioration and prohibitory legislation?

One way to approach this question is to consider places where drugs are not illegal, or at least not so illegal as in the United States. Most notably I refer to Mexico which is a major source for drugs coming into the States, and where all drugs are openly available. Yet the US State Department asserted in 1991 that Mexico 'does not have a serious drug problem' (Bureau of International Narcotics Matters, March 1991).

But for Americans and Europeans the most important example is Holland, where marijuana has been *de facto* decriminalised. Since this has happened, the use of cannabis has markedly declined. Certainly it is more available, but cheaper. And it has lost value as a 'protest drug.' Put simply, it is no longer so fashionable.

I would further predict that there will be a decrease in the crime rate and what one might term, the general 'paranoia level.' Less crime, means less intrusion, means more civil liberties.

Similar experiments are brewing in the States where Arizona effectively decriminalised marijuana in 1983 by making available a 'Cannabis and

Controlled Substances Dealer's License.' The state has even made handsome $10 tax stamps to affix to an ounce of cannabis (*International Herald Tribune*, 7 October 1996: 3).

In November 1996, California followed suit by voting with big majorities to legalise the sale and possession of cannabis for medical purposes (*International Herald Tribune*, 7 November 1996: 3). At the same time, Arizona held a comparable referendum. The outcome was almost identical, but with an extra proviso that heroin and LSD could be made available for pain relief. However, the forces that have sustained drug propaganda and persecution have not disappeared; nor has the 'war on drugs' begun to wind down.

Within a couple of months of the ballot in Arizona and California, President Bill Clinton approved a plan to combat the new state laws and prevent them from being utilised. The federal administration fears that the ballots are the 'thin edge of a wedge' that will lead to the legalisation of marijuana, and then all drugs. As a result of these and other unspoken 'fears,' the administration has decided to threaten doctors with loss of their medical privileges and criminal prosecution, not just for prescribing marijuana, but even for recommending it. Moreover, the Drug Enforcement Administration (DEA) intends to use surveillance and informers to catch what the DEA terms, 'Dr. Feelgoods,' physicians who support its use. (*The Times*, 30 December 1996: 7)

The proposed attack on doctors utilises a form of interdiction that was widely deployed in the years around the First World War and before the narcotics were formally banned. Doctors were simply threatened with prosecution if they prescribed them.

The President's battle plans are being coordinated out by a retired army general, and Vietnam veteran, Gen. Barry McCaffrey, chief of the White House drug policy office. Gen. McCaffrey claims that marijuana has no accepted medical use and that he will deploy all available means, including the facilities of the Internal Revenue Service and the Postal Service, to protect children from drugs and maintain drug-free workplaces (*International Herald Tribune*, 30 December 1996: 2).

The policy of challenging the referendums has had a chilling effect on the medical profession in California and Arizona. Doctors are frightened about losing their federal licence to prescribe, as well as of being excluded from the Medicare and Medicaid health programs. As one California oncologist put it, 'There is no way I can recommend it [marijuana] without risking my livelihood' (*International Herald Tribune*, 2 January 1997: 3).

This new battle reinforces the themes of this chapter – that conscious and unconscious fears of drug use, as well as political, bureaucratic and financial expediency, lead non-drug users to threaten and actually damage users of mood- and mind-altering substances. Or, to put it another way, we see how the paranoia (of the non-user) potentiates the persecution (of the user).

Paradoxically we have also seen how such threats lead to increased drug use, the exact opposite of intended policies. Whether the result of social defiance or social demoralisation, this increased drug activity leads to increased crime and other activities which persecute non-users. Here we can see how the persecution (of the user) potentiates the paranoia (of the non-user). In either case spirals of fear and hurt emerge which serve to justify the expectations and actions of users and non-users alike.

NOTES

1 Under the new California Cannabis Reform Act passed in November 1996, the use of cannabis has been authorised in the treatment of anorexia, cancer, Aids, chronic pain, spasticity, glaucoma, arthritis and migraine ('Cannabis law reformer plans mass production,' *The Guardian*, 14 November 1996: 14.).

2 In Vietnam tens of thousand of soldiers used large amounts of heroin. It was cheap and widely available. By conventional standards they were addicts. Yet almost all performed their duties well, and when they returned to the States, most of them stopped using it. This shows the power of the setting, not just the set, in determining drug practices.

   The Scottish Office of the British government is currently funding a study at Glasgow Caledonian University about the importance of set and setting in heroin use. Psychologists David Shewan and Phil Dalgarno are investigating the importance of factors such as the user's way of life, environment, character and the availability of the drug in order to assess the relative social and physical toxicity of heroin in comparison to legal drugs such as tobacco ('Taxpayers fund study into "respectable" heroin use,' *The Sunday Times*, 9 March 1997: 7).

3 However, Justice Black, in the epigraph from his dissent in *Turner v. United States*, did go on to say that even the horrors of drugs use did not justify repealing constitutional freedoms.

4 There exists direct evidence that Nancy Reagan, with the help of her advisors, deliberately and cynically created a cause, 'the scourge of drug abuse,' in order to change her media image and gain personal popularity ('Drugs really can fix up a president,' *The Sunday Times*, 10 August 1997: 4–7).

5 The original allegations of CIA involvement with the sale of crack were made by the *San Jose Mercury News* in a series called, 'Dark Alliance,' which caused shock, fear and outrage in the Los Angeles black community. Subsequently the paper acknowledged that although members of the drug ring did meet Contra leaders, there was no direct proof that CIA officials knew of the relationship. Both the paper and the CIA are continuing to investigate the allegations ('Newspaper backs down over CIA drugs deal claims,' *The Times*, 14 May 1997: 14).

6 As of 1986, lawyers face a felony conviction for accepting a payment of $10,000 or more that was derived from unlawful activity. In drug cases the government assumes that all property and money was illegally obtained, whether this was the case or not. So, persons so accused are not able to pay for counsel.

7 Bissell and his wife and associates had creamed off huge amounts of money to support luxurious lifestyles. Having been convicted on thirty counts of fraud,

tax evasion, obstruction of justice, abuse of power and perjury by a federal jury, he killed himself before being sentenced to a probable ten year gaol term ('The fugitive, with an unhappy ending,' *International Herald Tribune*, 28 November 1996: 2).
8 Of course, Clinton's 'get-tough measures' may have just been a political ploy to outflank his opponent, Bob Dole. Nevertheless, once started, the measures are difficult to stop ('The drug war: tougher than ever, still a bust,' *International Herald Tribune*, 31 October 1996: 9).

BOOK REFERENCES

American Bar Association (ABA) and the American Medical Association (AMA), Joint Committee (1963) *Drug Addiction: Crime or Disease?*, Bloomington: Indiana University Press.

Baum, D. (1996) *Smoke and Mirrors: The War on Drugs and the Politics of Failure*, New York: Little, Brown.

Berke, J. H. and Hernton, C. C. (1974) *The Cannabis Experience: An Interpretive Study of the Effects of Marijuana and Hashish*, London: Peter Owen.

Black, W. (1928) *Dope: The Story of the Living Dead*, New York: The Star Co.

Bureau of International Narcotics Matters (1991) *International Narcotics Control Strategy Report*, Washington, DC: US Department of State, March.

Conti, E.C. (1932) *A History of Smoking*, New York: Harcourt Press.

Duke, S. and Gross, A. (1993) *America's Longest War,* New York: A Jeremy P. Tarcher/Putnam Book.

Haldeman, H.R. (1994) *The Haldeman Diaries: Inside the Nixon White House*, New York: G. P. Putnam.

Himmelstein, J. (1983) *The Strange Career of Marijuana*, Westport: Greenwood Press.

Langston, J.W. and Palfreman, J. (1996) *The Case of the Frozen Addicts*, New York: Vintage Books.

Polo, M. (1875) *The Book of Ser Marco Polo, the Venetian,* trans. H. Yule, London; excerpts republished in *The Book of Grass* (1967) London: Peter Owen.

Pratt, G. (1991) 'Dissenting Opinion,' in *United States v. Hooper*, 935F.2d (2d. Cir.).

Reagan, R. (1982) 'Remarks on Signing Executive Order 12368, Concerning Federal Drug Abuse Policy Functions,' *Public Papers of the Presidents of the United States, Ronald Reagan, January 1–July 31, 1982*.

NEWSPAPER AND JOURNAL REFERENCES

Chicago Tribune, Chicago: 6 March 1988.

Guardian, London 'Cannabis law reformer plans mass production,' 14 November 1986.

International Herald Tribune, 'Licensed to Deal, Marijuana Sellers Put Arizona on the Spot,' 7 October 1996.

—— 'The drug war: tougher than ever, still a bust,' 31 October 1996.

—— 'Californians reject affirmative action,' 7 November 1996.

—— 'CIA chief faces hostile audience,' 18 November 1996.

—— 'The fugitive, with an unhappy ending,' 28 November 1996.

—— 'Clinton plan to combat laws legalizing marijuana targets doctors,' 30 December 1996.

—— 'Threats scare off doctors,' 2 January 1997.

Life, 'Justice revealed,' September 1987.

New York Times, 'Straight talk about children and guns,' 30 March 1992.

The Atlantic, 'More reefer madness,' April 1997.

The Sunday Times, London, 'Taxpayers fund study into 'respectable' heroin use,' 9 March 1977.

—— London, 'Drugs really can fix up a president,' 10 August 1997.

The Times, London, Letter to editor, 24 July 1992.

—— 'Clinton acts to prevent medical use for "pot",' 30 December 1996.

—— 'Newspaper backs down over CIA drug deal claims,' 14 May 1997.

USA Today, 6 September 1989.

Chapter 11

Between history and me
Persecution paranoia and the police

Calvin C. Hernton

The police stand between me and nearly four hundred years of history. I distinctly remember the police while living on Slayton Street as a child in Chattanooga, Tennessee, my home town. But I have no memory of the police prior to Slayton Street. Then – all of a sudden – boom! There they were, white men in blue with guns, in police cars, cruising up and down Slayton Street all hours of the day and night. They stopped often and talked with someone in the neighborhood, like Mr John, who was a fair complexioned, middle-aged Negro who owned 'The Joint'. 'The Joint' was the place where the juke box played, and the people indulged in spirits and partied way into the night, especially on weekends.

I was aware of the two-tone black-and-white patrol cars, cruising along the street, slowing down, idling on either side of the street in front of 'The Joint'. The people kept on partying, getting down! The white faces of policemen dressed in blue with guns on their hips were a fact of Negro life. They came with the territory.

One time I happened to go into another 'Joint', up on East Main Street around the corner from Slayton Street. I was standing off to the side just inside of the door. The door opened and in came several white policemen. There were probably only two or three of them but I remember that a depressive mood came over me and settled over the joint, which continued to jump but not so freely as before the cops invaded us. That was what I remember feeling at the time, as though we had suffered an invasion.

Then, suddenly, I remember being afraid of the police. We all were. I do not know exactly when I got that way. The fear, through the process of social contagion, must have been socialized in me by merely living on Slayton Street. It must have been normal to fear the police, the *white* police, for we always thought of them in terms of their being white and our being black. Our fear was not out of control, it was there like the weather and it lived deeply within us. But we controlled fear and kept on living as best we could. That was why we behaved the way we did, as though nothing was happening when the police showed up. For, deep within our psyches, we were immensely aware that it was possible for anything to happen.

Growing up, I felt the police had unfriendly feelings towards colored people, and if given the chance they would act out these feelings, simply because we were colored. That is what we were politely called during these times, 'colored,' and we used this term in referring politely to ourselves. But at this point I do not remember having witnessed the police behaving badly towards black people, I do not know if I had heard talk of such behavior or intentions, I think I might have, but from whom I have no recollection. I think my fear of the police was connected with my learning to fear all white men, to be guarded against them no matter how friendly they might behave. I was by now reacting or responding to the patterns of demeaning behavior and atmosphere of hostility from white people in general toward black people in general. It was white racism that I feared in the generic sense, and the cops were merely a manifestation of this more primal fear. The fear of whites was in the 'social air' that we all breathed. I know now that this fear was paranoia, the fear of being hated and persecuted, and it was learned or contracted by the blacks because it was engendered by all white men, especially if they were in some kind of official-looking uniform. I remember experiencing anxiety whenever I would see a postman, a bus driver, the conductor on a train, or even a waiter in a uniform. Similar to what I felt when I saw a cop in uniform: deep in my gut I would have a reflex of fear.

My first personal encounter with the police occurred when I was about eight years old, not long after we began living on Slayton Street. Another child about my age and I were walking along East Main Street on our way home from school. We had first met coincidentally there on the street a few days before. Some days we met and other days we did not. After a while we would fall in pace with each other and chat, before she turned off and headed down a side street to where she must have lived. I do not recall what we talked about, except on the occasion of our first conversation. I remember that she asked about the school I went to, since she never saw me or any colored children at her school, and I said I wondered about her too, and all white kids, because no white children were ever at my school. That is all I remember of our conversations. Then one afternoon the police suddenly appeared. I remember having the feeling that they 'swooped' down on us there on the street and 'arrested' me. The two of them put me in their patrol car and took me to my grandmother – in broad daylight down Slayton Street where all the neighborhood could see – and warned her and me against the crime I had committed, which consisted of walking beside a white schoolgirl. They must have stressed the fact that I was 'socializing' (talking) with the girl. They put the fear of God; or, rather, the fear of the Ku Klux Klan into my grandmother.

She scolded and chastised me in front of the police who insisted that she chastise me. My grandmother's warnings made reference to the 'Scottsboro Boys,' who at that very moment I believe were in jail and were probably going to be executed if not lynched for the accused crime of raping several white girls. The lives of the boys were completely destroyed and black men in general were vilified as 'rapists.' The situation happened in Scottsboro, Alabama. Many years later, during the 1960s, The 'Scottsboro Boys' were exonerated by the only remaining one of the women who came forward and confessed on national television that the police at the time had forced the white girls to falsely accuse the black boys. Although I did not understand the gravity of my 'crime,' the outraged attitude of the police and the fear exuded by my grandmother as she admonished me, conveyed the nameless horror that not only me and my grandmother but all black people could reap as a consequence of my transgression against one of the cardinal taboos of southern Jim Crow, socializing with a white female.

When I was fourteen years of age, the police arrested me on the playground. They ordered me into their car and drove up to East Main Street. They stopped in front of a house on a hill and took me inside to a white woman who had been burglarized. But she said I was not the colored boy whom she saw running from her house. By now there were two cars of policemen at the woman's house. They took me and the woman in separate cars to the police station, downtown Chattanooga. I remember being in a room with the cops, and I was scared, and they kept trying to get me to confess to burglary and to raping the woman. They threatened me but I maintained my innocence. At one point a policemen spilled coffee onto my lap. It burned but I pretended not to be offended. I was scared and I was crying and pleading with them. Finally they let me go. I was ushered out of the front door of the station at the same time that the woman was being let go, too. The harried expression on her reddened, tear-wet face shocked and dismayed me. I remember we looked at each other for a brief moment but it seemed like a lifetime. I became aware that we were sharing the experience that we had undergone. I knew then that the white policemen had been trying to get the woman to say that I was not only the burglar but that I had sexually attacked her. But she had refused to comply. She probably saved my life, or a good portion of it.

By now my fear of the police had become visceral. Not only in my neighborhood, but wherever I saw them anywhere in town, riding in their cars, a picture of them in the newspaper, walking their beats or directing traffic, a tightness would rise up in my chest, and I always felt like some ominous fate was going to befall me. One day they put me in their car and drove across East Main Street to the other side of Slayton Street. They drove down by the old trash dump where Buggle lived with a family of boys and girls and grown folks in a small shack on the corner over-looking the dump area. The white policemen kept driving by the house, asking me if I knew what went on in Buggle's house. But I had no idea what they were talking about. Then the policemen wanted me to say I had witnessed Buggle selling drugs, which I had not. Then they tried to get me to agree to hang out with Buggle and spy on him, and report back to the police. I refused to go along with any of this. When they brought me back to my side of Slayton Street it was night and my grandmother was worried out of her mind. She was praying, as she moved about the house gathering up my clothes and school books. She sent me to live with my mother and stepfather and stepbrother, across town way out on East Third Street in northeast Chattanooga.

The very first day in the new neighborhood the police arrested me. They were different ones than on Slayton Street, yet they behaved toward me exactly like the others. I had parked my stepfather's hauling truck in the driveway alongside the house and was coming around to the front to enter the house when the police drove by and spotted me. Their tires squeaked as they put on brakes. Out they came with their guns drawn. Now my fear had progressed to a fully fledged paranoia. I ran! I ran back around alongside the house to the back door and went in and locked the door. Outside I could hear them cursing and yelling for me to come out, as they banged on the doors and windows. I let them in and convinced them that I lived in the house by pointing to a family photograph of me and my mother and stepfather and brother. They handcuffed me anyway and took me about a mile away to a grocery store that had been robbed and got the proprietor to say I was the one who did it.

By now I had perceived that the police existed to persecute black people. I was being arrested because I was a Negro, and not because there was evidence of me breaking the law. Being a Negro was evidence enough of having broken the law. I knew that this applied not just to me but to all black people. The policemen were white. No black person could be a policeman. The reason was obvious to me: the police existed to persecute black people. They were supposed to protect property; or, rather, they were charged with protecting white property. All of us colored people knew that the Ku Klux Klan and the police were one and the same. Frequently sheriffs, mayors, district attorneys, and other officials openly boasted in newspaper articles of their relations with the Klan. In a phrase, the police were the paid agents of white racism. Their job was to patrol, enforce and promote the white system, its institutions, its mores and folkways.

To a modified extent this was the situation with the police and black people in both the southern and northern parts of the United States. But the South was the crucible of the deadliest malady: paranoia. In the Talladega Alabama bus station, my friend and I boarded a bus together.

We were students at Talladega College. There was never more than one or two white students at the College at a time, but Talladega College had always been an historical Negro college with a noticeably 'mixed' faculty. Sounds crazy but that is precisely what racism is, insanity. So my friend was white. He and I made our way through to the rear of the bus and took seats. Since we had not planned or had a prior discussion about it, I was surprised when Joe – my friend's name was Joe – sat down beside me. Everybody else noticed it too. The bus driver ran back and demanded that Joe move up front with the white people. When Joe refused, the driver ran off the bus and returned a few minutes later with some state highway patrolmen, three car loads of them eventually arrived. The patrolmen stormed through the length of the bus, they collared Joe and catapulted him all the way up front of the bus into a seat by the window. They demanded that he stay in that seat for the rest of the ride through the state of Alabama. To make sure Joe complied, a patrol car followed the bus until we crossed the state line.

The bitter relations between the police and black people in America originated during slavery. From the very beginning in 1619, despite the slaveholders' propaganda to the contrary, the slaves had to be policed because they did not like being slaves. They were prone to running away and sabotaging the system by various and sundry means: being lazy, getting sick, pretending to be pregnant, setting fires, poisoning masters, and many other creative strategies of resistance and rebellion.

By setting crosses on fire, wholesale horse-whippings, lynchings and burnings, the KKK reeked terror upon the black population. This way, through the perpetration of daily acts of intimidation and persecution, the poor whites came to serve as police for the system of slavery and later on the Jim Crow system of segregation and discrimination which followed slavery. The fear between whites and blacks intensified during the first quarter of the nineteenth century. Between 1800 and 1835, a conglomeration of slave uprisings and insurrections took place in the south. The most impacting of the uprisings was the Nat Turner Rebellion in 1831 in Virginia. Many lives were lost, including the lives of whites. Earlier, in 1829, David Walker, a free Negro in Boston, issued an incendiary pamphlet against the slave system, *Walkers Appeal* (1829).[1] The pamphlet so enraged the South that stringent measures were enacted against free Negroes and slaves alike throughout the South. The fear of the blacks, and the whites too, grew and turned members of both groups into volcanoes of paranoia. A price was placed on Walker's life. A year later he was found dead, probably from poison, in the hallway of his tailor shop. But the most feared black individual of the Abolition epoch was Harriet Tubman. She became a legend for leading slaves out of the South to freedom in the North on the 'underground railroad.' A $40,000 reward was offered for her capture, 'Dead or Alive.' But she was never captured.

She made dozens of trips into and out of the South with escaping slaves, and she succeeded in eluding the net of the 'patterollers.'

By the time of the Civil War there were over four million slaves, the overwhelming majority of whom were in the South. The official law enforcements were not enough to patrol, protect and control this large mass of abjectly oppressed people. A wide gulf existed between the rich planters class, which fashioned itself as the aristocracy, and the vast majority of poor, uneducated whites, derogatorily referred to as 'white trash.' Through the ideology of white supremacy and racism, the system positioned the poor white population in the South against the slave and free black population. Millions of poor whites were nurtured on hatred and fear of the blacks. It was from among these ranks that the loosely organized but brutal para-military system of patrolling the slaves came into existence. In large measures it was a freelance policing force, in that many poor whites took it upon themselves to become 'patterollers' of the plantation South. The poor whites did not seek an alliance with the slaves and free Negroes to overthrow the system that kept both of these populations in abject poverty and oppression. Instead, the poor whites behaved like crazed bounty hunters. For example, in the early 1860s, when the handwriting of Abolition was clearly written on the wall of history, poor whites organized the Ku Klux Klan for the purpose of wreaking violence on the blacks and beating them back into a subordinate status that might have been much worse than legal slavery.

The passage of the Compromise of 1850 strengthened the 'Fugitive Slave Law' by placing a price on the heads of fugitive slaves; and made it possible for slave catchers to travel across state lines into free territory and 'capture' anyone they designated as a runaway slave. The terror against black people – including those in the South and North who had never been slaves – became even more draconian.

Between 1865 and 1876 Reconstruction in the South took place. The blacks and poor whites were supposed to be integrated into the making of a more perfect democracy. Instead of welcoming the coming of democracy, the whites of the region grew more embittered, resentful, and fearful of what they termed, 'Black Domination' – simply because newly freed blacks were voting and some were elected to various local and state positions and a few were even in the national government.

The most devastating aspect of the situation was that after Reconstruction was betrayed and disbanded by a deal made between the Republican and Democrat parties in the national election of 1876, the South and the Negroes were handed back over to the very people against whom the Civil War had been fought, the former slaveholders and poor whites. It was at this juncture in the relations between the police and blacks that the police militia of the United States, eventually including the national guard and state troopers, became a legalized segregated enclave manned exclusively by poor white men. The white Negro-hating police were officially charged with maintaining, protecting, and promoting the system. To accomplish this they had to patrol the blacks, and intimidate, quash, and punish all behavior perceived as rebellious. Where the police were not explicitly charged with these duties, they took upon themselves the job of patrolling black communities and they exercised complete freedom to act out their misplaced resentment, anger, and hatred against black people, especially against black male youth, who the police felt posed the greatest 'threat' to the police, as well as to the system of slavery and later on to the system of Jim Crow and the entire southern way of life.

The resentment, hatred and brutality of the white police against black people in the United States – and the feelings of persecution and paranoia of the blacks, that the police are out to 'get' them – have continued to contemporary times. This is the legacy that makes the much-publicized brutalization of Rodney King by California policemen in 1991 a commonplace occurrence among black people everywhere in the United States. The names of Negro-brutalizing policemen, such as Birmingham, Alabama's 'Bull Conner' of the 1960s, have been legend. The Civil Rights movement of the 1960s – with Negroes and white sympathizers engaged in Freedom Rides, sit-ins, and public protest marches – revealed the entire white police force as Negro-brutalizers throughout the South. South and North, the view and use of Negro communities as colonial ghettoes for police exploitation was and is common practice. Throughout the 'inner cities' of the nation – Chicago's Southside, New York's Harlem, Cleveland's Westside, Los Angeles's Watts, and so forth – the white police criminalize the Negro neighborhoods; this way, they grant themselves license to perpetrate acts of intimidation, graft, extortion, drug peddling and other crimes against black people, including brutality and murder, with absolute impunity. Both inside and outside the ghettoes, black people carry in their emotions an ever-present fear of the white police: they feel they are never safe from the violence of the police; and the police feel and act as if black people are their recreation.

The police are especially keen on recreating themselves through violence against black males, for black males are perceived by the police as the most dangerous to the police. Black males are perceived as the real threats to the system: they hate white authority, they are the crazies, the dope pushers, the gang members, the rapists of white women, the insurrectionists and leaders of rebellions. The police believe all of this. Therefore they fear and resent black male youth with paranoid intensity, and when they do not 'criminalize' and 'fit them up' and incarcerate them, they brutalize and murder them. The leadership of the Black Panther Party, for example, was regarded in this manner and many of them were murdered by the police and the FBI. The fact of the matter was that the Black Panther Party was organized to counteract the brutality and pillage that the white police were perpetrating against the black community – the actual name of the Panthers was the Black Panther Party *For Self Defense* (against the police).

The historical white paranoia of the 'criminogenic' Negro rapist and spoiler of white civilization is a function of white people's guilt for the crimes they have perpetrated against black people. Whites actually fear that if blacks get into power they will retaliate by doing to the whites what the whites have done to the blacks. Thus, when a lone black person, particularly of the male sex, gets a good job or any position formerly denied to blacks, the whites fear that Negroes are 'taking over!'

Precisely, the paranoia of the whites is not founded in facts. Blacks have never been in a position to persecute and oppress whites on a systematic scale. In a phrase, black people have not historically enslaved, segregated, and discriminated against white people; black people have not oppressed, brutalized, and dehumanized white people.

On the contrary, the historical facts have been the other way around. Concrete acts of persecution against black people warrant fearing and being paranoid about white people in general, and white policemen in particular. Negroes have not written books describing white people as 'beasts.' But white people have written books claiming scientific proof that African peoples are less than human. In the title of his book, published in 1900, author Charles Carroll proclaimed, *The Negro A Beast*.

The Alabama state troopers who carted my friend Joe away up to the front of the bus undoubtedly felt they were protecting the white race and the mores of Jim Crow, and they were motivated by a deeply ingrained racist paranoia against black people and race 'mongrelization,' which has no basis in actuality. But what about my paranoia? What of my fear of violence from those state troopers? What about black people's sense of loss of dignity as human beings?

The incident on the bus occurred more than forty years ago. I have lived in many different places around the world since then. In Sweden I found myself rather tipsy as I wandered about the streets in a strange and completely empty town. I had mistaken the bright sun to mean it was daytime but it was in fact three a.m. in the 'night.' I was picked up by the police and driven thirty miles to where I was staying. Then the police came in and drank tea and chatted with me. I was relieved by their behavior, and I enjoyed their company and friendliness. Yet I was also shocked and apprehensive at such friendly behavior on the part of, of all people, the police! And, despite these and similar experiences abroad, I am still visited by paranoid feelings and impulses towards white policemen. I still experience an initial fear in the presence of white people in general; and over the mere thought of their existence in the world, my skin shivers. I still think of and feel the police to be enemies of black people; I feel they have it 'in' for blacks and are out to 'get' us.

It can be proved that the police have been responsible for untold brutalities and numberless murders of black men and women. White policemen mounted the stairs of a sixty-seven-year-old black woman, Eleanor Bumpers. They shot her hand off and blew a hole in her chest, simply because she was standing in her own kitchen nude with a cooking knife in her hand. Or so they said. New York transit policemen dragged Michael Stewart into a hole in the subway station and beat, tortured, kicked, and spat obscenities on him until he died. The Philadelphia's police force dropped incendiary explosives (bombs) on the roof of the residence of the Move Organization and killed men, women, and children, many of whom were on the street attempting to escape the fire when the police mowed them down with gunfire. The police have framed (falsified evidence) thousands of black men and women for crimes they did not commit, crimes, in fact, that the police themselves committed.

A Negro professor was sitting in his yard in Georgia during the summer vacation reading a book. The white police arrested him for 'vagrancy' – and they knew who he was. Indeed, historically tens of thousands of black men have been incarcerated for the crime of 'vagrancy' – the crime of being unemployed. Indeed, the infamous 'chain gangs' and 'work gangs' of the South consisted of black males whose only crime was being without a job.

The framing of black people by law officials is part of the history of black people in America. During the mid-nineteenth century free Negroes in border states were frequently framed as fugitive slaves by slave hunters and returned (sold) into bondage. A contemporary victim of police frame-up is Mumia Abu-Jamal, a news reporter now on death row, charged with killing a policeman that the police may have killed themselves through their own careless gun-fire. Between 1880 and 1920, thousands of black men and women were lynched and mutilated by members and sympathizers of the Klan. However, historically, more than the episodic violence of Ku Klux Klan, the police have been the foremost perpetrators of continuous violence and *menace* to the safety and well-being of black people and their communities.

It is 1997, three years from the twenty-first century.

Frantz Fanon from Martinique, was one of the first psychiatrists systematically to study the psychological reactions of oppressed people. In 1963 he published *The Wretched of the Earth*, which is a study about the mental disorders of prolonged oppression of Algerian natives engaged in a protracted freedom struggle against the French colonizers. In a section of the book headed, 'Colonial war and mental disorders,' Fanon describes 'reactionary psychosis' in terms of 'the events giving rise to the disorder,' which included 'the sum total of harmful nervous stimuli,' such as a blood-thirsty and pitiless atmosphere, and the brutality and torture wreaked upon the oppressed by the police. 'Mental pathology,' Fanon observed, 'is the direct product of oppression.'

Long before Fanon published *The Wretched of the Earth,* the African-American writer, Richard Wright published an essay in which he dealt with 'The psychological reaction of oppressed people' (1957). In this essay and a prior novel, *Native Son* (1940), Wright asserted that in the lives and minds of people oppressed by three centuries of American racism, the 'reality of whiteness' has become a cosmic force that produces paranoid feelings of ontological dread and delusions of grand endangerment. Therefore many black men have strongly promulgated the notion of them-selves as an 'endangered species' (1940).

The fact that people are regarded by the police, and by white society itself, as though their very color, the very blackness of their bodies is a crime, tends to create in them feelings of ontological ambiguity, feelings that make them scared – not merely of the police but scared of every-body and everything, including themselves. In *Mein Kampf,* Hitler's denunciations of Jews, blacks, gypsies and Ukrainians were based on his conception of them as 'unclean peoples who needed to be exterminated' (1930). A rage emanates out of the suffocating fearful feelings of perse-cution that, if no outlet is found, will explode. During the 1960s two black psychiatrists, William Greer and Price Cobb, published a book-length study about this phenomenon in black male youth, entitled *Black Rage* (1968). During the 1960s and 70s, the comic, Dick Gregory, tended to interpret every act of injustice experienced by black people as part of a larger 'conspiracy' to damage and destroy black people.

After the system of slavery was abolished, another apartheid-like system known as 'Jim Crow' segregation and discrimination against black people was established.[2] Out of this system of inequality and police brutality, which replaced slavery, the psyche system of paranoia between whites and blacks was solidified in the United States and is ongoing to this day.

Thus, despite having lived where the police are not a menace, whenever white policemen enter the space where I am, I experience anxiety and fear. I can be rational and control this 'pathology.' Yet, similar to black people everywhere in the United States, particularly the youth in their own neighborhoods, I too live with a measured sense of being persecuted by the police. And I strive to negotiate my fear and paranoia in ways that help me survive both the imagined and very real animosity and brutality of the police toward all people whose complexion and status in the eyes of the world are similar to mine.

NOTES

1 See also Richard Barksdale and Keneth Kinnamon (eds) *Black Writers of America*, pp. 150–4.
2 The Separate but Equal doctrine on which Jim Crow was based and instituted, was legally sanctioned by the Supreme Court of the United States in 1896 in the *Plessy v. Ferguson* decision.

REFERENCES

Barksdale, R. and Kinnamon, K. (eds) (1972) *Black Writers of America*, New York: Macmillan.
Brown, S. (1968) 'Negro Character as Seen by White Authors,' in James Emanuel and Theodore L. Gross (eds) *Dark Symphony,* New York: The Free Press. First published in *Journal of Negro Education*, January 1933.
Carroll, C. (1900) *The Negro A Beast,* cited in Brown 1968.
Fanon, F. (1968) *The Wretched of the Earth*, New York: Grove Press. First published as *Les Damnés de la terre*, Paris: Maspéro.
Greer, W. and Cobb, P. (1968) *Black Rage*, San Francisco: Basic Books.
Hitler, A. (1930) *Mein Kampf,* trans. J. Murphy, London: Hurst and Blackwell.
Walker, David (1829) *David Walker's Appeal, in Four Articles: together with a Preamble, to the Coloured Citizens of the World, but in Particular, and very Expressly, to Those of the United States of America*, Boston: published by himself.
Wright, R. (1940) *Native Son,* New York: Harper and Row.
—— (1964) 'The psychological reaction of oppressed people,' in *White Man, Listen!*, Ch. 1, New York: Anchor Books.

Chapter 12

Machine phenomena

Stella Pierides

Machines are an increasingly important part of our external and, there-fore, internal environment. Freud, while noting the positive aspects of culture in *Civilization and its Discontents*, wrote:

> with every tool man is perfecting his own organs, whether motor or sensory, or is removing the limits to their functioning. Motor power places gigantic forces at his disposal, which, like his muscles, he can employ in any direction; thanks to ships and aircraft neither water nor air can hinder his movements; by means of spectacles he corrects defects in the lens of his own eye; by means of the telescope he sees into the far distance; and by means of the microscope he overcomes the limits of visibility set by the structure of his retina.
>
> (Freud 1929: 279)

This description is particularly apt for the concept of the machine, which, in contemporary language, is described as 'a device, having a unique purpose, that augments or replaces human or animal effort for the accomplishment of physical tasks' (*Encyclopaedia Britannica*); and as 'an assembly of interconnected components arranged to transmit or modify force in order to perform useful work' (*Collins English Diction-ary*). In both definitions, machines are mainly thought of as tools used by us to manipulate, control, modify or change our environment; they are often seen, even more so today than in the earlier part of the century, as extensions of ourselves and available to soak up our mental and physical projections. At the touch of a button, they can be made to show, record or produce images. They can be made to reproduce our voice in our absence or entertain us by storing and reproducing our favourite music. They can work for us or with us, transport us to the other end of the earth, or beyond, provide knowledge and pleasure. As such, they are used to connect us to other people, places, the past, through enhancing our cognitive apparatus, our memory, knowledge, understanding, relating. In that, they embody ideas of power, constancy, reliability, regularity, objectivity, enormous memory storage, speed, intelligence, strength, spark, wisdom. It is no coincidence, therefore, that they are being advertised as 'man's best friend' in the form of cars or computers. 'Are you connected?', the advertisement for Internet use is telling. Further, we are said to be protected by the military machine, governed by the state machinery or even hoping to bequeath the earth to intelligent machines.

The concept of the machine is associated with a sense of modification, transformation and replacement. This is included in the dictionary definitions of the machine as a design that modifies something. A machine consists of an input, an output and a transforming device which may turn different kinds of energy into mechanical energy, or vice versa, or modify a force or motion. This particular property of the machine endows the metaphor of the machine with a specific sense of transforming ability, and therefore comforting power, as well as omnipotence and magic. We often wonder about the quality of life in pre-industrialised society, which had to make do without the comforts the Industrial Revolution brought about. The protecting, comforting, enriching, life-enhancing and, in medicine, life-saving properties of the machine make it into a coveted and admired object.

Given this multitude of machine imagery, it is not surprising that machines have entered our symbolic universe, our metaphors and collective thinking about the world (Asch 1991). From Andersen's *The Emperor and the Nightingale*, to Asimov's 'Robotics', to James Cameron's *Terminator* films, our imaginary world is populated by different kinds of machines. Everyday language is full of machine metaphors. To charge one's batteries, to have drive, to think like a computer, to program oneself to do something, to steel oneself, to electrify, are all expressions arising out of a view of machines as enhancing and empowering. Having accumulated this amazing array of connotations, machines are quite often linked in our minds with ideas of mastery and control. And yet, there is an aspect of the concept of the machine which conveys lifelessness, circularity, blind obedience, lack of creativity. There are expressions in everyday language which carry this sense of the latter aspect of the machine metaphor. To listen, walk, behave mechanically, to walk like an automaton, to be a 'motormouth', to 'obey orders' (of the military machine) denote a negative, lifeless, repetitive state of mind; a condition where life, thinking, creativity, humanity are denuded.

One of the first 'influencing machines' portraying the negative aspects of the metaphor appeared in Plato's simile of the cave. In this simile – predicting the cinema and television (machines) by two and a half thousand years – Socrates asks his interlocutor to imagine men chained from infancy in front of a screen which portrays shadows of passing men, animals and objects. As they had never seen any of the real world, and being unable to even move their heads, these prisoners had come to believe that the shadows they saw were the real world. Socrates skilfully leads his companion to the conclusion that, were one of these men to escape to the light of day, he would have – blinded by the light – great difficulty in seeing and trouble in accepting that what he now saw was real. Also, that upon his return he would be regarded by his companions – once again blinded by the change in the light – as behaving foolishly; and that his fellow prisoners would resist any change in their circumstances and in fact would prefer death to having to leave their chained abode in the cave. The effect of the contraption is to keep the men half alive, prisoners of a reality only partly illuminated by understanding. Dante's infernal descriptions of the mechanics of hell is a chilling literary image of the circular, hopeless, repetitive, driven, dehumanising turns of this state of mind.

On the other hand, in *Modern Times*, one of the most powerful icons of this century, Charlie Chaplin portrays the industrial worker caught in the cogs of his industrial machine and eventually being swallowed up by it. This film is an insightful comment on the personal, social and cultural losses incurred through industrialisation which the Luddites foresaw, when they opposed mechanisation a century earlier. This external, real persecution, and the 'dis-ease' and paranoia industrialisation engendered, have been carried forward to its present state. In stark opposition to the comforting and life-enhancing image of industrialisation and its wonderful machines, this view of men chained to automation and unthinking regularity, made redundant and driven mad by it, reinforces the negative aspects of the metaphor of the machine. Science fiction in particular, often develops and portrays this aspect of the machine metaphor in its images of machines (computers) threatening to wipe out the world.

In this chapter, using psychoanalytic ideas, I will be concerned with some of the more disabling aspects of this metaphor, and how they may come to underpin human relationships in the intra- and inter-personal, social and political environment, with particular reference to the notion of circularity.

The concept of circularity is central to our understanding of life itself. The twenty-four-hour cycle of the earth's rotation underpins the rhythm of the activities of the bodies of humans, animals and plants. The biological clock is basic to all forms of life. From cell cycles – e.g. individual nerve cells discharging regular electrical impulses over hours or days – to the circadian cycle of the human body, to the tidal cycles of shore-inhabiting invertebrates, all animals and plants are subject to one or more biological cyclical processes. It was the Cartesian idea of the human body, and brain, as a sophisticated machine that allowed science to study man as part of the natural world. The clockwork mechanisms and automata that Descartes admired in the Italian gardens he visited, became the models for the new sciences his work gave impetus to. We refer to these mechanisms, as underpinned by the model of man as a machine, when we speak of the life-cycle, of the biological clock ticking away, of the menstrual and hormonal cycles. These expressions include notions of necessity and inescapability, of the constraints of the human, embodied, existence. Indeed, attempts to go beyond these processes, to stop or delay them, take us into the realms of medicine as well as metaphysics and psychopathology.

Concomitantly, the notion of circularity is inherent in the concept of the machine. From the first wheel, to the cogs of the earlier machines, to the clock, to the computer program loops, it is the 'circle' that makes the machine possible, and limits it, at the same time. This limiting aspect is portrayed in expressions such as 'to go in circles', to produce circular arguments, to think circularly. Equated with following an absolute order as well as stickiness, this is a state that involves being like a machine, or a brain without a mind with the freedom of thinking, which cannot step outside its prescribed course. A person acting like a machine is seen as someone with no intelligence who acts with unfailing regularity and automatically. To 'go through the motions' or follow/obey blindly refers to a mechanical, repetitive behaviour with no involvement of feeling or thought. To 'go round the bend', 'to have a screw loose', or 'to be screwed up', 'to be twisted', 'bent' or 'loopy' are all indications of dis-ease with oneself and others. The circular motion of the hand by the temples is used to denote madness.

There is a wide range of situations along a continuum of machine manifestations in which the machine metaphor is made use of in a concrete way, producing clinical pictures of machine-like phenomena. Bion (1958) describes a patient who appeared to him to behave like an automaton, or clockwork toy, moving in unison with him. As therapists, we are all familiar with situations where patients, thinking concretely, take everything literally, like a machine would; or, who prefer to relate in a monotonous, repetitive, lifeless fashion and treat us as affectless, lifeless automata.

It may be said that autistic children display machine-like phenomena in their behaviour. Tustin (1986) describes how autistic children can, during periods of regression, behave like robots or zombies going through automatic motion; they feel that, having left their bodies, 'there is an armoured carcass which walks around automatically, and is hollow and empty, like the Tin Man in the Wizard of Oz'. The automatic repetition they display in the form of echolalia, of rocking movements, as well as the need for 'hard' sensations induced by the 'autistic' (sometimes metal) objects they employ may also be said to belong to this category of machine phenomena.

Further along the continuum of these phenomena, to be under the influence of a machine – whether it is spying, watching or controlling – is to be involved in a cycle of despair and desolation. A paralysis of thought, petrification, a cut-off and frozen psychic state is involved where one is completely ignorant of, or torn from, one's good objects. In Dante's *Inferno*, Hell is such a circular, desolate and desperate place; it consists of nine rings, each containing tortured souls that go in circular paths over and over and over again, for ever. For these unfortunates, no spiralling movement to a higher plane, turning back, or escape is possible. The final stage in the range of phenomena in this category is the full-blown delusion of an influencing machine, affecting the person's thoughts, feelings and behaviour. Tausk in his classic paper (1919) was the first psychoanalyst to describe the evolution in the continuum of the 'Influencing Machine' (IM) – which he saw as the final stage in the development of the symptom of estrangement in schizophrenia.

Before considering Tausk's ideas in more detail, along with other theoretical perspectives, I will briefly describe two machine manifestations which I observed in two of my patients. The first patient, whom I will call Arthur, 'suffers' from a machine in the form of a metal rod running straight through his back. It sometimes takes over his heart too, in that it replaces it with a pump that circulates various liquids in his body. Through our work together, we have come to understand the machine as offering him protection from weakness, vulnerability, human frailty. It convinces him that it is holding him together, holding him upright as an alternative spine, which, were it to fail, would result in his disintegration. Once it takes hold, the patient loses his sense of his human reality and he becomes the 'bionic humanoid', the other than human and entirely invincible machine which cannot be touched by affairs of the human mind and heart.

However, the machine also tortures him. In the form of a metal pincer, or a hook, it pierces Arthur in the head, eyes, hands and feet, it pulls and tears his flesh. It involves the patient in such horrific torturing and dehumanising processes that it becomes impossible for him to have a space for his human concerns. There is an attempt to engage me in the visual imagery projected by the psychotic side, and take my attention away from his internal world. Thus, the psychotic solution to the psychotic problem is to stop himself and me from using our eyes by omnipotently projecting images – hallucinations – through his eyes and by trying to blind me with colourful and very worrying imagery – the liquids, the machine, the pincers, the hook, tearing him apart – and stop me from thinking; furthermore, he tries to convince us both that, like Plato's prisoners in the cave, this psychotic 'picture' is his reality and that we should abandon hope.

The existence of the machine and its effects on my patient come close to Tausk's description of the Influencing Machine. What is also shown is the influence the image of the machine has on the nature of the delusion; the notion of circularity and repetitiousness are present in the delusion in different ways. Arthur is not only assailed by a machine, which in one of its forms pierces through him repetitiously; he can also 'see' the predictability of its appearing unfailingly, keeping its 'evil' promise. In its grip, the patient can only see himself as going round in infernal circles.

The second patient, Beatrice, occupies a different point on the continuum of machine phenomena. Beatrice experiences herself taken over by a self that makes her behave in violent ways which have dire consequences for her and which cut her off from meaningful, emotional contact. As these violent takeovers and outbursts occur at a particular point in her hormonal cycle, my patient is convinced, and tries to convince me, that she is the prisoner of her biological clock. No amount of pills and medication is spared to supplement, control, correct and balance this internal, physical 'clock'; attempts at understanding, however, and inter-pretations are rejected. Beatrice, after such a 'takeover' that had resulted in her becoming violent, came to one of her meetings with a glass of water visibly upset, huge tears rolling down her face. While I felt very sorry for her and close to tears myself, I noticed one of her tears falling in the glass. In a minute, with what looked like a mechanical movement of her arm, she drank. I understood her predicament then as her being taken over by the self that tells her that being sad is a waste, and recycles her tears by using her arm to collect them in the glass and feed them back to her. The glass of water also provides a container for diluting the tears – one tear lost in a sea of water. As such, it is an alternative feed to the one that she wants to get by coming to her session. Her wish to obtain help to get out of the state of mind that imprisons her is not being allowed to materialise, and her body is taken over by the psychotic her that believes in 'waste not want not', and is transformed into a robot or a tear machine.

These phenomena are discussed by Tausk in his paper on the Influencing Machine. Tausk (1919) distinguishes three main stages in the evolutionary history of the 'IM': a sense of internal alteration produced by the flow of psychic energy into a particular organ (hypochondria); a feeling of estrangement, whereby the pathologically altered organs or their functions are denied and seen as something alien by the ego; and finally, a sense of persecution arising from the projection of the pathological alter-ation on to the outer world. Such a projection takes place either by attribution of the alteration to a hostile power outside the self, or by the construction of the IM as a summation of some or all of the pathologi-cally altered organs (the whole body) projected outward.

In the final stage of the machine affliction, the machine

> consists of boxes, cranks, levers, wheels, buttons, wires, batteries and the like. Patients endeavour to discover the construction of the appa-ratus by means of their technical knowledge, and it appears that with the progressive popularisation of the sciences, all the forces known to

technology are utilised to explain the functioning of the apparatus. All the discoveries of mankind, however, are regarded as inadequate to explain the marvellous powers of the machine, by which the patients feel themselves persecuted.

(Tausk 1919: 186)

Tausk lists the main effects of the IM, which I have condensed as follows: The Influencing Machine makes the patients see pictures. It produces/removes thoughts and feelings by various means. It produces motor phenomena in the body that are intended to deprive the patient of his potency and weaken him. This is accomplished, Tausk notes, either by means of suggestion or by air-currents, electricity, magnetism, or X-rays. Furthermore, the IM creates sensations that, if they can be described, are sensed as electrical, magnetic or due to air-currents.

Tausk notes that a large number of patients complain of these symptoms without ascribing them to a machine; they consider them to be a result of a telepathic or other mental influence. These complaints precede the symptoms of the IM and the latter is a later pathological development serving the purpose of explaining the alien and pathological changes occurring. The former complaints may be linked to the idea of an influencing agency, where the patient experiences herself passively, merely as its tool, while the latter developments of the IM may be understood as the embodiment and complete takeover of the patient's mind.

One additional important component of the machine affliction not emphasised by Tausk ought to be noted: that which springs from the concept of circularity. This component is responsible for an inescapable circularity in thought or behaviour patterns, thereby convincing the patient of its power and her helplessness. Everyday language includes the expression 'it is a machine' to denote such a state of mind in which one feels trapped by the situation one is in. At the other end of the continuum, this 'machine' is experienced concretely as a machine physically doing things to the person – as I observed in some of my patients. It involves a repetitious working, a circuitous, monotonous, inescapable motion, which also springs from machine imagery. The patient both feels under the control and manipulation of a machine which continuously and methodically literally 'does' things to her, and feels under the influence of a machine which convinces her that she goes in circles. Often, there is a rhythm, pattern or cyclical process that is identified, as, for instance, when a patient complains that 'it is happening every spring', or the beginning of the week, or as in the example of Beatrice.

A more recent description of machine phenomena is one given by O'Brien (1976). O'Brien describes phenomena she experienced during her breakdown, as part of a whole internal world where hallucinatory characters, the 'operators', have access to and control people's minds to the extent that the latter are referred to as 'things'. 'Things' are manipulated like clockwork toys, they are wound up or down, they are used for entertainment, programmed, and so on. O'Brien subtitles her work 'The Inner Life of a Schizophrenic' to indicate the severity of the condition she is describing, as well as her ability to differentiate between what afflicted her from her ability to think about it. In a similar vein, Asch (1991) takes up the question of the animator of the machine. Asch concentrates on the 'mad scientist' issue, as illustrated in the Frankenstein story, to discuss the duality of the influencing machine fantasy: that of an evil operator and his tool, advocate, assistant or machine. As such, the fantasy not only links up, as Asch suggests, with the human conflict over passivity but, to my mind, with the issue of creativity. Frankenstein the scientist – unable to cope with his mother's death, reflecting Mary Shelley's difficulties with the death of her own mother who died of complications from giving birth to her – in a frenzy of omnipotent activity 'creates' a monster, which itself is remembered by its creator's name. Frankenstein has thus created out of dead bodies, under the influence of his ill self, a monstrous being which then persecutes him. Creativity under these conditions of disability, and inability to cope with the difficulties of the psychic world, springs from the psychotic world; it both reflects it, and its contents, and leads to further injury. Like a Trojan horse, it is a machination and it contains the seeds of destruction. Mary Shelley illustrates this process very clearly in her description of the scientist Frankenstein as the 'creator' using resources that can be said to spring from the psychotic world. Her ability to do so indicates her own capacity to differentiate in her own thinking between psychotic and non-psychotic creativity.

The development of mechanisms which split the ego and its functions to the detriment of the non-psychotic personality has been discussed by Bion (1957). Hatred of reality fuels the sadistic splitting attacks on consciousness of sense impressions, memory, attention, judgement, thought, which result in their fragmentation and expulsion from the personality to outer or inner objects. These objects, wrapped with bits of expelled ego functions, swell up and while continuing to perform their functions – seeing or hearing or judging – being denied their proper context, behave in an increasingly bizarre way. The 'watching television' or the 'listening radio' may be the simplest examples of this process. As a result, the patient experiences herself as the recipient of an enormous amount of bizarre and, mainly persecuting, attention coming from her internal and external environment which is increasingly made up of a bizarre mental furniture. Bion did not elaborate on the persecutory aspect of this attention in terms of dread of annihilation – he rather concentrated on the hatred of reality. But it would seem that such a predicament involves the patient experiencing this terror from two angles: as a result of her unconscious evacuation grown sour, and also in terms of her dread of annihilation arising out of the operation of the death instinct which, according to Klein (1946), takes the form of persecution. Segal (1993) describes a patient living in her internal world as in a state of permanent fall-out, full of persecutions, persecutory guilt, psychosomatic and hypochondriacal fears, and fears of nuclear warfare, and specifically worried about the question 'whose finger is on the button?'. In her analysis, Segal's patient becomes able to face the operation of the death instinct in herself, and think of her own pushing of her mental button, which, when combined with immediate projection, becomes a threat of death experienced as coming from the outside.

Rosenfeld (1964) describes a patient who dreamt that, while on a train, a machine landed emitting a ray of dangerous fire. The patient felt that the machine had been sent by someone bitter and revengeful, because of ill-treatment he believed he had received. Rosenfeld understands this as showing the omnipotent virulence of a narcissistic, enormously hostile part of the patient's personality which attacked him for submitting himself to situations – like the analysis or the relationship with the parents – where he felt humiliated and ill-treated.

Elaborating on his concept of a two-self model, a psychotic and a non-psychotic self co-existing in the same body, Sinason (1993), describes the nature of the 'cohabitee' as involving a hatred of the human, interpersonal environment. Within this concept, the machine could be seen at the core of the psychotic personality whose ambition is to evade being seen, to misrepresent the named patient so that her needs are not appreciated, and to create contact based on mechanical and abusive relating.

In sum, machine phenomena have been incorporated in psychoanalytic theoretical frameworks in various ways: in terms of projection and displacement of psychic energy (Tausk), splitting and projective identification within the ego, such as the psychotic part in the personality (Bion), or in narcissistic structures (Rosenfeld). Within the theory of a dual self (Bharucha 1989; Sinason 1993) I would consider machine phenomena to be at the core of the psychotic personality. Illusory relief from terror is afforded through submission to these constructions which promise to protect the patient from it.

A common element in all these views, which is particularly relevant to the more extreme and disturbing end of the continuum of machine manifestations, is the impoverishment of psychic reality with the resulting use of a concrete way of thinking. This can be fruitfully considered in the context of Rey's (1994) discussion of the mental functioning necessary for the processing and transformation of sensory and sensorimotor experience into meaningful perception. Rey points to a dysfunction in the schizoid organisation of the mind, with particular reference to the space–time continuum. The psycho-physical co-ordinates which are the result of transformatory processes have not developed in such a way as to allow for thinking to rise above concrete physical aspects – through internalisation, introjection, projection and symbolisation – to mental and psychic functioning. Thus, we might say that, where continuity has not been achieved, much like the isolated pictures in a movie film, the present object (e.g. the mother's breast) this moment in a particular position in space and time, is not the same one the next moment, when in a different position, or the absent object this moment is not the same as the one that was present a moment ago. Time and space interactions that have not developed enough to allow for constancy and continuity over the physical space, give the impression of rejection, even when the object is present, and of interchangeability and equalisation of objects.

Bion's (1962) view of the person who cannot discriminate between different sensory experiences due to under- or non-development of the ability to process, digest and transform experiences – what he calls alpha-function – adds to our understanding of this particular predicament. Without the experience of being understood by a human being (mother), without having one's hunger or pain transformed in a containing way by (m)other, one is left with a mass, and a mess, of undigested and indigestible paranoid and persecutory experience, fit only for evacuation for relief. The vacuum that this process generates for the person is enormous. Paradoxically, at the same time, Bion notes, there exists an immense amount of awareness of sensory stimuli – lack of discrimination between them results in a state of heightened awareness which does not allow contact with reality – and which cannot be repressed or suppressed or result in learning. I would think that this mass of sensory data is more akin to a passive computer memory than an organising human mind.

Further, some factors in the human environment of the infant result in a split between taking in material comforts such as milk, and psychical ones which would require acknowledgement of the feeding person. Breast and infant appear inanimate, preference and reliance on material comforts develop accelerating insatiable greed, since more and more material comforts are not what the person needs. Lacking understanding of her predicament, the patient remains stuck in a cycle of despair.

With such a meagre basis for a human world, the objects of desire do not make sense and never satisfy: quantity rather than quality, speed rather than considered work, power rather than understanding are sought. Automated, snap or machine responding is preferred to painful, painstaking thinking. The fascination with machines – and to a large extent the view of oneself as a Cartesian machine – becomes a way of patching the damage in the ego, of repairing without proper reparation taking place. On this level, machines are seen as the all-powerful, ever-available transformers of experience as part of a material world. The failure of the maternal/internal carer to transform her infant's experience need not be experienced; there is always a more powerful computer, as a transformer of data, one can buy, a rule-book manual to comply with, a religious or state machinery one can identify with. The latter is beautifully illustrated by Brian Keenan (1992), in his description of his four and a half years of imprisonment; while Keenan, the kidnapped and hostage, was chained to a radiator, he compassionately, as well as insightfully, understood his captors' predicament as being 'chained to their guns'.

The predicament of the concrete thinker then, ill-equipped for human, whole-object relationships, is one where transactions take place, where people or objects in the internal world are used, abused or misused, rather than related to; where 'operators' and 'things', or machines, replace people. To my mind, this is the machine-like aspect of human relating where the other – it being the sane self, non-psychotic personality or the person out there – is seen as a tool or as an obstacle to one's ends, in a unilateral using rather than a reciprocal relating. This use of the other as a thing, a machine or a tool to achieve personal ends, arising to a large extent from a misguided attempt to heal or protect, as well as out of envy, becomes a barrier to the development of symbolic thinking and the depressive position and thus to relating in a human and humane way. This is the situation where the soul or essence of humanity in oneself, one's offspring and society at large is being denied, or murdered (Schatzman 1973); where human creativity and potential in the person, or the other, are barred, where 'machines' wipe out one's humanity. This is paranoia becoming idealised and actualised and engendering a cycle of human, intellectual and emotional poverty and persecution.

REFERENCES

Asch, S.S. (1991) 'The Influencing machine and the mad scientist idea: the influence of contemporary culture on the evolution of a basic delusion', *International Review of Psycho-Analysis* 18: 185–93.

Bharucha, M.P. (1989) 'Understanding the patient through attending to perspectives'. Talk given at the Willesden Centre for Psychological Treatment.

Bion, W.R. (1957) 'Differentiation of the psychotic from the non-psychotic personalities', in W.R. Bion, *Second Thoughts*, London: Maresfield Library, 1984.

——— (1958) 'On hallucination', in *Second Thoughts*.

——— (1962) *Learning from Experience*, London: Karnac Books, 1984.

Freud, S. (1929) *Civilisation and its Discontents*, in *Civilization, Society and Religion*, Harmondsworth: Penguin Books, 1985.

Keenan, B. (1992) *An Evil Cradling*, London: Vintage.

Klein, M. (1946) 'Notes on some schizoid mechanisms', in M. Klein, *Envy and Gratitude*, London: Hogarth Press, 1984.

O'Brien, B. (1976) *Operators and Things: The Inner Life of a Schizophrenic*, London: Abacus.

Rey, H. (1994) 'The schizoid mode of being and the space–time continuum' in J. Magagna (ed.) *Universals of Psychoanalysis in the Treatment of Psychotic and Borderline States*, London: Free Association Books.

Rosenfeld, H. (1964) 'On the psychopathology of narcissism: a clinical approach', in H. Rosenfeld, *Psychotic States,* London: Maresfield Reprints 1965.

Schatzman, M. (1973) *Soul Murder. Persecution in the Family*, Harmondsworth: Penguin Books.

Segal, H. (1993) 'On the clinical usefulness of the death instinct', *International Journal of Psycho-Analysis* 74: 55–61.

Sinason, M. (1993) 'Who is the mad voice inside?', *Psychoanalytic Psychotherapy* vol. 7, no 3.

Tausk, V. (1919) 'On the origin of the "Influencing Machine" in schizophrenia', in P. Roazen (ed.) *Sexuality, War, and Schizophrenia: Collected Psychoanalytic Papers*, New Jersey: Transaction Publishers, 1991.

Tustin, F. (1986) *Autistic Barriers in Neurotic Patients*, London: Karnac.

Chapter 13

Paranoia and persecution in modern Japanese life

Hisako Watanabe

With its prosperous modernity, Japan enjoys the longest lifespan – over eighty years – and the lowest infant mortality in the world. But every day the news tells of men dying from overwork, of postnatally depressed women commiting suicide after killing their babies, of children 'protesting with death' against bullying at school, of adolescents murdering their parents in protest against vicious parental pressure for academic achievement and more and more high-school girls moonlighting in the sex industry. Who would have anticipated this modern tragedy when our parents set out to rebuild Japan from the ashes of the Second World War?

As a child psychiatrist for over twenty years, I have witnessed how ordinary Japanese families have pervasive persecutory fears about living up to society's norms and surviving the ratrace. People are intimidated by the total overall pervasiveness of modern technology, labouring relentlessly, driven like blindfolded horses just to survive.

Behind the charade of conformity and compliance, people crave the secure, simple life of good old Japan, harbouring a deep fear of further alienation which they dump onto their children. This yields mental difficulties: increasing cases of school phobia, child violence against parents and various psychosomatic problems, such as anorexia nervosa. This is but the tip of the iceberg, all the more complex and insidious in Japan with its deep repression, stunting the individual and society as a whole (Watanabe 1987; 1992).

In this chapter, I will consider the 1995 underground sarin gas attack by Aum in the context of the relentless fanatical wartime and postwar expansionism, driving contemporary Japanese thinking. I will argue that Japan's success-oriented competitiveness is part of a postwar national manic defence to ward off profound humiliation and grief about loss of the Second World War. The folly of attempting to fight the enemy with a bamboo spear, when confronted with superior technology represented in atomic bombs, was transformed into a technological and economic war. In my view, we must as individuals and as a nation scrutinise our history

and feelings about the past, in order to prevent the transmission of unresolved conflicts to the next generation.

AUM: A MINIATURE OF JAPANESE SOCIETY

When, in March 1995, the Tokyo subway trains were attacked with the
lethal nerve gas sarin by leaders of the Aum cult, killing 12 citizens and
injuring 5,500, people knew something was seriously amiss in Japanese
society. Aum is a neo-Buddhist sect led by Shouko Asahara, a forty-one-
year-old congenitally blind man, who professes to be the Priest of the
Ultimate Enlightenment with powers of levitation. He has won more than
50,000 followers in at least six countries among whom are Japan's best
and brightest university graduates. He preaches the Apocalypse and imminent Armageddon and worships Shiba, the God of Destruction. The sarin
attack was only part of Asahara's own wholesale plan to kill and destroy
whoever and whatever stood in the way of his ambition to dominate Japan
and to fulfil his prophecy.

This seemingly docile group's destructive plan had been known for
years, but neither the police nor the public had dared to speak out.
Parents who had lost their grown-up children to the Aum had actually
sued the sect for robbing them of family assets by way of harsh coercion
and brainwashing. Then in 1989 an anti-Aum lawyer, T. Sakamoto, suddenly vanished without trace with his wife and infant son. Police found
an Aum sect badge in his flat but did not follow the lead up.

It was only six years later, when the sarin attack took place, that a
thorough investigation of the Aum sect was launched, revealing an
amazing litany of atrocities and subversion. Asahara had lured young
followers practising weird mystical rituals using mind-altering drugs and
bizarre headgear fitted with electrodes to put their brainwaves in sync
with those of Asahara. He had kidnapped and murdered defectors and
opponents with lethal drugs, VX gas, and laser burners. His plan was to
attack the Diet in November 1995 and so spark off what he envisaged as
a world war. To triumph in this, he amassed assets of more than a billion
dollars to fund production of some of the world's deadliest weapons.
To this end his inner circle of PhDs was divided into groups to produce
conventional arms, chemical weapons, biological weapons and drugs.
Tsuchiya, considered the brains behind Aum's chemical weapons,
produced many kilograms of the deadly nerve gas, sarin, at the cult's
chemical plant in Kamikuishiki, at the foot of Mount Fuji. Hayakawa,
who masterminded the cult's nuclear armament, meanwhile visited Russia
to recruit nuclear scientists, buy Russian nuclear warheads and set up a
laboratory in a ranch in Australia to make atomic bombs from uranium.

Asahara's destructiveness was clearly fed by his deep-seated resentment
and inferiority complex. As a congenitally blind boy from a poverty-

stricken background, he had been humiliated, harassed and ostracised from the family and the community, uprooted and sent away at the age of eight to a distant boarding-school for the blind. Interestingly, the emotional deprivation of his childhood was graphically inflicted onto his followers: families were separated within the sect compound of Kamikuishiki near Mount Fuji and all assets confiscated as contributions to the religious fund.

Aum created a self-contained society with its own government and ministries of health, finance and transport, claiming to compete with and take over the Japanese System. The word 'System' here denotes the relationships which embrace the inscrutable complex society called Japan, as coined and studied by Karel Van Wolferen in his book *The Enigma of Japanese Power* (1993).

It is interesting to note the striking similarities between Aum and the contemporary as well as the wartime Japanese System. They highlight the notion that the nation still lives in the same fanatic frame of mind.

1 Conformity principle: this is reminiscent of the Japanese wartime imperial army demanding that people never complain of deprivation until the country wins the war.
2 Authorisation by bogus deity: Asahara, the guru with his duality of an outer docile facade and inner grandiose narcissism, deceived his people, pretending to be an enlightened Buddhist priest of the highest rank with supernatural powers of levitation. This is reminiscent of the Japanese imperial army forcing people into the war, declaring that Emperor Hirohito, the living God, possessed the supernatural powers of Kamikaze, the invincible Wind of God.
3 Enforced stereotype: the Aum followers have to chant the guru's words by rote, just like the stereotyped rote learning in Japanese schools, stifling creative thinking. Their enthusiastic striving to survive the supposed Armageddon looks like the fanatical diligence of Japanese men and their families driven by groundless fears of impending doom: a typical, all too common example being entrance examination applicants and their parents who firmly believe that passing into a good high school or university is the best guarantee of wealth and status.
4 Aum orders its followers to put loyalty to the guru first, to sever family ties and live apart, and forbids them to dine together or converse. This caricatures the fragmented nuclear Japanese family today, with company men posted alone to remote cities or working long hours outside the home, while mothers endure the tense lonely life of child-rearing in a fiercely competitive climate.
5 Exploitation of its own people: Aum has amassed millions of yen for the acquisition of military weapons. This is reminiscent of the charge that the Japanese government, land retailers, banks and companies are

colluding to exploit the ordinary citizens and amass money, for example by raising the land price, manipulating the market and loading people with lifelong housing loans. Aum orders its followers to fight against the enemies in the Armageddon to the death and preaches sacrifice as a way to salvation. This is an exact repetition of the wartime education in which people were taught to fight against the 'demons' and 'beasts' of America each with a single bamboo spear. Just then the two atomic bombs were dropped in Hiroshima and Nagasaki and put a decisive end to the war. These bombs were perceived as some sort of natural disaster from heaven and strangely expunged people's guilt for their past wrongdoings.

6   Massive denial and unaccountability: even after his arrest, Asahara flatly denied the charges against him, saying 'How could a weak blind man like me commit such a terrible act?' Asahara was known to his followers as the gentlest man, incapable of killing a fly. This supremely enlightened Buddhist monk could not possibly have committed such a savage crime! But it is this very duality that seems to me to be so typical of the Japanese leaders' mentality, whose warmongering and fanaticism led to the atrocities of the Second World War.

7   Inferiority complex, envy and resentment: one can view Asahara's greed, dishonesty and envious craving for power as embodying the deep-rooted inferiority complex and resentment of prewar Japan, when threats of European invasion and colonisation confronted a poor Asian nation blinded and retarded by three centuries of self-complacent isolation.

Thus in many ways Aum Shinrikyo reveals a deeply flawed trait in modern Japanese society, dramatically caricaturing its fanatical aspects. The facade of prosperity, the so-called 'miracle' of postwar economic progress in Japan, can be better construed as a manifestation of the nation's manic defence against the festering wound of defeat. The degree to which the humiliation of defeat has been warded off, and massively denied, is evident in the way Japanese people think and manage life in what amounts to the same wartime mode. A pervasive fear of persecution and invasion by the West persists, so we have to struggle ever harder to win. If we look closely, such fanatic zeal is everywhere in everyday life, in the national drive towards material success, and in the harsh competition to enter prestigious schools and universities.

CHILD EXPLOITATION IN THE NAME OF EDUCATION

The 40,000 children who toil every year to get into private schools with little sleep and free time to play may be said to share some of the fanatic zeal of the followers of Aum: while the latter blindly worship the guru and rigorously practise his teachings with the aim of surviving impending Armageddon, the former singlemindedly believe a diploma from a prestigious school is the ticket to a successful promised life. The following vignettes from my practice illustrate the result of such beliefs:

It was one March morning. A twelve-year-old boy staggered into my office and collapsed at my knees. 'Help me. I am so exhausted that I'd rather die,' he gasped. 'Don't tell my mother'. Clearly, he was on the verge of a serious nervous breakdown.

This mother had pressured her preadolescent son into competing academically, to the point of psychotic breakdown; indeed she was so fanatical that my persistent warnings of his impending breakdown went unheeded, until he virtually exploded into psychomotor excitement and had to be hospitalised. Only then, after much soul-searching, did she realise that she had been obsessed with the desire to win her parents' favour by producing a 'golden egg'.

This pressure is particularly prevalent in the well-to-do upper middle classes. When another twelve-year-old boy, the only son of an elite company man, presented with uncontrollable violence towards his family, prompted by his failure in an entrance examination, I insisted that the father attend a second consultation on his own. He was reluctant and fumed: 'How dare you take sides with a pampered boy who cannot cope with what forty thousand other children of his age can manage! Shame on him!'

'You sound just like an advertisement for expensive crammers,' I replied. 'You talk like the brainwashed follower of some fanatical cult intimidating innocent people with imminent disaster. Yet you are the only father your son has. He has worked day and night, deprived of ordinary childhood happiness, believing your words to be the only way to his happiness. Why not stop being the parrot-like spokesman of the exploitative examination business and reflect on your part in depriving your son of his individual freedom? Is this the kind of father–son relationship you envisaged when he was born? Isn't it your own fear of failure, rather than his, which drives you into such panic and rage?'

How often we hear young people criticise our tight-knit stereotypic society, yet they succumb and give in to circumstance, saying '*SHIKATA-GANAI*' [It cannot be helped] without ever trying to change things. Every day in my child psychiatry practice I witness children in silent despair over expectations of higher academic performances. The parents themselves are the product of the cramming practised in the 1970s and 1980s, when Japan tried madly to catch up with the West and even overtake it. They had to study by rote and were not allowed to discuss or reflect. This practice was inculcated in them to such an extent that they are repeating what they learnt with their own children. A similar trend can be seen in the patterns of wartime military behaviour acted out by present-day company chiefs. Indeed, I argue that the dramatic increase in juvenile psychopathological problems in the Japanese is in part a consequence of the unresolved primitive fanatical drive to devour the envied prosperity and social achievement of the West .

A CULTURE IMBUED WITH PARANOIA AND PERSECUTION

Why the fuss and rush to achieve? Why all the denial and reticence? What drives people to such hard, silent diligence? Underpinning this manic defence is a highly political and bureaucratical Japan which enforces silence through many means.

As Chie Nakane elaborated in her book *Japanese Society* (1970), the Japanese population is structured, vertically and hierarchically, to facilitate competition. This allows for tight control of power by a central bureaucracy which stifles individual freedom of speech and action. For example, there are many taboos respected even today. An old proverb says that 'a recalcitrant nail will be hammered in' meaning those who break the taboo will be ostracised. A recent example is the exposure of sumo scandals: when the ex-sumo-wrestler Onaruto exposed rampant match-rigging, tax evasion and *yakuza* [mafia] involvement, he and his co-author suddenly died simultaneously of a mysterious cause. Evidently the *tatemae* [facade] of sumo, with its 1,500 years of history and spiritualism, should never be tainted by the *honne* [hidden truth] of sumo. Hence death for whistle blowers and minimal police investigation.

Those in power in Japan cover up their failures, abusing religious authority to justify their intense greed, sometimes resorting to utter savagery in their hunger for power. Although there is some slow, steady progress towards liberalisation and democratisation in parts of Japanese society, the vast majority remain frozen under the fear of structural intimidation. Conformity and the emphasis on unity are excessive in Japan, frustrating frank confrontation and discussion or simply the expression of ideas and thoughts, so hampering individual psychological growth. From an early age, people are trained to stifle their feelings and thoughts, to rule out the possibility of harm by superiors who disagree or disapprove. Silence is proverbially golden while the mouth is said to be the source of calamity. Any straightforward, negative, critical opinion runs the risk of being taken personally as a verbal attack, remembered in resentful silence and insidiously stored up for subsequent retaliation by power-holders within the group. Thus, people rarely voice their opinions, hiding their real thoughts behind stereotyped conversation, while slyly spying on others' true meaning.

As a counterpart to this trend, there is the politicisation described by Van Wolferen (1994) in which any decision, expression or plan needs to be vetted by the powerholder of the group, leaving no room for individual freedom. This politicisation of group workings and condemnation of individual expression as defiant mirror the Japanese propensity for conformity and ostracism. For example, Asahara mystified and allured alienated young people into an excessive longing for utopia, portraying himself as a blind, long-haired hermit, dressed like a male deity in Japanese mythology.

Historically, people have been mystified, exploited and abused by despotic rulers, especially since the Edo Period (1603–1867). Indeed, conflicts have been passed down the generations, suppressed and neglected. Samurais had such a frightening reputation that a child would stop crying, at the sight of them, knowing how they could hit out unpredictably with their swords against anyone who annoyed them. This is all too reminiscent of Japanese soldiers killing Asians during the Second World War.

It is, of course, difficult to believe that with such a long history of sophistication and spiritualism, the Japanese could commit such atrocities. But the army of old exploited people's good nature and decency, as they did later in the Second World War, when they forced young Kamikaze [God Wind] attackers to make suicidal landings and the population of Okinawa to kill their families. In fact this fanaticism permeates daily life now, extending from school sports clubs right through the education system.

Such military coercion may have stemmed from the soldiers' own dread of humiliation and torture by the enemy which might be inflicted with the same brutality they themselves had exercised on the enemy. Perhaps they needed to hide all evidence of such inhumane conditions as malnutrition and deprivation, and feared popular rebellion against their brutal domination, exploitation and non-acceptance of defeat. Maybe they took their narcissistic rage out on the people. At any rate, the group dynamics of both Aum and the System seem to be self-destructive, both betraying their own people, their followers, consumers, patients and supporters.

One is reminded of oppressed, compliant children who win favour with their immature narcissistic parents, performing like dolls until, at the onset of adolescence they become violent within the family with a sudden explosion of long-repressed resentment.

Lebra (1984) describes Japanese boys swaddled in their mothers' love in early life and gradually manipulated to become ambitious and successful. But there is no healthy scope to develop self-esteem and the social skill required in adolescence. Maternal possessiveness is often a manifestation of tacit grief about perinatal loss or abuse by in-laws; to the child the oppressed, depressed mother may well seem to be psychologically dead and vacant, like the mother of the dead mother complex described by André Green (1986).

The shock of *Kurofune* [the Black Ship] probably lingers in Japanese consciousness today. People had been kept in the dark about the world outside Japan until Commodore Matthew Perry landed in Yokosuka in 1853. The Edo Shogunate had successfully maintained the *TENKA TAIHEI* [peaceful rule] with an extremely sophisticated, tightly knit system of control in which any dissident was decapitated on the spot and absolute obedience was rewarded with heavenly protection and favour. People submitted to this despotic manipulation for three long centuries, in such a way that the submissiveness became second nature, even 'a unique Japanese value' by which one denied oneself individual thought and freedom of speech and gave in to a powerful dominant figure, saying *SHIKATAGANAI* [it cannot be helped]. This attitude is deep-rooted and continues today: people rarely discuss politics with family or friends and accept obfuscation, making it all too easy to manipulate them, both in commerce and education. Clearly, the pathological seclusion of the Edo period hampered people's individual growth in an insidious way and the sudden arrival of the Black Ship may have prompted in such a naive, ignorant population an untoward terror of an outer enemy invading Japan.

Historically, *Kurofune* ended the three centuries of Japan's peaceful isolation, heralding the premature arrival of modernisation, and threatening invasion. Surprisingly, a similar style of coping with threat as in the Edo period persists today: the so-called democratic government exercises totalitarian control over the Japanese population.

How could such serious atrocities as the Rape of Nanking, Unit 731's secret wartime human experimentation programme (Gold 1996), and the scandal of comfort women (Hicks 1995) be hidden from the Japanese for so long, despite the world's loud protests, especially by Asian victims? Personally, as a member of the postwar generation, I was never officially taught in school about this dark side of wartime history. Why has the suppression of the truth worked so efficiently?

Sameroff and Emde in *Relationship Disturbances in Early Childhood* (1989) proposed three levels of regulation, namely micro-regulation, mini-regulation and macro-regulation within the infant caretaking environment system. In Japan, people seem to be caught up in the web of micro- and mini-paranoia, believing that the more you struggle the more you get entangled, and the best way is to succumb to helplessness. This learned helplessness destroys a person's individuality and morale. Drawing from the authors' model of infant development, I perceive three different dimensions of paranoia at work in the individual and his living system: micro-paranoia within the infant and mother system, mini-paranoia within the child and family system and macro-paranoia within the individual and his social system. While the Aum followers represent the macro-paranoia of Armageddon, micro- and mini-paranoia entail more private, tacit workings of the mind, pervasive in the everyday life of the Japanese.

Some examples of micro- and mini-paranoia are the following. The number of children suffering from anorexia nervosa is increasing rapidly and understandably as their character tendency fits in with the morbid aspects both of the disease and the culture. They are obsessed with fear of abandonment, exclusion and denigration to such extent that they constantly spy on their parents, teachers and significant others. We witness anorectic inpatients' tension as they try to comply with the staff's expectations: when a therapist or attending paediatrician encourages them to express their feelings, they try hard to do so in the expected way without any actual feelings, producing endless sequences of pretence and false self. Interestingly, it is usually the younger paediatric patients in the ward who facilitate them to acquire genuine expression of feelings of anger, sadness and craving for attention.

People are usually unaware or only dimly aware of micro-and mini-paranoia until they deviate from the expected cultural norm and meet with harsh, silent, persistent persecution. Many mothers who have either lost their babies or have given birth to handicapped babies confide to me during perinatal bereavement work their persecuting guilt and fear of ostracism by their own husbands and mothers, despite their truly sympathetic stance. For example, a wife of an elite salary man, who had lost her long-wished-for infant daughter from stillbirth, agonised that her loving husband must harbour silent hatred towards her for failing to produce a healthy baby.

For a Japanese person to become an individual in his own right, he has to emancipate himself from the micro- and mini-paranoia which deprive him of autonomous thinking. The appearance of submissiveness may give rise to the false impression of the person having reached a stage of maturity, which in psychoanalytic thinking has been termed the 'depressive position'. In fact, this position is motivated by fear and enforced by silent intimidation: if you speak out you will be abandoned and retaliated against.

Seated in the Toshogu Shrine of the Tokugawa Shogunate in Nikko are three famous wooden monkeys carved by the leading wood sculptor of the day. The first monkey, with its hands over its eyes, is the *MI-ZARU* ['won't-see' monkey]; the second, with covered mouth, is the *IWA-ZARU* ['won't-speak' monkey]; the third with covered ears, is the *KIKA-ZARU* ['won't-hear' monkey]. In fact they are neither blind, dumb nor deaf; they are physically intact but voluntarily deny their ability to see, speak and hear in deference to the ruler. So the oppression is subtle and masks the ruler's gross attitude. The identification with the aggressor in Japan often takes the form of pre-empting his wish and appeasing him to mitigate or ward off any potentially untoward outcome. Today's Japanese children are well-trained: like the monkey trio of Nikko Shrine. They behave well to appease their parents and teachers but at the cost of developing their inner sense of autonomy and freedom.

In *Understanding Japanese Society*, Joy Hendry (1987), a noted Japanologist, writes of the deeply rooted village mentality inculcated from early childhood by tense oppressed mothers who constantly discipline children with humiliation and subtle intimidation: 'You will be scorned for such behaviour', 'People will think you are mad', they say, and train them to distinguish between inside and outside. Highly perceptive children, who sense their mothers' loneliness and miserable marriages, pre-empt their mothers' desire for a perfect child to mitigate their unhappiness and take on the role of parenting their mothers by behaviour more appropriate to adults.

Perhaps some aspect of the Japanese psyche fails to develop the basis for forming the bond with mother, without which there can be no separateness. When it comes to relating to the group, family, company or country, a Japanese person instantly becomes mute, dumb and obedient, as if spellbound.

It seems that for the Japanese the prototype of relationships starts in the womb, where life is secure and fulfilled provided there is acceptance of such a parasitic symbiotic relationship and no thought of leaving it. But it can become a persecuting world if one starts to question its credibility and wonder about getting out. Most Japanese share the fantasy that they owe their existence to their womb-like family and country and will be punished if they so much as suggest there is any flaw in the System. With this tacit acceptance they idealise the womb and worship it.

Unlike dishonest bosses and administrators who dissimulate their wrongdoings, ordinary people are tormented with guilt about past secrets and are only too ready to confide in a sympathetic listener and and so gain peace of mind.

So when I hinted that a miserable-looking father might want to tell me about his family history, he sent his wife out of the consulting room and became totally absorbed in describing his own father's plight in the Second World War as a POW in a Siberian concentration camp. It was like opening Pandora's box, out of which poured his witnessing of his father's sufferings of being ostracised as a communist returnee. The father apparently kept going by venting his rage on his long-suffering wife, who bore his atrocious explosive violence in silence. But police surveillance of him was so relentless that he was driven to suicide and even this fact was completely hushed up. Imagine the man's relief on finally disclosing such a terrible story.

The extent of postwar violence committed by returnee soldiers towards their families is indicated in a recent letter from a middle-aged housewife published in the *Asahi Shimbun* (September 1996). Mourning her father's recent death, she recalls the painful memories of her mother enduring his incessant violence. Her mother told her 'We must forgive him. He has been harshly victimized in the war.' In large meetings, say, of teachers, parents and ordinary citizens, whenever I touch on the issues of women's suffering during and after the war, in the context of the marital rift caused by wartime separation, I see several women collapse and become silent.

A DAWN OF CONFRONTATION: GRASSROOTS DEMOCRACY

Where are the resilience and strength of the Japanese to counter this heritage of massive denial? Fortunately, both during the Second World War and since then, there have always been conscientious individuals who have silently and anonymously questioned our society's morbid traits. Now their number is steadily increasing.

One such person was Saburo Ienaga, a Japanese history professor, who for thirty years until his death, brought his School Textbook action against the Japanese government for concealing all facts about the Japanese wartime invasion by strict censorship.

Another example is Tadashi Kosho (1995), professor at Kowazawa University. He and his colleague at the Centre for Research and Documentation on Japanese War Responsibility continue to investigate the responsibility of Japanese companies and civilians in actively colluding with the Japanese imperial army in their wartime atrocities. So, increasingly, ordinary citizens living under covert and overt oppression begin to stand up and speak out (Watanabe, R. 1992).

More locally, in the spring of 1994, when Dr Joseph Berke (1995) was visiting Yokohama to talk about humane mental care at the Arbours Crisis Centre, a mental health charity, in London, an audience of 400 gathered to listen: psychiatric patients and their families, community psychiatric workers, volunteer workers, housewives and ordinary citizens. Indeed, the talk was so captivating and lucid that a man stood up and identified himself as a schizophrenic patient. He sincerely asked how to handle his psychiatrist's disturbed behaviour. Such a question, and so direct, was unheard of from a mental patient. The anti-psychiatry movement in Japan died out in the 1970s with the defection of its most active supporters, and the stigma of psychiatry remains as strong as ever. Fortunately, the 1994 meeting led to the formation of the MIND CLUB, an open forum for mental health in Yokohama. With 300 members, it has built a group home for psychotic patients in the community and a day-care bakery.

There has been another impressive development created by mothers of children suffering from school phobia in Niigata prefecture, a remote repressed rural area, steeped in tradition, where serious ostracism awaits deviant children and their families. Most of the housewives have been cruelly treated by their mothers-in-law and other in-laws during their children's early childhood and many are depressed in the wake of losing babies by abortion, miscarriage and cot death. Furthermore, the more delicate children who have silently witnessed their mothers' physical and mental suffering have eventually become mentally ill. Their mothers' unhappiness amounts to what André Green called the dead mother complex in which despair, death and rancour are the mothers' major pre-occupations (Watanabe, H. 1996).

The women and children have travelled all the way to Yokohama and after seven years of working with me they have become mature, resilient people, capable of speaking out and standing by their children and supporting each other in the struggle for emancipation.

It was poignant to hear such silent, submissive women describe the terrible oppression they have suffered at home and their repeated suicide attempts and plans to run away when their children were small. Since they had nothing to lose, they were ready to open up to prevent further suffering by women and children in the area. One girl who refused to attend school for nine years, hating the cold strict atmosphere, but now finding home in a liberal boarding high school, told the *Asahi Shimbun* in an interview (13 May 1993):

> After many years of distancing myself from the school, I realise that I chose the right path to grow into a healthy individual, for by becoming school phobic I was able to encounter so many wonderful people who led creative lives of their own. I would never have had this experience had I been attending school. Children should have the right to choose the way of life which best facilitates their sense of self-esteem and individuality.

Iri and Toshi Maruki are an elderly couple of artists. Iri, the husband, paints in ink; Toshi, the wife, paints in oil. Together they are known for their powerful murals featuring human atrocities and subversion (Dower and Junkerman 1985). Their first work was a sequence of murals entitled *Hiroshima*, painted immediately after the explosion of the atomic bomb, and after they had cremated their dead relatives and tended the injured. Hiroshima and Nagasaki are generally remembered in Japan with self-pity and feelings of victimisation. But the Marukis insist that victims and victimisers are intertwined in a complex entanglement; from their own researches, they discovered that all twenty-three American prisoners allegedly killed by the Hiroshima bomb were in fact beaten to death in the streets in the aftermath of the bomb, by ordinary citizens egged on by the military police. This prompted them to look at the tragedy of Hiroshima in the context of all the atrocities of the mid twentieth century that have transcended national boundaries, in the multifarious instances of warfare, nuclear destruction, racist and ecological devastation made worse by modern technology – tragic manifestations of the dark reality of the human mind.

Further, they have extended their scope outside Japan, to cover such horrors as the Rape of Nanking and Auschwitz concentration camp.

In 1979 they painted a panorama linking past and present entitled *From the Axis Pact To Sanrizuka* featuring six symbolic events of modern history: the 1940 Axis alliance in Germany, Italy and Japan; Auschwitz; the annihilation of the 'Himeyuri Brigade' of Okinawa schoolgirls, conscripted as nurses in the Second World War; the atomic bombs; the Minamata mercury poisonings; and the Sanrizuka struggle by farmers dispossessed by the construction of Japan's new international ariport at Narita. In this litany of modern fascism and state oppression of its own people, such tragic victims of reckless economic growth should not be forgotten; in the case of the villagers of Minamata on the islands of Kyushu, the Chisso fertiliser factory's effluent destroyed an entire community with mercury poisoning, killing many, crippling others physically and mentally and damaging foetuses in the womb with fetal Minamata disease.

Set in the Maruki museum adjoining the artists' house, on a quiet country hillside in Saitama to the north of Tokyo, are the murals of *Hiroshima*, a series of twelve panels depicting the aftermath of the bomb. The fifth panel, subtitled 'Water', shows an injured mother embracing her dead baby. Fleeing the flames in search of water to soothe her scorched face, she comes upon mountains of corpses piled on all sides, and she offers a breast to her child only to find it is dead. Her brooding eyes, fixed onto her beloved one seem to say:

Who killed my baby? Not an outer enemy, but an enemy inside us: greed, deceit, conceit and all the other dark aspects of our mind. Stop embracing impossible, unattainable dreams. Come down to earth and embrace with me the irrefutable truth of our mortality. Our lives are equally in the hands of Mother Nature: we have to abide by Her law. How long could She put up with our relentless misuse of life on earth? Our material prosperity has merely scored to expand our greed, rage and fear, diminishing our capacity to trust, share and live in harmony together. No more monkey-like Nikko Trio: we Japanese must stop appeasing our aggressors, keep our eyes, ears, mouths wide open, to be true to ourselves, and to examine our past experiences. How many more mistakes must we make and how many losses must we incur before we can save 'our baby'? The future and the hope of mankind are indeed at stake. Will we accept this injured mother with her dead baby as the Madonna and Child of our times? How far we have moved away from our original selves! We must stand up to face the enemy within us, or we will not save 'our baby'. The clock is ticking fast.

REFERENCES

Asahi Shimbun, May 1993. Tokyo: Asahi Shimbun.

Berke, J. H. *et al.* (eds) (1995) *Sanctuary: The Arbours Experience of Alternative Community Care*. London: Process Press.

Dower, J.W. and Junkerman, J. (eds) (1985) *The Art of Iri and Toshi Maruki*. Tokyo: Kodansha International.

Gold, H. (1996) *Unit 731 Testimony*. Tokyo: Yen Books.

Green, A. (1986) *On Private Madness*. London: Hogarth Press and the Institute of Psycho-Analysis.

Hendry, J. (1987) *Understanding Japanese Society*. London: Routledge.

Hicks, G. (1995) *The Comfort Women*. Tokyo: Yen Books.

Kosho, T. (1995) 'The responsibility of the Japanese companies under the situation of enforced recruitment', in *The Report on Japan's War Responsibility* (Japanese, quarterly), no. 7: 47–54, Center for research and documentation On Japan's War Responsibility.

Lebra, T. S. (1984) *Japanese Women: Constraints and Fulfillment*. Honolulu: University of Hawaii Press.

Nakane, C. (1970) *Japanese Society*. Tokyo: Tuttle.

Sameroff, A. J. and Emde, R. N. (1989) *Relationship Disturbances in Early Childhood*. New York: Basic Books.

Van Wolferen, K. (1993) *The Enigma of Japanese Power*. Tokyo: Tuttle.

—— (1994) *The False Realities of a Politicized Society* (Japanese). Tokyo: Mainichi Shimbunsha.

Watanabe, H. (1987) 'Establishing emotional mutuality not formed in infancy with Japanese families'. *Infant Mental Health Journal*, vol. 8: 398–408.

—— (1992) 'Difficulties in Amae: a clinical perspective'. *Infant Mental Health Journal*, vol. 13: 26–33.

—— (1996) 'Alienation and retrieval: cases of a male foetus and a nineteen-month-old boy whose mothers had been abandoned in infancy', unpublished paper presented at the Sixth International Psychoanalytic Association Research Congress, March 1996.

Watanabe, R. (1992) 'How people remember being victims but forget being aggressors'. Critique Column, 7 August: Asahi Shimbun. Tokyo.

Chapter 14

Peace and paranoia

Stanley Schneider

In the Editor's note to Freud's 'Why War?' we find an interesting historical footnote. In 1931, the International Institute of Intellectual Co-operation was asked by the League of Nations to arrange for an international exchange between intellectuals on subjects that would serve 'the common interests of the League of Nations and of intellectual life' (Freud 1933: 197). Albert Einstein, who was approached by the League, suggested communication with Freud. In 1932, Einstein wrote to Freud: 'Is there any way of delivering mankind from the menace of war?' (Freud 1933: 199). Freud wrote back: 'war is in the crassest opposition to the psychical attitude imposed on us by the process of civilization, and for that reason we are bound to rebel against it; we simply cannot any longer put up with it. This is not merely an intellectual and emotional repudiation, we pacifists have a *constitutional* intolerance of war ...' (215).

During this period, in the 1930s, pacifism as an ideological movement drew its support from the world's intellectuals. The aftermath of the First World War, and the economic collapse in the United States and in many parts of Europe, forced many to look for a newer life-style with an emphasis on suppressing anger, aggression and conflict.

I chose this historical vignette as my branching-off point for a look at the concept of peace. When we hear politicians presenting their skewed views of a particular situation, it is hard to comprehend that they are all talking about the same thing. How, then, can we understand such completely opposite views? Must we say that one party is out of touch with reality? Need we revert to labeling those who differ from us as rightists, leftists, doves, hawks, communists, fascists, religious, non-religious, etc.? Or, even more importantly, must one look over one's shoulder all the time for fear of a fifth column that will break down all ideals and belief systems? As a clinician, I might be pressed to consider one side or the other as paranoid. If so, then the next question is: which side? In order better to understand the above, we need to look at the concept of paranoia and how it interweaves with the concept of peace as a process. In order to make peace with a former enemy, one needs to bear in mind that both sides view themselves as being persecuted, the 'victim,' and want to extract as much as possible in the negotiating process.

PARANOIA AND PARANOID ANXIETY

One of the reasons that we have difficulty in clinically defining the term paranoid is because its definition is based on the particular group that gives it 'consensual validation and political respectability' (Erlich 1994: 3). Emotional 'fuel' is garnered from ideologically based convictions that sound and appear as logical. By branding others as paranoid, we define them as the bad ones, the enemy. By doing this, we project into/onto them those displaced parts of ourselves. In fact, there is a part of us that really identifies with them on some level. However, for various reasons, we cannot/will not or choose not to be associated with such views. Hence the need to extrude those views from ourselves.

These projections into/onto others allow us to feel safe and good. Having an enemy, an 'other,' another in whom to project, expunges from us feelings of badness. So why would we want to get rid of the enemy? In effect, war and conflict enable us not to have to deal with these conflictual parts within us. So why make peace?

In analyzing group psychology, Freud (1921) established the identification processes by which group formation occurs. He defined identification 'as the earliest expression of an emotional tie with another person' (105); 'the ego has enriched itself with the properties of the object, it has "introjected" the object into itself' (113). Freud based his theoretical formulations on the work of Ferenczi (1909) who wrote about 'the first "object-love" and the first "object-hate" [as] ... the roots of every introjection' (49). In group situations, group members identify with a uniting theme, sometimes manifest and sometimes latent. This is the original form of an emotional tie with an object. While early on Freud did not distinguish too carefully between the terms identification and introjection, he later was clearer in stating that in introjection qualities from the outside are taken inside. By an interesting process, the ego boundaries which had once been felt as external are now experienced as internal. Freud's thoughts have important implications with regard to the concept of the perceived enemy. In trying to bridge the gap between the enemy's position and our own, there is a need to become closer to a position that, on the surface, appears as diametrically opposed to our own. As we begin to understand the 'other' position, we become closer to it and begin to experience some of the underlying feeling aspects of that position that seem to associate to our own position. This resonance causes us to introject some of these feelings into our own position. This confusion of 'inner' and 'outer' positions eventually creates a paranoiac feeling; it makes us want to reject those hostile parts of ourselves.

Some followers of Melanie Klein's theories expanded upon Freud's ideas and applied them, together with more sophisticated projective mechanisms that they developed, in order to understand the underlying archaic mechanisms that operate in groups and organizations. Every group, according to the Kleinian view, regresses unconsciously to defend against psychotic paranoid and depressive anxiety. Jaques (1955), in a pioneering paper, set forth a Kleinian view of social systems and organizations as a necessary ingredient that individuals need in order to project outwards their inner feelings of anxiety: 'all institutions are unconsciously used by their members as mechanisms of defence against ... psychotic anxieties' (496).

In other words, the social system or organization is a convenient vehicle for one to project anxieties upon/into. In the Kleinian view, this meant that we would expect to find in group behavior manifestations of depersonalization and unreality, hostility, suspicion and other forms of maladaptive behavior. What's interesting to note here is 'that projective and introjective identifications take on a fixed or psychotic quality' (Jaques 1990: 363). Bion held similar views with regard to what group members experience (1959). In the Kleinian view, the regressive mechanisms mimic the regression of the psychotic.

Following the Kleinian thesis of paranoid psychotic anxieties that are inherent in us, 'wars break out because real difficulties are dealt with in a psychotic manner' (Fornari 1974:101). Money-Kyrle (1937) extended the theories of Melanie Klein and applied them to the study of war and political life. Money-Kyrle felt that in the developmental process, the child often times internalizes frightening external objects (monsters, witches etc.). The child feels persecuted by this internal enemy that has now been created. In order to avoid the internalized bad object, the child identifies with it in a manic sense of strength in order not to be afraid of it.

> According to Money-Kyrle, this manic process in the child seems to be the prototype of war psychology in the adult ... According to the paranoiac theory of war, these conflicts are transformed into war because real differences are not dealt with by realistic procedures, but rather through distortions of reality and through the assumption of a radically destructive attitude toward the other.
>
> (Fornari 1974:100)

What drives man to war is the paranoid psychotic anxiety that is felt. This is not necessarily related to aggressive feelings but rather connects to the earliest object relations with the mother and other mothering objects. Incorporating Freud's view (1921) that every herd needs a leader, political leaders, through ideological fiery rhetoric, can connect to the group members' underlying anxieties and push them into a 'fear of the enemy' posture.

In the Freudian view, which does not deal with extreme unconscious primitive dynamics as in the Kleinian system, one can have one's ego identify with an object or one can replace the ego-ideal by an external object. As Freud states: 'the ego divided, fallen apart into two pieces, one of which rages against the second ... some such agency develops in our ego which may cut itself off from the rest of the ego and come into conflict with it. We have called it the 'ego ideal,' and by way of functions we have ascribed to it self-observation, the moral conscience, the censorship of dreams, and the chief influence in repression' (Freud 1921:109–10). We have here an Elmer Gantry-type of situation: the preacher who engages in illicit sexual behavior, yet preaches vehemently against it from the pulpit. This would mean that we all have both positive and negative feelings about objects and situations. The hawk or dove at heart has elements of the other side's point of view. One has one's own view but there is a part of oneself that has the view of the other side. So when one feels or acts, the attitude is tempered by the opposite view. Or, in a reaction-formation sort of manner, one acts/talks the opposite – but in extreme terms.

What causes groups to become paranoid? Why do some leaders become dictators and fascistic and others less pathological yet not much less paranoid? Is there an impairment in the ego function of judgment? The *Diagnostic and Statistical Manual of Mental Disorders*, the *DSM-IV* (1994) defines a paranoid personality disorder as: 'A pervasive distrust and suspiciousness of others such that their motives are interpreted as malevolent' (637). However, I think that for our purposes it is best to look at paranoia as a breakdown in the tenuous balance of 'inner' and 'outer'; where there is difficulty in being able to discern the delineated boundaries of what is felt as inside and/or outside.

Let us look at the enemy. The enemy can be from within or from without. How do we relate to these two different types of enemies? The enemy from without is easier to deal with because he is directly in front of us; we know who the enemy is. However, the enemy within is a fragmentation within the self. Parts of the self fuse towards one direction and parts of the self are foreign and need to be extruded. These projected-off parts of the self are the conflict within the self. In order to avoid such internal conflicts, an external enemy is chosen and is vehemently abhorred. The enemy outside can be a political foe, different religious viewpoints or other conflictual issues or objects (Volkan 1988). Fornari (1974) sees 'stranger anxiety of the infant in its eighth month of life ... as the original emergence of the other as enemy' (161). We see here the externalization of the bad internal object described earlier as being projected onto the stranger.

Developmentally, as the child matures, the ego is capable of integrating contradictory 'pictures in the mind' called self representations (images that relate in some way to one's self) and object representations (images that bring to mind objects that one has contact with or relationship to). Volkan (1988) feels that the integration doesn't always coalesce into a unified conceptual corpus. These unintegrated self representations and object representations become laden with aggressive drive derivatives. This leaves one with an incomplete picture of one's feelings and thoughts about oneself and a confusing picture of the different objects in one's repertoire. This incomplete merger interfaces with the development of the super-ego, the development of a value system, which skews the way self, object, self representations and object representations are viewed. This gives rise to what Volkan (1988) called 'the concept of the shared enemy' (30). We are not only dissimilar to the enemy but also have similar feelings. This is because there is confusion regarding feelings and factual reality.

This is where the plot thickens. Feelings and perceptions are the potential enemy on the boundary between inner and outer self. This gives rise to existential anxiety (Kierkegaard 1946; Soloveitchik 1965) which is not easily containable, and therefore the need for projective and intro-jective mechanisms. We all have within us the primitive reaction to difference. The one whose values, perceptions, appearance, etc. appear as different can easily be scapegoated as the carrier of the projected and introjected impulses. The one whose opinions are different is seen as a threat to our identity (Turquet 1975). Thus the need to have an enemy in order to be able to rid ourselves of our inner conflicts and difficulties. The paranoia arises when our self becomes aware of the split that is occurring – between inner and outer – between our real feelings and our denying our real feelings.

In effect, we are experiencing both sides of the conflict. However, rather than dealing with this split and the questions that it brings up, it is easier to blame it on an external source rather than deal with the source of the paranoia. The peace process brings up both sides of the conflict – one is expressed externally and one is experienced internally. The internal feeling experience, as soon as it is viewed as being in conflict with the external reality, is projected outwards in order to rid oneself of any doubt. What we need to do is to listen to both sides of the conflict and try to arrive at a compromise formation rather than a paranoid way of dealing with conflict. We need to learn 'to be able to cope with different points of view, [with] other living spaces' (Resnik 1985: 243).

WAR AND PEACE

Whenever we look at the concept 'peace' and see how it manifests itself in various places in the world, we inevitably see a polarization of views. All viewpoints are represented as logical, coherent and ideologically correct and an outsider could be influenced to agree with many of these disparate views. This must mean that there is a common thread that permeates throughout and can serve as a uniting rather than a dividing force.

One way to look at this seemingly paradoxical situation is to try and understand what opposing sides see in themselves and in the other. If I am fearful of making peace with another, it is because I perceive a threat to my self, to my integrity. It is easier for me to hold on to my individuality or uniqueness when I am vastly different from another. By accentuating my separateness I feel that I am able to strengthen my position. Making peace with another forces me to relax my strict boundaries, which were set in place in order to separate me from opposite views, in order to meet the other side. The meeting point ought to be somewhere in between our former two opposite positions. Meeting another with opposite views from me, enables me to give up my overt hostility.

In the last twenty years, only world leaders who held and were willing to forgo extreme political positions could make peace with 'the other side.' Interestingly, those who did make the effort (some may call it 'sacrifice') were individuals who were not only charismatic but also very extreme in their former positions. To wit: Sadat and Begin; de Klerk and Mandela; Nixon and the Mao leadership in China. Each of these protagonist personae held extreme positions and were even called 'terrorists' by 'the other side.' Yet, they were able to find a common ground with the former enemy. It would seem that strong, extremist leaders can 'afford' to offer and accept a compromise solution.

I am reminded of the famous interchange between Henry Kissinger and Golda Meir during the Sinai disengagement talks. After a heated session when Kissinger pressed Meir for Israeli concessions, Meir balked. Kissinger called her 'paranoid' and Meir was forced to remark that 'even paranoids have enemies.' The implication in Meir's statement was that Israeli fears and behavior were based on real feelings of persecution and potential annihilation. To the outside world (non-Israelis), the Israeli position may be viewed as paranoid since peace talks were in progress. However, to the Israelis who needed to concede territory and pull back to potentially less defensible borders, they weren't paranoid – they were only wary of the enemy.

It is very important for us to have this 'other' on whom we can project all our fears and bad feelings. Why look at ourselves when it is easier to blame 'the other'? In effect, the enemy allows us the opportunity to rigidify our boundaries thereby avoiding closeness. By staying within my own views and feelings, I deny legitimacy to others.

As mentioned earlier, paranoia arises when our self becomes aware of the split that is occurring between 'inner' and 'outer.' In a strange sort of way, this is the psyche's protective mechanism in order to avoid conflict.

We need the extreme, polarized division in order for us to avoid looking at our position – to avoid looking at our selves. Having the external enemy, the enemy on the outside, the 'outer' one, makes it easier for us to deal with reality. We close off other views; only our opinions, ideas and feelings are to be considered. All other views are opposing and, therefore, threatening to our inner stability. We do not want to threaten our position by opening up questions and possible opposing thoughts, feelings and ideas. However, if we want to make peace and decrease hostilities, we will have to come closer to the outside enemy. We will be left, however, with the enemy within; we still have to deal with our selves.

Interestingly, while the two terms, peace and paranoia, seem so different from one another, they are very much related. Note the following definitions:

> *paranoia*: systematized delusions and the projection of personal conflicts, which are ascribed to the supposed hostility of others.
> *peace*: an agreement . . . between warring or antagonistic nations, groups etc. to end hostilities.

> (*Random House Dictionary* 1967)

Both definitions contain the word 'hostility.' Historically we have seen how during the Second World War, pacts with Hitler and Mussolini were illusory. Yet, those who did enter into such agreements did so out of feelings of despair and persecution. In order better to understand the idea of peace between opposite groups, we need to explore the concept of war.

Freud (1933) saw war as an inevitable reaction to civilization, which he saw as repressive to man's innate sexual and aggressive drives. Violence was seen by him to be related to a decrease in the culture of society of opportunities to find socially acceptable outlets for sexual and aggressive expression. Freud felt that with regards to war, 'we are bound to rebel against it' (215). He felt that we should not allow ourselves to be influenced by the culture of those who are 'behaving in an uncivilized way' (1915: 286). There seems to almost be a contradiction in terms. A cultured person should be behaving in a civilized manner, yet we find that as man has advanced in civilization, he has become increasingly more violent and warlike (Gumbel 1973).

Why do we have cultures that contain intelligent people and who are aware of the dangers involved in waging war (loss of life, injury, economic hardships, loss of property, as some examples) that are so self-destructive? In spite of the intellectual understanding, the emotional response leaves much to be desired. We may have cultures with kind people (as individuals) and yet they may still be part of 'violent cultural contexts' (de Maré, Piper and Thompson 1991: 77). There must be some underlying instinctual reason that drives people to war. This goes against the grain of expecting that in the 'process of civilization ... [there is a] strengthening of instinctual life and renunciation of instinct' (Freud 1933: 215, n.).

Menninger (1938) tried to find an answer as to why war is raged in spite of the awareness of the dangers, by relating to Freud's hypothesis of the death instinct: 'a consideration of war and crime, no less than of sickness and suicide, leads us back to a reiteration and reaffirmation of the hypothesis of Freud that man is a creature dominated by an instinct in the direction of death' (412). We know historically, that Freud's disciples and successors had difficulty accepting the death instinct, while Melanie Klein and her colleagues incorporated it into their theoretical formulations. Nonetheless, there is underlying pressure that comes to the fore with regards to the individual and society struggling to wage wars and perpetuate social violence in order to further political and ideological thoughts, ideas and feelings. Searles (1979) called this a 'realistic "paranoid" threat' (238). Something is hovering over us, according to Searles. He sees this as the potential, ever-present nuclear threat. But we are also looking for an underlying, *internal* feeling of threat: something that propels us forward in order to split off these internal bad feelings from the outside reality.

Flugel (1945), in a brilliant chapter on 'The problem of war and peace,' tried to delineate the 'psychological appeal of war' (303). One needs to bear in mind when reading Flugel that this chapter was written, in its early form, in 1940. The impact of the beginnings of the Second World War were slowly being felt. Flugel felt that 'war ... opens up unknown possibilities and opportunities'(303). War helps change a bored routine and adds excitement to life. So while war is a terrible thing for mankind, there are underlying emotional reasons for fueling aggression and hostilities. This is quite similar to Melanie Klein's thesis that while separation and grief in the depressive position are painful, they are a necessary part of life and are, therefore, growth experiences (1935). Flugel (1945) enumerated four main reasons why people need war:

1. adventure: war takes the worker out of the dull, mundane, repetitive life of the farmer, factory or office worker; war forces us not to rest on our laurels but become more actively involved, physically as well as mentally; risk-taking spurs mankind forward and involves greater gratification; the thrill of excitement is greater when pain and sacrifice are in the air;

2. social unity: war allows people to 'rally around the flag' and there is a common cause that unites people and stifles their usual dissident feelings and activities; fighting the enemy is the task at hand and this coalesces a nation by uniting individuals and group factions in pursuit of the common goal; war enhances the feeling of belonging so that

each person can contribute; 'war makes the activities of the individual more ego-syntonic, it reduces the tension between the ego and the super-ego, and tends to raise the ego to the level of the super-ego ... Herein lies ... the most essential element in the *moral* appeal of war' (307–8);

3. freedom from individual worries and restrictions: the common danger of war drives away individuals' anxieties because war provides employment and there is reduced economic worry; there is less class fighting as everyone is exposed to the same dangers and competition is no longer a relevant variable;

4. aggression: war provides a sanctioned moral outlet for aggression. Can one imagine a better way to gratify instinctual impulses without feeling guilty? The enemy becomes the focus of our scapegoating and projected aggressive feelings, thus reducing our aggression towards other members of our own group.

Ladan (1989) deals with man's refusal (I think reticence would be a more appropriate term) to know anything about the underlying wish for war. Ladan clearly points out the contradictory feelings of aversion to and wish for war. He feels that the mechanism of splitting is not sufficient to explain this phenomenon and we must look to the wish for war as an expression of underlying instinctual feelings.

> War is an attempt to solve an internal conflict ... connected with our impotence ... A state of peace, of non-war, is psychologically burdensome ... In peacetime ... we have no alternative but to seek less destructive outlets and tolerate our impotence. But there is one consolation: the prospect of a forthcoming war.
>
> (Ladan 1989: 336)

The above ends on a somewhat pessimistic note as it makes the prospects of peace seem so remote due to the underlying wishes and feelings for war and the benefits that accrue to the war-wagers versus the peace-makers. It is this latter point that we need to look at more closely. As an illustration, I would like to focus on the peace process in Israel and the recent assassination of the Prime Minister of Israel, Yitzchak Rabin, as the theoretical and psychological meeting point between peace and war.

THE PEACE PROCESS IN ISRAEL

The right-wing Likud Party in Israel was responsible for signing the first peace treaty with an Arab country, Egypt, and for attending the first Peace Conference with all the Arab protagonists in the continual protracted battle with Israel, the Madrid Conference, in 1991. Yet, when the Labor

Party, formerly a centrist political group, merged in a coalition government with the left-wing political parties, it was credited with being the
party that brought peace to Israel. I start with this brief historical note in
order to underline how ideological views can become skewed when they
are attributed to one group or another.

The Labor Party had their own in-fighting and bickering that finally led
to the election of the late Yitzchak Rabin as party leader replacing Shimon
Peres. In July 1992, Rabin was elected Prime Minister and he appointed
Peres as his Foreign Minister. Because of the need for a majority in the
Israeli Parliament, the Knesset, Rabin had to rely on 'strange bedfellows'
as coalition partners: the left-wing parties which also included, for the first
time, reliance on an Arab party.

Over the next three years Rabin moved at break-neck speed in order
to complete as much of the Peace Process as possible before the end of
his four-year candidacy. In September 1993 he shook hands with PLO
Chairman Yasser Arafat at the White House, sealing their joint
Declaration of Principles which provided the framework for the phased
granting of autonomy to the Palestinians of the West Bank and Gaza.
This was formal recognition of the entity known as the Palestinians and
acceptance of the need to provide a political settlement to the continuous
war atmosphere that has been in existence since the founding of Israel in
1948. In May 1994 the Oslo I accord, granting self-rule to the Palestinians
of Gaza and Jericho was signed. In October 1994, Rabin and King Hussein
of Jordan signed a formal peace treaty ending the forty-six-year state of
war between Israel and Jordan. At the year's end, Rabin together with
Peres and Arafat were awarded the Nobel Peace Prize. In September
1995, Rabin signed the Oslo II agreement expanding Palestinian autonomy
in the West Bank.

On 4 November 1995, Rabin was assassinated by a law school student,
Yigal Amir, who was identified with extreme right-wing activists. In the
two years prior to the assassination there was a deepening of the ideological rift between two opposing groups: those *in* the government and
those *outside*. Slogans abounded with those who stated *they* were *for* peace
and the *others* were *against* peace. Positions became polarized and enemy
camps solidified their positions. Verbal assaults become the norm – not
just in the street but also in the Knesset. Physical threats were 'in the air.'
In between the unrelenting verbal violence which fragmented the nation
into two warring camps, there were vicious terrorist bombings which left
scores killed and many more wounded physically and psychologically.
These acts of violence by Arab terrorists against innocent children, women
and men, served to unite the country for a brief respite from the continuous in-fighting and argumentative atmosphere.

Rabin, together with the other architects of the Peace Process, had
committed one fatal error: they moved too quickly and without trying to

unite the population. What they succeeded in doing was to polarize the country into two camps. Each side then proceeded to delegitimize the other. The media and educational and religious institutions began taking sides. The venomous hatred that was erupting from the inner bowels of the population was not being contained. Those who were not part of the government felt that there was no way that they could have their point of view acknowledged. Moderate positions were pushed to extreme positions in the hope that their voice would be heard. The religious establishment was called in in order to stem the tide of what the right-wing parties felt to be a groundswell of leftist support together with Arab propaganda. Another error was that religion was now being identified with a particular ideological position rather than being a useful tool in trying to defuse a volatile situation.

Rabin was perceived as being intolerant of difference and disrespectful of positions held by others. The ideological positions of the two opposing political groups intensified in the extreme. The leaders could not prevent the escalation of verbal violence; physical threats and eventual violence were the inevitable result.

Political murder is, unfortunately, not a foreign concept to the Middle East. Since Israel and her Arab neighbors began to move towards a peaceful resolution of their age-old conflict, extremist groups became violent as a way of expressing their dissatisfaction with any overtures toward peace. President Anwar Sadat of Egypt was assassinated by Moslem extremists who were opposed to his making peace with Israel. Prime Minister Yitzchak Rabin was assassinated by a Jewish extremist because of Rabin's overtures to the Palestinians. Volatile tempers in the Middle East are not a new phenomenon. A bit before the establishment of the State of Israel in 1948, King Hussein's grandfather, King Abdulla, was assassinated by Moslem extremists. Abdulla's willingness to seek peaceful coexistence with the Zionists was not viewed favorably by some of his constituents.

In the Bible we see that after the destruction of the First Temple in 586 BCE, the Babylonian-appointed Jewish governor of Judea, Gedaliah the son of Ahikam, was assassinated by Ishmael, the son of Netaniah, who considered him to be a traitor (Jeremiah 41). The event is remembered to this day by Jews as the Fast of Gedaliah. Clearly, political murder needed to be recorded in the national psyche as heinous and reprehensible. What better way to do this than by having a Fast Day which falls on the day right after Rosh HaShanah, the Jewish New Year!

Yigal Amir felt that Rabin was leading his people down a road with a point-of-no-return and therefore, in his mind, something needed to be done to stop the Peace Process. Amir saw Rabin as a dictator who was unwilling and possibly unable to stop a process that was, in Amir's eyes, already out of hand. As Meltzer (1988) states: 'The dread felt in relation to the tyrant is fundamentally a dread of loss of the illusory protection against the terror' (237). Amir felt that Rabin and his government were no longer able to protect him. The internalized mother's breast represented in the transferential situation by the protector of Israel, in the guise of the Prime Minister, the leader, was not able to do the job. Amir's mixed feelings of fear and aggression were projected onto Rabin. In order for Amir to be able to deal with these noxious feelings they needed to be projected onto the leader (Rabin) and the group-as-a-whole (the Rabin government). Since some of the people in Israel were disillusioned with the Rabin government, the unconscious and conscious functioning of the group (those following Rabin) was no longer the majority. The 'containing envelope' (Anzieu 1984) which should have served the protective function as 'envelope' to the group psychical apparatus, was not sufficient to hold and contain the feelings of fear, dread and aggression. Rabin, following Amir's logic, had to be eliminated.

Everyone felt that Rabin had undergone a major personality transformation and metamorphosis. Within the space of a few short years, his centrist – with a shade to the right – position, had moved sharply to the left. One could argue that only a truly great leader could be flexible enough to change deeply embedded views. Yet, there were those who tried to show that Rabin, the former army chief-of-staff and hero of the Six Day War of 1967, had been brainwashed by his leftist coalition partners egged on by his 'former' arch-rival, Peres. For these pessimists, Rabin was not only misguided but dangerous and a traitor. As Greenacre (1969) stated:

> Treachery ... is the special product of human rivalry and implies the ability to scheme and to deceive ... The explanation of the traitor that he has been driven by a high motive – that of a benevolent wish for greater harmony and peace, the salvation of the country or the world – is a constantly recurring one. This appears, however, in a spectrum of intensity – varying from the most superficial rationalization to the most fanatical belief in a sacred mission. Examination of the qualities of significant traitors brings out rather clearly their relationship to those of leaders.
>
> (Greenacre 1969: 365, 396)

Interestingly, the above quotation can be the rationale for Amir for assassinating Rabin. In Amir's eyes Rabin's treacherous behavior qualified him for the death penalty. With ideological 'religious backing', Amir felt that he was destined in history to be the one who removed Rabin from the national and international stage. Amir would have seen Greenacre's comments as referring to Rabin's wish as a traitor to change the face of Israel in the eyes of the world. On the other hand, it is my wish to utilize Greenacre's words to typify Amir as the traitor who by the use of his gun killed a democratically elected political leader and who wanted by that maniacal act to change the course of history. This fanatical belief, fueled by years of intemperate, extremist verbal vilification by many people including leaders from across the political spectrum, led to a terribly tragic act.

Several months later the Labor Party, now under the leadership of Shimon Peres, lost in the general elections to the Likud Party and Binyamin Netanyahu. Both Labor and Likud utilized in their pre-election campaign the Rabin assassination as ideological propaganda. Labor stressed the need to continue along the path of Rabin in order to save the country from the catastrophe of stopping the peace process. In addition, how could the country elect Netanyahu and his cohorts. As the campaign ads read: 'You killed and also inherited?' (I Kings 21:19). The Likud appealed to the emotions of the masses: an end to violence and bloodshed; 'peace with security.' Both parties tried to speak to the raw emotions of a country split almost equally, both sides earnestly desiring peace but with drastically different platforms on how to achieve that elusive goal. Peace, as an election issue, was used by both sides. Both parties spoke to the paranoiac elements in the souls of the people.

Pressures began to mount within the right-wing Netanyahu government to take a stronger security position with the Palestinians. Netanyahu tried to *listen* to the different voices in his cabinet but he wasn't *hearing* what they were saying. Netanyahu didn't understand that he needed to unite the different voices, both in and out of his government, by concentrating on how to deal with the Palestinians and continuing the 'peace process.' In the space of several months, Netanyahu covered 'all ends of the political spectrum.' He tried to 'satisfy' everyone and really satisfied no one. At the end of September 1996, he authorized the opening of the Hashmonean Tunnel. This led to Arab violence against citizens and the security forces. For the first time, Arab policemen opened fire against Israeli soldiers and police. Here we have a perfect example of Netanyahu unilaterally creating 'facts-on-the-ground.' While Rabin and Peres tried to forge a link between the opening of the tunnel and expansive building by the Arabs at Solomon's Stables, under the Temple Mount, they failed to carry this out. Netanyahu did not discuss the issue with the Palestinians as he needed to show strength through forceful decision-making since the issue, in his eyes, was Jerusalem. However, the lesson of not listening to the other side, which provokes paranoia and violence, was not heeded.

In October 1996, Netanyahu, in spite of his protestations, eventually shook hands with Arafat on the White House lawn in the presence of President Clinton, King Hussein and President Mubarak. Rather than spending the previous months talking to avoid paranoia and violence, actions took place in the hope of obviating the need to communicate. This led to a feeling of underhandedness, increased paranoia and a quick jump to violence.

In December 1996, Israel redeployed in Hebron, and for several months both sides began to try and develop trust, one in the other. Then in March 1997, Israel decided to build in Har Homa (Jebel Abu Renaim, to the Arabs). Israel felt that there was no need to seek permission to build in what they view as undivided Jerusalem. The Arabs felt that this was a test case for the final status of Jerusalem. Rather than both sides seeking a way to work together with one another, fear and mistrust magnified.

It seems that politicians find it easier to create and fight an enemy rather than look for ways to deal with internal conflict. With the possibility of peace on the horizon, the outside enemy no longer is the danger. The danger now comes from within. As Money-Kyrle (1961) states: 'the major impediments to political agreement by rational argument alone spring far more from the distorted pursuit of ends, and from the wrong choice of means, because of misassessments of facts – especially psychological facts – than from any irreducible conflict of interest' (141).

In conflict, we need to be able to hear both the external (the enemy) as well as the internal (our selves), otherwise we will have feelings of paranoia and persecution. We all need to be able to contain oftentimes contradictory feelings and attitudes. This tolerance of difference need not necessarily be at the expense of one's own deeply felt values. However, under situations of internal feelings of persecution, we sometimes feel our position to be slowly eroding. We feel an internal conflict between various opposing forces. In order not to have to deal with this split, which we are now becoming aware of, we become paranoiac. The only way out of this situation of terrible anxiety is to blame the other – to project outwards. What complicates the situation even more is that these feelings of paranoia dovetail with feelings of persecution. On one hand, if I persecute then I feel relieved in my own internal psyche because I am on the offensive rather than on the defensive. On the other hand, I can feel persecuted because the contradictory feelings that I am feeling are too strong for me to bear. I feel this internal persecutor as so strong that I use it to help destroy my internal enemies. This allows me to blame others – the enemy.

As the peace process between Israel and the Palestinians continues, trust and confidence between the two sides are supposed to become stronger. However, what really is occurring is that both sides are learning to accommodate one another. In the Piagetian scheme of things assimilation and equilibrium (the acceptance and internalization of thoughts, ideas and values) can only occur after a phase of accommodation (learning the boundaries and parameters of the new item to be learned after contrasting and comparing it with previous learning and experiences). So what we really have as the peace process proceeds is a willingness to try to bridge positions. This means that each side needs to give something of their 'self' in order to accommodate the 'other.' The 'enemy' is still there but in a more acceptable manner that no longer brands him as the enemy. The accommodation helps to modify the split and reduces the feelings of paranoia and persecution. What we are left with is a 'healthy dose' of paranoia. While the split has been contained and reduced, we still have healthy paranoid feelings regarding the trustworthiness of our former enemies. This helps each side keep on its toes. By being more tolerant and willing to contain all types of feelings and attitudes – sometimes different from ours – paranoia and persecution can stay within the bounds of culturally determined norms.

REFERENCES

American Psychiatric Association (1994) *Diagnostic and Statistical Manual of Mental Disorders*, fourth edition (*DSM-IV*), Washington, DC: American Psychiatric Association.

Anzieu, D. (1984) *The Group and the Unconscious*, London: Routledge and Kegan Paul.

Bion, W.R. (1959) *Experiences in Groups*, New York: Basic.

de Maré, P., Piper, R. and Thompson, S. (1991) *Koinonia: From Hate, through Dialogue, to Culture in the Large Group*, London: Karnac.

Erlich, H.S. (1994) 'Enemies Within and Without: The Sad Tale of Paranoia and Regression in Groups and Organizations,' paper presented at the National Conference on Group Psychotherapy, Tel Aviv, March.

Ferenczi, S. (1909) 'Introjection and Transference,' *First Contributions to Psycho-Analysis*, New York: Brunner/Mazel, 1980.

Flugel, J.C. (1945) *Man, Morals and Society*, New York: International Universities Press.

Fornari, F. (1974) *The Psychoanalysis of War*, New York: Anchor Books.

Freud, S. (1915) 'Thoughts for the Times on War and Death,' *Standard Edition*, vol. 14, London: Hogarth, 1981.

—— (1921) 'Group Psychology and the Analysis of the Ego,' *Standard Edition*, vol. 18, London: Hogarth, 1981.

—— (1933) 'Why War?' *Standard Edition*, vol. 22, London: Hogarth, 1981.

Greenacre, P. (1969) 'The Nature of Treason and the Character of Traitors,' in *Emotional Growth*, vol. 1, New York: International Universities Press, 1971.

Gumbel, E. (1973) 'Notes on Some Psychic Motives for War,' in H.Z. Winnick, R. Moses and M. Ostow (eds) *Psychological Bases of War*, New York: Quadrangle.

Jaques, E. (1955) 'Social Systems as a Defence against Persecutory and Depressive Anxiety,' in M. Klein, P. Heimann and R.E.T. Money-Kyrle (eds) *New Directions in Psycho-Analysis*, London: Maresfield, 1977.

—— (1990) *Creativity and Work*, Madison, CT: International Universities Press.

Kierkegaard, S. (1946) *The Concept of Dread*, Philadelphia: Saunders.

Klein, M. (1935) 'A Contribution to the Psychogenesis of Manic-Depressive States', in *Love, Guilt and Reparation*, London: Virago, 1988.

Ladan, A. (1989) 'The Wish for War,' *International Review of Psycho-Analysis*, 16: 331–7.

Meltzer, D. (1988) 'Terror, Persecution, Dread – A Dissection of Paranoid Anxieties,' in E.B. Spillius (ed.) *Melanie Klein Today*, vol. 1, London: Routledge.

Menninger, K. (1938) *Man Against Himself*, New York: Harcourt, Brace and World, 1966.

Menzies Lyth, I.E.P. (1988) 'A Psychoanalytic Perspective on Social Institutions,' in E.B. Spillius (ed.) *Melanie Klein Today*, vol. 2, London: Routledge.

Money-Kyrle, R.E. (1937) 'The Development of War: Psychological Approach,' *British Journal of Medical Psychology*, 16: 219–36.

—— (1961) *Man's Picture of his World*, London: Duckworth.

Random House Dictionary (1967) New York: Random House.

Resnik, S. (1985) 'The Space of Madness,' in M. Pines (ed.) *Bion and Group Psychotherapy*, London: Routledge and Kegan Paul.

Searles, H.F. (1979) 'Unconscious Processes in Relation to the Environmental Crisis,' in *Countertransference and Related Subjects*, New York: International Universities Press.

Soloveitchik, J.B. (1965) 'The Lonely Man of Faith,' *Tradition*, 7: 5–65.

Turquet, P. (1975) 'Threats to Identity in the Large Group,' in L. Kreeger (ed.) *The Large Group*, London: Maresfield.

Volkan, V.D. (1988) *The Need to Have Enemies and Allies*, Northvale, NJ: Jason Aronson.

Name index

Abdulla, King of Jordan 213
Abu-Jamal, M. 174
Ahikam 213
Ahlquist, J.E. 129, 138
Amati, S. 105, 109
Amir, Y. 212–14 *passim*
Andersen, H.C. 178
Anslinger, H. 146, 152
Anzieu, D. 93, 98, 214, 217
Arafat, Y. 212, 215
Artaud, A. 18
Asahara, S. 190–2 *passim*, 195
Asch, 178, 184, 187
Asimov, I. 178
Auerhahn, N.C. 48, 49, 57

Balint, M. 57
Ball, B. 23, 24
Bamber, H. 37
Barksdale, R. 176
Barnes, M. 15, 75, 76, 79, 81, 82
Baudelaire, C. 146
Baum, D. 152–4 *passim*, 158, 164
Begin, M. 208
Bennett, W. 153–4, 156
Bergmann, M.V. 49, 57
Berke, J.H. i, vii, 7, 8, 75, 79, 82,
    141–3 *passim*, 149, 164, 199, 201
Berman, A. 99
Bernstein, C. 75, 82
Bharucha, M.P. 185, 187
Binswanger, L. 21
Bion, W.R. 18, 24, 30, 32, 34, 90–1,
    93, 94, 98, 180, 184–6 *passim*, 187,
    205, 217
Bissell, N. 159, 163
Black, H. 153, 163
Black, W. 164

Blake, W. 118
Bleuler, E. 13, 21–3 *passim*, 34
Bleuler, M. 63, 65, 70
Blum, H. 4, 9
Boss 65
Bowers, M.B. 63, 67, 68, 73
Bowlby, J. 38, 46
Branson, R. 135
Breuer, J. 16, 21
Brooke, E.M. 112, 124
Brown, B. 152
Brown, S. 176
Buford, B. 104, 109
Bukovsky, V. 80
Bumpers, E. 174
Burns, G. 75, 76
Bush, G. 153, 154

Cameron, J. 178
Cancro, R. 70, 73
Canetti, E. 72, 73, 92, 99
Capras, J. 29, 35
Carroll, C. 173, 176
Carter, J. 153
Chaplin, C. 179
Chasseguet-Smirgel, J. xii, xiii
Clark, D.H. 119, 123
Clinton, H. 75, 78
Clinton, W.J. 154, 159, 162, 164, 215
Clunis, C. 122
Cobb, P. 175, 176
Cohen, J. 50, 57
Coleridge, S.T. 76
Conti, E.C. 146–7, 164
Cooper, D. 81, 118, 121, 123

Dalgarno, P. 163
Dante 36, 181

Subject index